The Death of Josseline

The Death of Josseline

Immigration Stories from the Arizona-Mexico Borderlands

Margaret Regan

BEACON PRESS

BOSTON

Beacon Press
25 Beacon Street
Boston, Massachusetts 02108-2892
www.beacon.org

Beacon Press books
are published under the auspices of
the Unitarian Universalist Association of Congregations.

13   12   11   10   8   7   6   5   4   3   2   1

This book is printed on acid-free paper that meets the uncoated paper
ANSI/NISO specifications for permanence as revised in 1992.

Text composition by Wilsted & Taylor Publishing Services.

Library of Congress Cataloging-in-Publication Data
Regan, Margaret.
The death of Josseline : immigration stories from the Arizona-
Mexico borderlands / Margaret Regan.
p. cm.
ISBN 978-0-8070-4227-4 (hardcover : alk. paper) 1. Immigrants—
United States—Biography. 2. United States—Emigration and
immigration. 3. Immigrants—Government policy—United States.
I. Title.
JV6456.R44 2009
305.9'0691209227917—dc22   2009018752

For my parents

Mary G. Regan,
great-granddaughter
of Irish famine refugees

&

William L. Regan,
grandson of Irish immigrants
who died young, poor,
and far from home

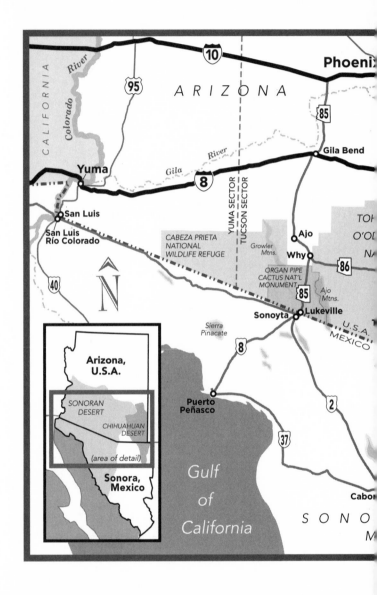

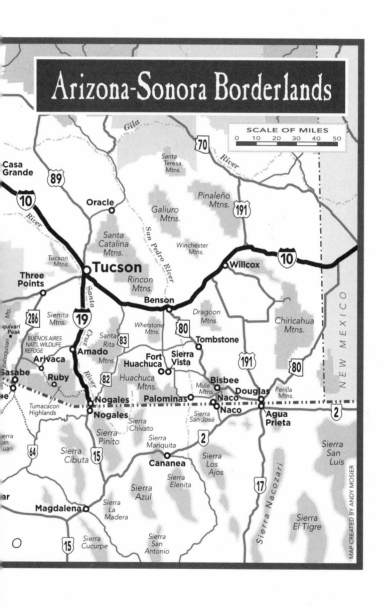

Arizona-Sonora Borderlands

SCALE OF MILES
0 10 20 30 40 50

Gila River

70

Casa Grande

89

10

Oracle

Santa Teresa Mtns.

Pinaleño Mtns.

191

Galiuro Mtns.

Santa Catalina Mtns.

San Pedro River

Winchester Mtns.

Tucson Mtns.

Tucson

Willcox

10

NEW MEXICO

Three Points

Rincon Mtns.

Benson

Santa

286

Sierrita Mtns.

19

quivari Peak

Whetstone Mtns.

Dragoon Mtns.

80

Chiricahua Mtns.

Mts.

BUENOS AIRES NAT'L WILDLIFE REFUGE

Santa Rita

83

Tombstone

Sierra Cruz River

Amado

Arivaca

Santa Rita Mtns.

Fort Huachuca

Sierra Vista

191

80

Sasabe

Ruby

82

Huachuca Mtns.

Mule Mtns.

Bisbee

Douglas

Perilla Mtns.

Nogales

Palominas

Naco

2

Tumacacori Highlands

Nogales

Naco

Agua Prieta

erra an uan

64

Sierra Chivato

Sierra San José

Sierra Pinito

Sierra Mariquita

Sierra Los Ajos

Sierra San Luis

15

Sierra Cibuta

2

Cananea

17

ar

Sierra Elenita

Sierra Azul

Sierra Nacozari

Sierra El Tigre

Magdalena

Sierra La Madera

15

Sierra Cucurpe

Sierra San Antonio

The terms used to refer to border crossers run the gamut, from the Border Patrol's "bodies" and "UDAs" (undocumented aliens) to the reverential "pilgrims" of Tucson writer Demetria Martinez. In between are "illegal aliens" and "entrants." In this book, I have chosen to use the neutral term "migrants."

I reconstructed Josseline's journey from multiple interviews, from the data in the Pima County medical examiner's autopsy report, and from my own hike into Cedar Canyon, where she died.

Contents

The Death of Josseline

She was just a little girl. She was on her way to her mother.

—*Kat Rodriguez, human rights activist*

Josseline shivered as she stepped over the stones and ducked under the mesquites. She was in Arizona, land of heat and sun, but on this late-January day in 2008, it was cold and damp. The temperature was in the 50s, and the night before it had dropped to near freezing. A winter rain had fallen, and now the desert path was slippery and wet, even more treacherous than it had been before.

Josseline was seven miles north of the Mexican border, near the old ranching town of Arivaca, in prime Sonoran Desert. It was a wonderland of cactus and mesquite, beautiful but dangerous, with trails threading through isolated canyons and up and down hills studded with rocks. She had to get through this perilous place to get to her mother. A little girl with a big name—Josseline Jamileth Hernández Quinteros—she was five feet tall and a hundred pounds. At fourteen, young as she was, she had an important responsibility: it was her job to bring her little brother, age ten, safely to their mother in Los Angeles. The Hernández kids had never been away from home before, and already they'd been traveling for weeks. Now they were almost there, just days away from their mother's embrace.

The family hadn't been together in a long time. Their father, Santos, was living somewhere in Maryland; their mother, Sonia, in California. Both parents were undocumented, working in the shadows. Back home in El Salvador, the kids lived with relatives, and in the years their mom was gone, Josseline had become a little mother to her brother. Finally, Sonia had worked long enough and hard enough to save up the money to send for the children. She'd arranged for Josseline and her brother to come north with adults they knew from home, people she trusted.

The group had crossed from El Salvador into Guatemala, then traveled two thousand miles from the southern tip of Mexico to the north. The trip had been arduous. They'd skimped on food, slept in buses or, when they were lucky, in *casas de huéspedes,* the cheap flophouses that cater to poor travelers. In Mexico, the migrants feared the *federales,* the national police, and now, in the United States, they were trying to evade the Border Patrol, the dreaded *migra.*

But here in the borderlands they were in the hands of a professional. Like the thousands of other undocumented migrants pouring into Arizona—jumping over walls, trekking across mountains, hiking through deserts—their group had contracted with a coyote, a smuggler paid to spirit them over the international line. The coyote's fee, many thousands of dollars, was to pay for Josseline and her brother to be taken from El Salvador all the way to their mother in Los Angeles. So far, everything had gone according to plan. They had slipped over the border from Mexico, near Sasabe, twenty miles from here, and had spent a couple of days picking their way through this strange desert, where spiky cacti clawed at the skin and the rocky trail blistered the feet. The coyote insisted on a fast pace. They still had a hike of twenty miles ahead of them, out to the northbound highway, Interstate 19, where their ride would meet them and take them deep into the United States.

Josseline (pronounced YO-suh-leen) pulled her two jackets closer in the cold. She was wearing everything she had brought with her from home. Underneath the jackets, she had on a tank top, better suited to Arizona's searing summers than its chilly winters, and she'd pulled a pair of sweatpants over her jeans. Her clothes betrayed her girly tastes. One jacket was lined in pink. Her sneakers were a wild bright green, a totally cool pair of shoes that were turning out to be not even close to adequate for the difficult path she was walking. A little white beaded bracelet circled her wrist. Best of all were her sweats, a pair of "butt pants" with the word HOLLYWOOD emblazoned on the rear. Josseline planned to have them on when she arrived in the land of movie stars.

She tried to pay attention to the twists and turns in the footpath, to obey the guide, to keep up with the group. But by the time they got to Cedar Canyon, she was lagging. She was beginning to feel sick. She'd been on the road for weeks and out in the open for days, sleeping on the damp ground. Maybe she'd skimped on drinking water, giving what she had to her little brother. Maybe she'd swallowed some of the slimy green water that pools in the cow ponds dotting this ranch country. Whatever the reason, Josseline started vomiting. She crouched down and emptied her belly, retching again and again, then lay back on the ground. Resting didn't help. She was too weak to stand up, let alone hike this roller-coaster trail out to the road.

It was a problem. The group was on a strict schedule. They had that ride to catch, and the longer they lingered here the more likely they'd be caught. The coyote had a decision to make, and this is the one he made: he would leave the young girl behind, alone in the desert. He told her not to worry. They were in a remote canyon that was little traveled, but the Border Patrol would soon find her. Nearby, he claimed, were some *pistas,* platforms that *la migra* used as landing pads for their helicopters. Surely they'd be by soon, and they would take care of her. Her little brother cried and begged to stay with her. But Josseline was his big sister, and Josseline insisted that he go. As he recounted later, she told him, "Tú tienes que seguir a donde está Mamá." *You have to keep going and get to Mom.*

The other travelers grabbed the wailing boy and walked on, leaving his sister alone in the cold and dark. She had only her clothes to keep her warm. On her first night alone, the temperature dropped below freezing, to 29 degrees. By the weekend, when her brother arrived safely in Los Angeles and sounded the alarm, Arivaca had warmed up—to 37 degrees.

Three weeks later, Dan Millis was getting ready to go out on desert patrol. He was filling up a big plastic box with nonperishables for migrants—granola bars, applesauce, Gatorade—and new socks, something the weary walkers always seemed to need. He tossed the box into his car and then loaded up dozens of gallons of water. A former high school teacher, Dan, twenty-eight, was an outdoors enthusiast who was spending a year volunteering with No More Deaths, a Tucson group determined to stop the deaths of migrants in the Arizona deserts. As the United States clamped down on the urban crossings, desperate travelers were pushing into ever more remote wilderness and dying out there in record numbers. So the No More Deaths folks began hiking the backcountry in the Arivaca borderlands, an hour and a half southwest of Tucson, setting out water and food in the rugged hills. Sometimes they'd meet up with migrants who were lost or sick, and they would provide first aid. But sometimes they found a body.

Before he left town, Dan studied the trail map. He could

see that several heavily traveled Arivaca trails converged on a single ridge, and he wanted to drop his load there, where it would do the most good. Three buddies were coming along to help, but the goods they were packing would be heavy—each gallon jug of water weighed almost eight and a half pounds—so he wanted to get his car as close to the ridge as he could. The map showed that a dirt ranch road edged near the drop spot, but the volunteers would have to hike up Cedar Canyon, where they'd never been before. Dan didn't know whether the canyon would even be passable, but he decided to give it a shot.

He had heard about Josseline Hernández. When the girl's little brother arrived in LA without her, her distraught family had called the Salvadoran consul in Nogales, a border town, and the consul connected them with Coalición de Derechos Humanos, a human rights organization in Tucson. Derechos compiles annual lists of the desert's dead, and tries to help the families of the missing. The coalition's Kat Rodriguez gets two or three reports of lost migrants a month. Josseline's mother couldn't even talk to her—"She was coming undone"—but the uncle gave Kat a description of the teenager and her clothes, including the distinctive green shoes Josseline was so proud of. Kat always asked for pictures of the loved one smiling; teeth, after all, can be used to identify a corpse.

The family sent Kat photos that pictured Josseline in uniform and cap, banging the cymbals in a parade with her high school marching band; Josseline posing in fashionable capris and a tank top; Josseline standing forlornly in her church, with flowers, lit candles, and a statue of the Virgin Mary behind her. The pictures showed her black hair and eyes and her warm brown skin—*morena,* the consul called it—but in every one she was serious and unsmiling, a young girl with heavy responsibilities. Kat organized the images and identifying info into a color flyer headlined "*Menor detenida o desaparecida"* (Female minor detained or disappeared). Kat sent her report to the Pima County medical examiner, in case he had a matching body in his morgue, and activists from the Samaritans immigrant-aid group checked the hospitals and detention centers. Other volunteers went out looking for her. They didn't have much to go on. The coyote had told the family Josseline was near *pistas,* or platforms; no one was quite sure of what he meant since there were no structures in the desert. And the flyer stated, erroneously as it turned out, that the girl had last been seen near Nogales, miles from where she'd been walking.

Dan Millis hadn't gotten involved in the searches. Hunts for missing migrants are needle-in-a-haystack affairs, typically conducted by well-meaning amateurs who don't know search-and-rescue techniques. Sometimes the volunteers get injured themselves. Even BORSTAR, the Border Patrol's search, trauma, and rescue unit, can't help when there's too little information. Far better, Dan thought, to stick to the work he knew would do some good, putting out food and water for the living. So he and his companions drove down to Arivaca and started into Cedar Canyon, lugging the water jugs and the box of goodies, traipsing a narrow path between looming rocky walls. There was an old dam back in there, along a wash, and he and his buds had to scramble up over the concrete. They'd been walking maybe twenty minutes when up ahead Dan spotted a pair of bright green shoes.

He didn't think of Josseline at first. Or of death. The owner of the shoes had to be around, he reasoned, maybe hiding. He began calling out the standard No More Deaths chant, designed to reassure fearful migrants. "¡Hola, hermanos! Somos amigos de la iglesia. Tenemos comida y agua." *Hello, brothers! We're friends from the church. We have food and water.*

Then, suddenly, he saw her. She was lying on a rock, under a bush, her hands raised up near her head, her feet plunged into water that had pooled in a cavity in the stone.

"I saw her teeth," he said months later. "I knew she was dead. It was a horrible feeling. I told my friends to stop.

"The body was intact," he went on, reciting details of the scene in a monotone. "She had taken off two jackets and hung them on a rock. She had a tank top on and sweatpants. Her feet were in the water." The little pearl bracelet was on her wrist. But Josseline's little brother had said his sister was wearing jeans, and this girl had on sweatpants.

Dan used his cell phone to call Sarah Roberts, a nurse active in No More Deaths who had helped coordinate Josseline's case. He told her about finding the body and the telltale green shoes and the sweatpants that didn't match up. Sarah got the message to Kat Rodriguez, who called the uncle, who questioned the brother one more time. This time, the little boy said, No, now he remembered, Josseline had put on her Hollywood butt pants. The news flew back over the cell phones to Dan. But the body was face up, and he couldn't see any writing. He knew enough about police procedures not to disturb the scene.

Dan telephoned the sheriff. Then he and another volunteer, Clint, drove the hour into Arivaca, marking down their route through the tangle of ranch roads so that they could give the police detailed directions back to the canyon. It was getting cold, so they picked up some hot soup in town for the two volunteers who had stayed behind with the body. In the meantime, that pair, a Frenchwoman named Marie and a refugee-rights worker named Max, had twisted some branches into a cross and planted it in a pile of rocks. When Dan and Clint got back, all four volunteers held a vigil, sitting by the body and the makeshift shrine, waiting for the authorities to come.

In the late afternoon, two sheriff's deputies finally arrived. They gently turned the body over. On the back of the pants was a single word: HOLLYWOOD.

———

Josseline completed her journey in a white plastic body bag. The deputies dragged her out along the trail, and lashed her corpse to a platform on the back of their SUV. It was dark by then, and they had to follow Dan's car out on the dirt roads, the two vehicles caravanning in an impromptu funeral procession. Once they hit Interstate 19, going north to Tucson up the broad Santa Cruz Valley, Dan noticed something strange in the sky. "It was the night of the full lunar eclipse," he remembered. "It was eerie to have the orange moon disappearing."

Josseline's father flew in from the East Coast in a panic. Hollywood pants don't carry much weight in the world of forensic identification, and her body was too far gone after three weeks in the elements to be identified by sight. So Josseline's dad paid a private lab to put together his DNA profile. The testing took weeks. In the interim, a coyote kept calling Josseline's mother, insisting that her daughter was not lost. If the family would only send him money, he promised, he would bring the girl to her alive and well. Sonia hesitated, not wanting to believe that her child was dead. But the DNA test, when it came in, was unequivocal. The probability that Santos was the father of the dead girl in the morgue was 99.988 percent. Armed with those results and a copy of the birth certificate, Pima County forensic anthropologist Bruce Anderson determined once and for all that this was the body of Josseline Hernández.

She was taken to California for burial. Her mother had no plans to return to El Salvador, and she wanted her daughter close.

Two months later, in the heat of late April, Father Bob Carney, a Catholic priest from Tucson, scrambled into Cedar Canyon to say a Mass for Josseline. He brought up the rear of thirty mourners, among them Josseline's aunts, uncles, and cousins. Her parents were unable to grieve at the place where their daughter had died, and neither was her brother;

as undocumented immigrants, they feared arrest. Tucson activists had turned up in large numbers. The death of the teenager had hit them hard. ("That case was hell," Kat Rodriguez would later say. "Every step of the way was agony.") The slow climb up the canyon was a reminder of what border crossers regularly endured. "People were getting scratched," Father Bob said later, "stumbling over the rocks. This is what she went through."

Josseline's relatives were the first to arrive at the rock where the body had been found. "All of a sudden this wail went up through that valley and echoed," Father Carney said. "When I got there they were truly grieving, and blaming themselves at the same time. All the emotions came pouring out in a heartrending wail."

The priest laid an altar cloth and his chalice on the rock, and said Mass among the prickly green plants, the canyon walls rising up behind him. As he broke the Communion bread, he intoned the biblical words "Do this in memory of me."

The No More Deaths Phoenix chapter had made a pretty new cross for Josseline, all pink and white, painted with flowers and entwined with ribbons. After the service, Father Bob anointed the cross with oil, and told Josseline, he would later say, "How sorry I was, that we as a people, as a nation, would do this."

Josseline's mother had written a poem in Spanish for her daughter, and her words were transcribed on the base of the cross. They began with encouragement to other migrants who might come this way: "When you feel that the road has turned hard and difficult / Don't give yourself up as lost / Continue forward and seek God's help." But it ended with a lament for her daughter: "Te llevaremos siempre en el corazón." *We'll carry you always in our hearts.*

The priest had seen many horrors in the ten years since he'd first blessed the bodies of eight young migrants piled up in an Arizona morgue, but for him, Josseline's tragedy stood out.

"For all of us, those who saw her, or saw her picture, she became so alive, so real," Father Bob said, beginning to cry as he spoke, months after the Mass in the desert. "We called her our sister, our daughter, our child. Every migrant is dear to us. But she was everybody. She was all of those thousands of people who suffered and died."

Introduction

> We did believe that geography would be an ally
> to us. It was our sense that the number of people
> crossing the border through Arizona would go
> down to a trickle.
>
> —*Doris Meissner, commissioner of the United States*
> *Immigration and Naturalization Service, 1993 to 2000*

It was evening in Naco, Sonora. Grandmothers and grandfathers, parents and kids were out enjoying the summer air in a plaza that was *puro* Mexico. White wrought-iron benches were arranged around a red-roofed band shell, and scraggly eucalyptus trees stood in patches of dry grass. A street vendor was doing a good business selling cold *aguas frescas* (fruit drinks) and hot *elotes* (corn on the cob). Kids were chasing a friendly black dog everyone called La Negra.

Scores of outsiders also packed the plaza, but they kept themselves apart from the locals. Most of them were men, but there were a few women and even children. Dressed in dark T-shirts, jeans, and sneakers, they sat on the ground and on the low wall that ran around the plaza. They were tense, unsmiling. Taxicab drivers idled nearby.

Suddenly, as if on cue, the strangers stood up. The sun had

dropped: it was time to cross the border. They slung daypacks over their shoulders, small satchels just big enough to hold a sweatshirt and clean clothes to wear at journey's end, and maybe a prayer scrawled on a scrap of paper for luck. Then they set out, striding purposefully to the east, to the west, abandoning the plaza by the dozens. I saw one group of thirteen hurrying off together. A father carried his six-year-old daughter on his back; a mother held a year-old baby in her arms. Another woman grasped a toddler by the hand.

A few got into the waiting cabs, but most kept walking, heading for the outskirts of the little border town. A Border Patrol fence cut the town off from its sister city of Naco, Arizona, but beyond the metal barriers, in the open grasslands, only flimsy barbed wire marked the international line.

The walkers were on their way to America, crossing into Arizona.

The year was 2000, and the Arizona-Sonora line had suddenly, dramatically, become the busiest border crossing in the United States. Migrants by the hundreds of thousands were slipping across Arizona's 377-mile border with Mexico, and trying to make their way through its inhospitable deserts and mountains. They were already starting to die out there in the wilderness, on blistering summer afternoons and frigid winter nights, succumbing to exposure and dehydration, to hyperthermia—death by heat—and hypothermia—death by cold.

The same July night I watched the travelers stream out of Naco, a young man from Guatemala crossed over from Agua Prieta, the next Mexican town down the line. By noon the next day, he was dead, his body lying in the desert outside Douglas, Arizona. Silverio Huinil Vail, twenty-three, was the fifty-fifth migrant to die in the U.S. Border Patrol's Tucson Sector in 2000.

The deaths of would-be migrants in Arizona were fast becoming a public health disaster—and a humanitarian crisis. All through the 1990s, annual migrant deaths in the state could be counted on one hand, maybe two, and the few who died typically lost their lives in car accidents. Suddenly, late in the decade, the body count shot up. Dr. Bruce Parks, the Pima County medical examiner, was one of the first officials to notice. Parks handles migrant bodies recovered from two of the four Arizona border counties, Pima and Santa Cruz. In calendar year 1999, 17 migrant bodies were brought to his morgue. The next year, Parks's caseload more than tripled, to 65. By 2001 it was 75, and by 2002 it was 146. All through the decade, the deaths continued. Parks's worst year to date, 2007, yielded 218. From the time he started keeping close track in 2000, and on up through April 2009, his office had processed 1,415 migrant corpses.

Kat Rodriguez's numbers escalated just as dramatically. Kat, the activist who helped Josseline's family, collects migrant body tallies from the medical examiners in all four of Arizona's border counties, Cochise and Yuma as well as Pima and Santa Cruz. In her first year of counting, from October 2001 through September 2002, Kat documented 163 bodies found. (Like the Border Patrol, she counts by fiscal year.) The next year, 2003, she listed 205, and the year after that, it was 234. Her worst year yet was 2005, when she counted 279. Josseline was one of 183 who made Kat's list in fiscal 2008.

She's quick to point out that her numbers represent only the bodies that have been found. Others waste away in remote deserts for years, never to be found, bleached by the sun and ravaged by animals, turning to leather, then bone, then dust. The true number of deaths will never be known, but in the first decade of the new century, between October 2001 and April 2009, Rodriguez tallied 1,588 migrant bodies found in southern Arizona.

Arizona had become a killing field.

What happened?

Put simply, the United States had switched to a border policy that funneled migrants away from easy urban crossings and into the deadly Arizona outback. In the mid-1990s, undocumented migrants were pouring into California and Texas, particularly through San Diego and El Paso. Jobs in the United States were plentiful, and would-be workers from poor villages all over Mexico and Central America were slipping illegally over the line. One government study estimated that every single week, ten thousand crossers were sneaking into San Diego from Tijuana. It got so bad, signs were posted on Interstate 5 to alert motorists to migrants darting through traffic.

No one has exact numbers on how many migrants enter the United States illegally each year. Economist Judith Gans of the University of Arizona's Udall Center for Public Policy puts the number at 800,000 in peak years. The only hard data are the Border Patrol's apprehension figures—those who've been caught—but even those numbers are slippery. Many border crossers are arrested multiple times before they either give up or get through, and every arrest is counted as a separate apprehension. Even so, the San Diego numbers are revealing: in 1992 agents made more than 565,000 arrests.

Responding to the political outcry, the Clinton administration resolved to plug up the porous borders. The Hold the Line project in Texas, initiated in 1993 by an enterprising Border Patrol chief, helped tighten *la frontera* between El Paso and Ciudad Juárez. The next year, Operation Gatekeeper clamped down on San Diego, walling off the most-traveled crossing points, flooding them with stadium lights and policing them with new boots on the ground. The Arizona cities of Nogales and Douglas also got stretches of wall. The crackdown was meant to stop illegal immigration once and for all. With the cities sealed off, the countryside would take care of itself. The harsh landscape of the Southwest would serve as a natural barrier.

"We did believe that geography would be an ally to us," Doris Meissner, commissioner of the Immigration and Naturalization Service under President Clinton, told the *Arizona Republic* in 2000. "It was our sense that the number of people crossing the border through Arizona would go down to a trickle, once people realized what it's like."

Their sense was wrong, tragically wrong. The abrupt sealing of the urban crossings did not stop impoverished migrants from trying to get into the United States. It only pushed them into the wild. Migrant routes rapidly shifted to blazing Arizona, and almost overnight the Border Patrol's Tucson Sector became ground zero for illegal immigration. In 1999, agents in the sector made 380,293 arrests. The next year, when I saw the small town of Naco teeming with hopeful migrants, Tucson Sector arrests had ballooned to an astonishing 616,346. (That same year, the San Diego Sector dropped to 153,134 arrests.)

Deaths likewise skyrocketed. A federal Government Accounting Office (GAO) study found that the annual border deaths doubled in the years after Gatekeeper's launch, and Arizona accounted for most of the increase. (By one calculation, five thousand migrant bodies have been found in all the Southwest borderlands since 1994.)

The U.S. government "intentionally redirected hundreds of thousands of unauthorized migrants away from previously busy crossing points in California and Texas into Arizona's perilous and deadly landscape," a 2006 report by the Binational Migration Institute (BMI) at the University of Arizona charged. "BMI's findings unambiguously confirm previous evidence that such U.S. policies did create the 'funnel effect' and this is indeed the primary structural cause of death of thousands of North American, Central American, and South American unauthorized men, women and children who have died while trying to enter the U.S."

In 1997 Father Bob Carney, the Catholic priest who later led the desert service for Josseline, got his first glimpse of the carnage that was to come. He was the pastor at Sacred

Heart Church in Douglas, in Cochise County in southeastern Arizona.

"I was called to the border," he remembered. "The last segment of the first wall with bars had been in place less than a week. Eight young men had scaled the wall and dropped into a storm drain. There had been heavy storms to the east of us. Douglas is a low spot and there was a flash flood. All eight perished in the storm drain."

He went down to the mortuary to bless the dead, all of them teenagers or men in their early twenties. "I asked to be let in to pray, to bless the bodies so the families could find comfort. When they opened up the door to the cooler, they were all lined up, four on top, four below. All the debris and mud was still on them. I pretty much lost it. I'm not sure how good my prayer was."

The Tucson Sector of the U.S. Border Patrol stretches 262 miles along the border, from New Mexico to the Yuma County line in western Arizona. It includes the big cities of Tucson and Phoenix, but its 90,000 square miles are mostly rugged terrain. The landscape alternates between towering mountain "sky islands" and wide-open deserts. Migrants from the cool green highlands of Mexico and Central America find themselves traipsing through the Sonoran and Chihuahuan deserts, waterless wildernesses full of rocks and cacti, and crawling with scorpions and rattlesnakes. Or they hike steep trails into mountains that soar seven thousand or nine thousand feet into the sky. They swelter in temperatures up to 112 or 115 degrees on the desert floor in summer, and shiver in winter when the mercury drops below freezing.

After Gatekeeper, this dangerous landscape was under siege. In 1998 the feds launched Operation Safeguard, deploying thousands of Border Patrol agents to the Arizona borderlands. In 1999 the Tucson Sector had 1,328 armed agents.

By 2009 that number had more than doubled, to 3,300. The agents brought with them all the hardware available to a military superpower, from Black Hawk helicopters to infrared cameras, from stadium lights to unmanned aerial vehicles, to platoons of SUVs capable of off-road travel. "Battlefield management," Tucson Sector chief Robert Gilbert proudly called it in 2008.

Southern Arizonans were already reeling from throngs of migrants running through their backyards, trekking through their ranches, cutting fences, and casting off trash. Now the locals had to endure the militarization not only of the border but of their neighborhoods. Helicopters clattered overhead in the formerly tranquil countryside, and Border Patrol SUVs rumbled down the roads. Border Patrol agents began stopping citizens at will, without cause, at enforced checkpoints on the highways. They still do.

A kaleidoscope of characters roamed the borderlands at cross-purposes: *la migra* and *los inmigrantes,* international journalists, coyotes, drug smugglers, angry ranchers. Humanitarians outraged by the migrant deaths turned up to try to save lives, and Minutemen mustered "citizen patrols" to guard American territory against the foreign invasion.

The 9/11 attacks of 2001 made a volatile situation infinitely more complex. The old Immigration and Naturalization Service was subsumed into the new and ominously named Department of Homeland Security. Now the Border Patrol saw every economic refugee, every campesino and shopkeeper, as a potential terrorist.

With immigration newly defined as a threat to national security, Congress passed the REAL ID Act, allowing the secretary of Homeland Security—an unelected official—to abrogate any and all environmental laws in pursuit of homeland protection. Fragile public lands and delicate ecosystems, like the Buenos Aires National Wildlife Refuge and the San Pedro Riparian Area, had already been cut up by new roads bushwhacked by the Border Patrol, and soiled by the trash left behind by the migrants. The government began erecting walls along the border, cutting wildlife habitats in half and triggering flooding and erosion. As of June 2009, 625 miles of walls and barriers had been built along the 1,969 miles of Southwest border. Almost half of those miles were in Arizona. More than three hundred miles of wall sliced off 80 percent of the state from Sonora, its Mexican neighbor.

The hardening of the border had some unintended consequences. For years, Mexican migrants had had an easy relationship with the border, traveling north to work and then back home to visit their families. Now, unwilling to go home and risk being caught reentering, they paid traffickers to bring in their wives and children. Women began taking to the dangerous trail in growing numbers, and more women than ever before were among the migrant dead. Josseline was only one of many young women to die *en camino*, on the migrant trail. The GAO report found that the percentage of female fatalities "more than doubled from 1998 to 2005."

In turn, Arizona hardened itself against the newcomers. By 2004, Arizona had 615,000 "noncitizens"—both legal and illegal—living within its boundaries, or about 10 percent of its population of 6.3 million. Gans estimates that 400,000 to 500,000 of those noncitizens are undocumented. (Demographers believe that 11 million to 12 million undocumented residents as a whole live in the United States.) Arizona voters, enraged and overwhelmed, enacted a series of increasingly onerous propositions targeting illegal immigrants.

The 2008 Employer Sanctions Law, considered the toughest in the nation, threatened to shut down businesses that hired undocumented workers. The use of a fake Social Security number to work was converted into a felony by another new law, and any undocumented immigrant charged with a felony was denied bail. The noncitizen children of immigrants, even those who had lived most of their lives in Arizona, could no longer get in-state tuition at the three state universities. Up in Phoenix, Joe Arpaio, sheriff of Maricopa County, became notorious for his immigration sweeps of Latino neighborhoods and his nighttime raids on workplaces.

In 2008 and 2009, murderous drug wars exploded in northern Sonora. Migrant travel routes became even more dangerous, and reports of rape soared. Drug smugglers added a sideline to their marijuana trade, and moved on to the lucrative business of people smuggling. With the Border Patrol sealing up the border ever more tightly, migrants paid anywhere from $1,500 to $8,000 to human traffickers in smuggling rings.

In the wake of the economic downturn late in the decade, as jobs dried up, migration began dropping. A Mexican government study released in May 2009 found that outmigration from Mexico had tumbled by 25 percent from the previous year, and remittances—money sent home by family members working in the United States—plummeted. Economists expect that migration will pick up again when jobs open up, but even in the hard times some are still coming. In the first eight months of fiscal 2009, the Tucson Sector made 140,000 apprehensions. And in June 2009 Dr. Parks's migrant-corpse count for the first four months of the year was 39, on target to supersede his tally of 174 for all of 2008. Kat Rodriguez was up to 104 recovered bodies by mid-June 2009, counting from the fiscal year starting October 1, 2008.

"There's no easy solution to the problem of illegal immigration, nothing short-term," said Paul Hirt, an Arizona State University historian and an activist who works on environmental issues of the borderlands. "As long as people who are poor can find work in a country that's rich, they'll come."

A powerful motive drives the trips, and it's beyond the reach of U.S. immigration law. Debbi McCullough, a Tucson artist who makes mixed-media pieces out of migrant belongings dropped in the desert, asks this question in one of her sculptures: "How far would you walk to feed your children?"

This book begins with a death and ends with a birth, both in the desert. Drawn from ten years of reporting, it covers a decade of migrants crossing Arizona, zeroing in on northern Sonora and the Border Patrol's Tucson Sector. It's about the tragic journeys of migrants, and about what happens when the wretched of the earth are criminalized for their poverty, when armed agents of the state can wrench mothers from their babies, when people risk dying in order to live. It's also about the impact of immigration on communities on both sides of the border, about the devastation border enforcement wreaks on the environment, and about the ways a military occupation on American soil erodes the civil liberties and human rights of Americans and immigrants alike. One chapter looks at the precarious lives of illegal low-wage workers in Arizona; another charts the progress of a small Mexican coffee co-op that tries to keep workers at home by paying them a living wage.

I first came face to face with the migrants whose stories this book tells in the summer of 2000 when I traveled to Douglas to report on the Arizona immigration crisis for the *Tucson Weekly*. The town was a war zone, occupied by the Border Patrol and overwhelmed by migrants. Human beings were dying in the fields and in the desert, two hours away from my comfortable home in Tucson, while ordinary American life continued all around them. Agents of my own government were chasing down farmworkers and busboys and cleaning ladies with helicopters and infrared cameras, and hauling these poorest of the poor off to jail in handcuffs.

I couldn't help but connect the plight of these migrants to

my own family history. My father had died the year before, and for Saint Patrick's Day 2000 I wrote a lengthy piece for the *Weekly* on his life and family. His Irish grandparents, Timothy O'Regan and Mary Comey, had fled rural Ireland for Philadelphia in 1872. They made an arduous voyage across the Atlantic, only to watch two of their small children die, before dying themselves, in extreme poverty, in a strange city, at the ages of thirty-six and thirty-four. My orphaned grandfather, Jeremiah T. Regan, was left to raise himself on the streets. My editor gave the story the title "Up from Desperation."

I had immersed myself in this Irish immigration history just months before I drove down to Douglas. So when I met the Guatemalan man whose young cousin, Silverio, had just died in his arms, I thought of my great-grandparents' deaths in a foreign land. When I glimpsed a lone migrant purposefully trekking north through the desert, I was reminded of their determination. And when I saw brown-skinned women and children behind bars, I remembered the discrimination the Irish and other earlier immigrants suffered when they arrived in America. The stories of these new dispossessed foreigners may have been different in the details from my great-grandparents', but they were the same in all the ways that matter.

Like my forebears, these Mexicans and Central Americans had given up their homes to go where the work was. They were doing whatever they could to survive and to keep their children alive. We sometimes forget that the American immigration saga, cheerfully celebrated every Thanksgiving, does not always have a happy ending for those who risk everything to cross the sea or desert, though it may for their descendants. My great-grandparents' journey ultimately was as much a failure as Josseline's and Silverio's, but it had a saving grace. They had two children who survived them, and their own suffering gave way to a better life for their children's children and generations beyond.

CHAPTER I

Children of the Water

At this time of year they don't understand how
dangerous it is. They've never walked a long
distance in the desert. This is a death warrant.

—*Janice L. Fields, assistant to the medical examiner,*
Cochise County, Arizona

Ismael Vasquez Vasquez sat on a chair in the Border Patrol
headquarters in Douglas, squinting in the glare of the fluo-
rescent lights. It was a summer evening, but the windowless
room was freezing. Ismael trembled in the air-conditioning,
holding his arms to his chest. It was a lot colder in here than it
had been out in the desert a few hours earlier. That afternoon,
the temperature in the broad valley had topped one hundred degrees, and in the sweltering heat, his cousin, twenty-
three-year-old Silverio Huinil Vail, had died in his arms.

Ismael had spent a night and a day in the nearby Chihuahuan Desert, where mesquite thorns rip open the skin
of migrants running from la migra, where rocks trip them
up, and where the sun scorches the life right out of them.
Now, inside, the icy office was all metal and concrete. Agents
wandered casually by in their dark green pants and shirts,
guns and radios strapped to their black belts. These guys were

used to seeing undocumented migrants. Their station had been picking up six hundred every single day in Douglas and Naco during this summer season of 2000, and they had long since grown accustomed to their tragic tales.

But it was all new to Ismael. He was a campesino, a farmworker, who had lived all his life high in the forested highlands of Guatemala. In his thirty-two years, he had never felt anything like the heat of the Arizona desert. His home was in the tiny Maya village of San Francisco La Unión, seven thousand feet up in the Sierra Madre, a place of cool temperatures and abundant rainfall. His cousin Silverio was from the nearby pueblo of Santa Cruz Cajolá, a Spanish-Maya name that translates as Holy Cross–Children of the Water. San Francisco and Santa Cruz were in coffee country, ten miles from the nearest city, Quetzaltenango, so remote that even Spanish was a foreign tongue. Like many migrants trying to enter the United States, Ismael and Silverio were *indígenas*, Indians. Their first language was K'iche' Maya.

Ismael spoke quietly in Spanish, looking down dejectedly at his hands. He was cleaned up, dressed in a cap and polo shirt, but he was numb with grief over the loss of Silverio. He was the one who'd have to make the call to the family back home to tell them the younger man was dead. Then there was the matter of his own surrender earlier in the day to the Border Patrol. His arrest was more than a personal disaster. In San Francisco La Unión, he had a wife and four children—ages one, three, five, and eight—and he had hoped to pull them up out of poverty with the big wages he'd send back from America.

"I just wanted to get to the United States," he told me and photographer Héctor Acuña. We were down in Douglas to report for the *Tucson Weekly* on the immigration crisis, and Ismael had agreed to talk to us, even though he was exhausted from the day's ordeal. At home, he and his family had a small plot of land, but it yielded only enough food for them to eat, nothing extra, he said. "There's just not enough money."

No one from his village had ever made the trip to the United States that he could remember. He didn't want to go, either, but as a father with a passel of hungry kids, he didn't see that he had a choice. Anyway, he was used to hard times. When Ismael was eight years old, back in 1976, his country was ravaged by an earthquake. *El terremoto* was a natural disaster, no one's fault, but it was followed in the 1980s by a human-made disaster. The government had waged a bloody counterinsurgency campaign against its own people, leaving more than one hundred thousand dead or disappeared. By 2000, the year of Ismael's epic journey, there was no more war in Guatemala. But there was no money either.

The cousins made their way out of the mountains slowly, on buses overstuffed with passengers and bundles and squawking chickens. Descending through narrow passes, they rode northwest into Mexico, through Chiapas and on into Oaxaca. Past Mexico City and central Mexico they traveled, and on into Chihuahua and finally Sonora, changing buses all along the way. It took them twenty-five days to go the 2,750 miles to the Arizona line. The two Guatemalans were never beaten up on the road, as migrants often are, but the Mexican police shook them down for money every chance they got.

Once in Agua Prieta—"dark water"—the ragtag factory town across from Douglas, the cousins found themselves in a throng of migrants trying to cross la frontera. Ray Borane was the mayor of Douglas then (in 2009 he joined the Southwest Border Task Force as an adviser to Homeland Security secretary Janet Napolitano). In that busy summer of 2000, he estimated that on any given day, anywhere from two thousand to three thousand would-be crossers congregated in his town's Mexican sister city. Like the rest, Ismael and Silverio stayed at a flea-bitten flophouse, one of the grandly named casas de huéspedes that rented out floor space or a dirty mattress for the night. They connected with a coyote in the central plaza in front of Iglesia Sagrada Corazón, a white mission-style church named for the Sacred Heart. The smuggler's underling, a *pollero*—"chicken wrangler"—would guide them over the border fence and then through the Arizona desert. A van would be waiting to drive them deep into America. If all went well—a big if—and if their coyote fulfilled his end of the bargain—another big if—the Guatemalan pair could walk to a road and the ride within about five miles. Ismael had no idea of their final destination. "Maybe Los Angeles," he said vaguely.

Five miles sounded like a cinch to young men without cars who had walked miles over the mountains all their lives. They started out at about 7 p.m. on Wednesday, July 19, 2000, in a group of about twenty-five people. Their first hurdle was the border wall in the center of Douglas; its vertical iron bars were fourteen feet high. Spaced a couple of inches apart, the bars allowed breezes to pass through and afforded residents on International Avenue a crosshatched view of Mexico. Painted a pale peach, the fence was meant, halfheartedly, to be attractive. Borane said the government even called it the "aesthetic fence." But for the Douglas homeowners sitting on their porches and in their gardens, the wall looked like prison bars.

Just beyond the central city, though, all pretense of beauty disappeared. The fence was made of sheet metal colored the purples and rusts of a bruise. The sharp-edged panels were military discards, flats that had once been used as helicopter landing pads in the deserts of Kuwait and the jungles of Vietnam. But in the ranch country east and west of town, barbed wire strung between fence posts was the only barrier. A guide wearing gloves could hold open a few strands while the walkers, one by one, did a border limbo, bending over and stepping between the wires. (By 2008 the barbed wire had been replaced by an intimidating wall of metal and concrete.)

The fence wasn't the only military hardware to be negotiated by Ismael, Silverio, and company. High-intensity lights, cameras, and infrared sensors cast Uncle Sam's eye on both sides of the border. Miles out into the desert, mobile surveillance towers were equipped with more of the same. And every few hundred yards along the fence, a Border Patrol agent sat in a big white SUV, his binoculars trained on the line.

No matter. The migrants had already traveled too far, and invested too much, to be deterred. They managed to sneak through the fence undetected and then began the nighttime hike. The land around Douglas is flat, making it attractive to crossers, but it's hazardous. If walkers don't trip on the rocks, they can crash into tree branches or brush their hands against needle-sharp cacti. Ismael's group did get a piece of good luck in the weather. There was a light cloud cover in the evening and even a sprinkling of rain. Yet shortly after beginning their trek *en el otro lado,* "on the other side," Silverio fell ill.

"We were only out one hour and he started to feel bad," Ismael remembered. "He was tired and we sat down to rest." The group didn't bother waiting. The smuggler and the rest went on, abandoning the cousins to the darkness. Survival of the fittest is the typical coyote MO, as Josseline's family would learn years later. Polleros hustle the travelers to walk fast, even run, and the weak are left behind. Ismael shook his head at the memory. "I had no idea I'd be left," he said. Fortunately, the cousins had paid no money upfront. The guide fee was strictly cash-on-delivery.

The two Guatemalans struggled along on their own. The temperatures were moderate during the night, but by midday Thursday the hundred-degree heat and monsoon's humidity had become unbearable. There was *mucho calor,* Ismael said—"a lot of heat"—and Silverio collapsed. Ismael hoisted him onto his back and tried to make his way back to Mexico. But it was hopeless.

Silverio began to have *dolor de corazón*, Ismael said, clutching his own chest to demonstrate his cousin's heart pain. And *dolor de brazos*, he added, gripping his arms. He laid the young man on the ground and held him, until finally, simply, painfully, Silverio died. It was one month to the day since his twenty-third birthday.

Ismael could have left the body in the dirt and gone on alone. Maybe he could have found his pollero and managed to get past Phoenix, where the Border Patrol presence almost disappears. He didn't, though. Going for help would guarantee his own capture, but Silverio was family. Ismael had to make sure his cousin's body made it home to his parents in Santa Cruz Cajolá. And he was in no condition himself to continue the trek. Overcome with grief, overwhelmed by the heat, Ismael was having chest pains of his own.

He trudged a mile out to the road. Local residents were out driving, going shopping, picking up the kids, oblivious to the tragedy playing out in the nearby fields. He didn't have long to wait for la migra. Border Patrol vehicles were a constant on the roads around Douglas. Ten years later it's quieter, but in 2000, on one twenty-minute drive from Douglas to Bisbee, Héctor and I counted seven vigilant Border Patrol SUVs parked roadside or hurtling toward still another capture. It was a rare drive that we didn't see a migrant being cuffed.

The agents took Ismael to the hospital, where he was treated for dehydration. After the nurses pumped a couple bags of IV fluids back into him, he was returned to Border Patrol custody. Six hours later, huddled up at the Douglas station, he appeared healthy. Silverio's body had been recovered. Following his cousin's directions, the agents had hiked into the brush and carried him back out. They drove to the nearby military town of Sierra Vista, and dispatched his corpse to the Cochise County morgue.

An autopsy conducted later by Dr. Guery Flores, the county medical examiner, determined that he had been "a very healthy young man," said Janice L. Fields, Flores's assistant. Silverio was robust, with a "well-developed musculoskeletal system." Had he not tried to cross the desert, he wouldn't have died. "The cause of death was exposure," Fields went on. "It doesn't take any time at all in the desert." Chest pains mimicking a heart attack are a common symptom of dehydration, she explained, and sighed. "Unfortunately, yes, we've had a lot of these [deaths]. At this time of year they don't understand how dangerous it is. They've never walked a long distance in the desert. This is a death warrant."

The noontime death of Silverio Huinil Vail was announced at Border Patrol headquarters at the 2 p.m. roll call. Dozens of agents, the boys in green, as the locals called them, listened soberly to the report that a migrant—in patrol parlance, a UDA, undocumented alien—had just died. But the supervisor quickly moved on from Huinil's tragedy to the more mundane matter of shift assignments. The agents had ranches to scour, streets to screen, captives to process.

Buses were pulling up to the station with the last hour's yield, and prisoners were being herded by the dozens into jail cells. Tired, dirty, and thirsty from their time outside, they were dressed in the dark clothes they had put on in the vain hope of eluding detection. They sat together on benches in the crowded cells, shoulders slumped and gulping water. Metal sheeting covered three walls of their sex-segregated cells; the fourth wall, open to the agents' watchful eyes, had Cyclone fencing instead of prison bars. The impression of humans in cages was inescapable. Many had been captured before, and they knew the routine: they would be fingerprinted and photographed, their data entered into a computer, and then released. Most of them would be bused back to the border before long, free to try the crossing again.

Eliseo Marques Trejo, twenty-five, from Querétaro, a pretty colonial city north of Mexico City, had been caught twice in three days, he told us. He wanted to live in the United States, because "la vida aquí es mejor." *Life is better here.*

Through no fault of its own, Douglas, a town of fourteen thousand souls, had become a pedestrian highway for Eliseo, Ismael, and all the others in the great migration of 2000. (The Tucson Sector made a staggering 616,346 arrests that fiscal year.) The town sits in a wide-open valley between the Huachuca Mountains on the west and the Perillas on the east. Two good Mexican roads, east-west Highway 2 and north-south Highway 17, connect Agua Prieta to every point in Mexico, and from Agua Prieta, it's just a hop over the wall and a skip to Douglas's flat grasslands. If it weren't for the little matter of the torrid Chihuahuan Desert, it would be the perfect place for a hike north.

Once upon a time, Douglas was a busy smelter town, melting down the copper mined in nearby hills on both sides of the border. Phelps Dodge, the mining company, shut down the last of the two smelters in 1987. Since then the biggest thing going had been the west-side Wal-Mart, where day-tripping Mexican shoppers stocked up on cheap goods. Then, without warning, the dusty little town became center stage for an international immigration drama.

"Obviously the Tucson Sector is the busiest sector in the nation," Border Patrol spokesman Rob Daniels said that crazy summer of 2000. And "the most active points in the country are at Douglas."

It was impossible to ignore the Border Patrol SUVs barreling around the city streets, the helicopters whirling overhead, the planes swooping through the sky, the agents positioned around town, keeping a close watch on everything and everyone that moved. The bright lights and noise kept townsfolk awake at night, and some said they could hear migrants hurrying past their houses in the dark. Hundreds of Ismaels and Silverios were clambering over fences, running through backyards, trekking through ranches outside town. Local ranchers were up in arms, some of them literally, over what they saw as an invasion of migrants trespassing on their lands, cutting wire fences, leaving trash and plastic water bottles behind. One rancher, Roger Barnett, had begun rounding up migrants at gunpoint and holding them until the Border Patrol arrived.

Migrant deaths were becoming so commonplace that they "don't even make the headlines here," said Linda Morales, a social worker in Naco, Douglas's nearest neighbor to the west. One day after Huinil's death, the *Douglas Dispatch* ran a page-one piece on the Border Patrol. Headlined "Bees Attack Border Patrol Agents," the story detailed the misfortunes of a clutch of agents-in-training who'd accidentally encountered a swarm of Africanized bees. The article never mentioned a Guatemalan dying in the desert north of town.

Most of 2000's dead, like those every year in the decade since, died of exposure and dehydration. Nine were killed in accidents, mostly rollovers on Arizona's secondary highways; two drowned. Five were ruled homicides. Most of those victims had suffocated after being squeezed into vans by their coyotes. One migrant would be piled atop the next until the bottommost migrant had the breath squeezed out of him.

Silverio, number fifty-five for the year, wasn't the last of the July casualties. Days after he died, on the twentieth, three more migrants perished. Two were found on Monday, July 24, one near Sasabe, a tiny border settlement in the Sonoran Desert 120 miles west of Douglas, the other in Organ Pipe Cactus National Monument, a furnace-like wilderness preserve 200 miles west. A week later, on Thursday, July 27, the decomposed body of a man was found near Three Points, a cowboy town west of Tucson. The three new fatalities pushed the Tucson Sector toll up to fifty-eight deaths. With two months left to go in the fiscal year, the total was already double the twenty-nine deaths in the sector for the whole of fiscal 1999 by the Border Patrol's tally.

If some border residents—and reporters—had grown inured to the carnage, plenty of Arizona residents found it appalling. Already in 2000 activists were arguing that U.S. border policy was causing the deaths of desperate economic refugees. Up in Tucson, Lupe Castillo, an activist with Derechos Humanos and a history professor at Pima Community College, blamed the carnage on the clampdown on the Texas and California borders. The blockade there, she said, "forc[ed] people into forbidding areas."

David Aguilar, then chief of the Tucson Sector, proclaimed the strategy to contain San Diego and El Paso a big success. "We sealed the border in San Diego," he said proudly in 2000. (A few years later, he was promoted out of the Tucson Sector and shifted on up to Washington, D.C., to head the Border Patrol nationwide.) Aguilar read the deaths differently.

The fatalities were the fault not of government policy but of smugglers, the coyotes and polleros despised by agents and activists alike. They were the ones callously leading migrants into danger and abandoning them when trouble hit. The story of Silverio, he noted, followed this precise pattern.

"Smugglers manage about 90 percent of the immigrants," Aguilar said. In response, in 1998, the Border Patrol had initiated Operation Safeguard to beef up enforcement in Arizona. Safeguard, he said confidently, is "denying smugglers the use of our communities as staging areas."

Mayor Ray Borane wasn't buying it. "This policy is not working," he told me angrily in his office the day after Silverio Huinil Vail died. "They're forcing people to go into the desert and lose their lives."

A popular Democrat who had recently won reelection, Borane was critical of the Clinton administration, which formulated a border policy that would endure all the way through the presidency of George W. Bush, becoming more militaristic, more punitive, as the years wore on. "We're solely doing border enforcement. Our only option is more-more."

He didn't want to knock the Border Patrol, but with Operation Safeguard in full swing he'd seen the number of agents in his town increase geometrically. The Douglas station had 58 agents in 1994, 200 in 1998, and 450 in 2000. "Absolutely, it's an occupied town," Borane said. "It's like a militarized zone."

The mayor thought he'd figured out a reasonable solution. He was an early proponent of a legalized guest-worker program, an idea that was heard often over the following decade. Opposed by labor on the left and anti-immigration activists on the right, it became a component of the doomed federal immigration reform bill of 2007. Obviously, Borane said, it would have to be better managed than the exploitative bracero program of a half-century ago, when workers were cheated of their wages. In a *New York Times* op-ed piece, he'd written that the United States should increase the number of work visas to match the demand for workers.

"I walk over to Agua Prieta and sit in the park or restaurants and just strike up a conversation [with people waiting to cross]," said the bilingual Borane, a Douglas native whose own grandfather was a Lebanese immigrant with "illegal" status his whole adult life. "They want to work. They want to send money to their families."

If there were no jobs for the migrants in the United States, they wouldn't be coming, he pointed out. Undocumented workers are heavily concentrated in the service industry, making beds in hotels and busing restaurant tables. They clean homes and offices, work in construction, pick fruit in orchards and crops in fields. They pack chickens in factories in the Southeast and butcher animals in the meat-packing plants of the Midwest.

The economic implosion of 2009 threatened many of these jobs, particularly in new-home construction, and migrant numbers dipped accordingly. But in 2000, the economy was humming, with so much work available that worker shortages were a problem. Isabel Garcia, a Tucson attorney and an activist with Derechos Humanos, argued that, in a hot economy, "we need their labor."

But the nation doesn't make it easy for them to get to those low-paying jobs. If they can get to the border, hop the fence, slip through a superpower's military arsenal, elude armed ranchers, drink enough water to outlast a desert trek, cough up enough money for a coyote, maybe they'll be rewarded with a job cleaning toilets in a motel. If they're really lucky, they might even get minimum wage.

Garcia put it this way: "We say to them, 'Yes, come through this deadly obstacle course and we'll employ you.'"

Agent Edmundo Erik Moncayo was one small hurdle in that obstacle course. A Mexican American who grew up in El Paso, by 2000, Edmundo had been holding the line at Douglas as a Border Patrol agent for five years. He was a supervisor, a working agent, and an information specialist. One of his many jobs was escorting reporters, like Héctor and me, who wanted to ride shotgun on a Border Patrol shift.

He'd had a busy summer. The international media had descended on Douglas, attracted not only by the record migrant deaths but also by the Wild West stories of armed ranchers like Roger Barnett. The BBC had been in town and so had CNN, as well as a Knight-Ridder reporter based in Mexico City and a trio of German magazine journalists. Assorted press from American dailies, newsmagazines, and television had also made the pilgrimage.

By July, intensive outreach had calmed most of the ranchers down, Edmundo said. (Barnett would get into some legal trouble a few years later, after apprehending some Mexican American citizens hunting on his land.) "We have a unit patrolling the ranches, the Ranch Patrol. Part of it is enforcement, part of it is liaison. We ask them, 'Are there problems?'"

Some community cleanups had also helped ease the ranchers' complaints of litter on their land. Discarded plastic water bottles marked the migrant trails all around Douglas; even a casual glance roadside uncovered dozens of empties. Cows are not exactly discerning. They'll eat almost anything, including plastic, and the sharp edges of the chewed containers can tear up their innards. Fleeing migrants leave behind food cans, backpacks, and clothes too, a yellow sweatshirt encrusted with dirt here, a pair of brown kneesocks there.

Edmundo was an expert on the military hardware, and on the maneuvers that so upset activists and civil libertarians, and had critic Lupe Castillo declaring, "We are using low-intensity warfare techniques along the border."

The Constitution, Edmundo said by way of a joke, has an "asterisk" for the border. If elsewhere the Bill of Rights prevents unreasonable searches and seizures, in the borderlands the Border Patrol can legally enter anyone's land—but not buildings—without a warrant. In their search for migrants, they can set up checkpoints along the road, stopping any and all drivers without probable cause.

At headquarters, Edmundo showed off a bank of computer screens, each displaying images from the Border Patrol surveillance cameras all over town. We could see people's front yards and backyards and walkers wandering the Douglas streets. And far out in the desert he took us up into a surveillance tower. Its long pole bent in half at a giant elbow, gently bringing the little tower room to the ground. We stepped inside and rode it back up to the sky, the better to see the land all around. An infrared camera on top transmitted images to a computer screen inside. The pictures were in negative—dark scrub at night becomes light—and hot bodies showed up brilliantly. On this particular day, only a cat, a deer, and some jackrabbits, but no humans, could be seen making their way across the desert.

As knowledgeable as Edmundo was about the hardware taxpayers had been buying for his remote border station, he was positively brilliant when it came to old-fashioned tracking. On the afternoon of Silverio's death, while we were driving around with him on patrol, a call came over his radio. A rancher had spotted twenty migrants making their way across her property, in the ranch country east of town.

We were off on the chase. Edmundo steered his SUV expertly into a dirt road cutting through the ranch in question, stopped to confer with another agent who was on foot, and then swung around to the east. He got out and crouched to examine footprints in the dust. Suddenly he was on hyperalert. "See these footprints?" he asked excitedly. "You can see that they're fresh. They're different from the ones made this morning."

He strode off into the high desert grass, intently following tracks that were barely discernible to a less practiced eye. And then, in an instant, he was gone. He was in the brush somewhere, but he was invisible, as if the earth had swallowed him up. Later we learned that he'd jumped soundlessly into a dry streambed sheltered by mesquites. He followed the tracks around the bend in the creek, and suddenly came upon no fewer than twenty-three migrants who'd just dropped their weary bones for a rest. The cry went out: "¡La migra!" They scattered into the desert, dropping a trail of sweatshirts, water, potato chips. Héctor and I, doing a little tracking of our own, came upon the discards minutes later. One man had lost a small leatherette case. Inside was a pair of eyeglasses, some stomach medicine, and several printed prayers. An *Oración a San Cristóbal*, prayer to St. Christopher, patron saint of travelers, had been hand-sewn—by a wife? a mother?—into a paper cover.

Edmundo's romp through the desert lasted almost two hours. He was running in the heat the whole time, along with a team of fellow agents he'd summoned. These guys were fit, but they caught only a dozen of the migrants. Nine got away, vanishing into the trees, but the agents picked up a consolation prize. Deep in the field, they happened upon three bales of marijuana—a whopping 131 pounds—so dried out, they concluded it had been baking out in the desert for a week.

Héctor and I were convinced that Edmundo had ditched us. He showed up laughing, exclaiming, "You guys missed the whole thing!" But a few things had happened in the field while he was gone. Before he came back, we had stopped by the arroyo one more time. We could tell that a migrant had been there in the last few minutes. He had taken a blue sweatshirt that had been left behind by his fleeing countrymen, and helped himself to their abandoned jugs of water. When we scanned the horizon, we could see him in the distance, a slow, steady, determined figure, trudging alone to the North.

It was a long shift for Edmundo, from 2 to 10 p.m., and he was never anything less than unflappable. He didn't stop for dinner, eating only a couple of snacks he picked up at a Circle K, adding only a few dollars of his federal pay to local coffers. He prowled relentlessly through town in the dark, shining his lights in gutters, in bushes, looking in the shadows at the dull edge of the Wal-Mart with the same single-mindedness that had powered his adventurous dash through the desert. Late in the evening, swinging by International Street downtown, he didn't flinch when three sassy Mexican boys dropped down over the wall in plain view and taunted him from across a ditch, shaking their hips provocatively and calling out "Fuck you." He stared them down silently until they scampered back over the border. He was just as stoic back at the office that evening when he impassively listened to Ismael tell us the sad saga of Silverio.

"Not to sound jaded," he sighed afterwards, "but I've heard the stories so often I can tell them before they do." The tales are always the same: "I just want to work, I want to feed my kids, I'd rather stay home but I don't have a choice."

Edmundo is a native Spanish speaker, so he easily aced the Spanish requirement at the Border Patrol academy. And he grew up along the Texas border, where the feared migra is part and parcel of song and folklore. As the night grew late, I asked a question I'd been pondering all day. What's it like for a Mexican American to spend his days chasing Mexicans through the brush? To work for la migra?

"I used to get more of a reaction," he admitted. "Not so much anymore. My mother was a little upset at first but I think she was more worried about my being in law enforcement than anything else. I'm just doing a job."

The evening before Silverio's death, Gabriel Hernández Cortez, a twenty-four-year-old from Guanajuato in central Mexico, stood in the central plaza in Naco, Sonora, watching migrants depart for the border. He had already been over the line four times, and four times he'd been caught. He wasn't going to join the hordes of crossers again until he nailed down a plan for a friend to pick him up on the other side, he told Héctor and me. One time Gabriel had gotten four kilometers into the United States, but he got caught as he was scrambling through a barbed-wire fence. An agent dragged him back by his hair, and the barbs ripped open his leg. He pulled up a pants leg, proffering a twelve-inch scar on his calf as proof. He shrugged off the injury. "I don't blame la migra. They're just doing their jobs, enforcing the laws that come down from above."

Gabriel had been living in the open in the plaza for four months, sleeping on the hard pavement in a blanket that he shared with a buddy, Juan Antonio Perez Hernández, a thirty-six-year-old from Chihuahua. The pair was mis-matched, Gabriel small and Juan Antonio tall, and the Guanajuatan jokingly shaked and shimmied to show how they played tug-of-war with the blanket at night. Juan Antonio could easily top his friend's border-hopping tales. He boasted of twenty crossings and just six captures, but he had no scars to show. La migra had never hurt him.

The men didn't like the so-called hospitality houses of Naco: too expensive, too dangerous. For five dollars you'd get the privilege of putting your blanket down on the concrete floor, and you'd get no food. Some other migrants had told us that the night before they were robbed at gunpoint in a *casa de huéspedes*. But the open plaza had its own dangers. The same night as the casa robbery, another migrant got angry at Gabriel and stabbed him with a sharp stick. The new wound festered alongside the old barbed-wire scar. "You never know who's going to be drunk," he said. The police occasionally locked up the troublemakers, or hit the migrants up for a *mordida*, a bribe, but mostly they left them alone.

Héctor and I invited Gabriel and Juan Antonio to take a taco in Naco at a taquería, an establishment of orange Formica tabletops and jukebox pop. The pair dug into some carne asada, the classic Mexican dish of roasted beef chunks, and gobbled up the condiments of onion and cucumber, laughing at their own hunger. They refused a second helping, grandly explaining that they didn't want to get used to too much food.

Gradually their life stories came out. Juan Antonio had a wife and two children, ages ten and twelve, back home in Chihuahua, the Mexican state southwest of Texas, but he had plans to join a sister living in Phoenix. He wanted to work in construction, a booming business in those days of the housing bubble.

The gregarious Gabriel also was married, with two kids. He had his heart set on Salem, Oregon. Back in Guanajuato, he had been earning about four dollars a day in construction. A fifth-grade dropout, he'd been working since he was eleven or twelve. One of five children of a cabdriver, the entrepreneurial young Gabriel and his fifteen-year-old brother secretly started their own commercial enterprise.

"We decided to drop out of school and start a little business selling popsicles," he related in Spanish. "We did it on our own and kept it from our papí. We gave the money to our mother. It was quite a while before our father found out. He finally realized there were no more school expenses. Papí said, 'Great. You can start buying your own shoes and clothes.'"

When he was seventeen and she was fifteen, Gabriel ran away with his future wife, Carolina. They married a few years later and now had two boys, Juan Pedro, four, and Carlos Ernesto, two. The year before, little Carlos had fallen seriously ill and had to be hospitalized. Though the baby recovered, the crisis ruined the family financially. The bill, Gabriel said, came to about $650. He had to sell everything they owned. Carolina and the kids moved back in with her parents, and he struck out for the border.

"If I could do anything, if I were president, I'd improve the quality of jobs in Mexico," he declared. "I prefer to stay home. But the only way to make it is to come north." There's an imbalance, he said, in the relations between the United States and Mexico. "Americans are free to cross the border at will, but it doesn't work the other way around. They're friendly tourists here, but as soon as I cross the border it's a different story. I just want a very tiny slice of pie. I just want to work for a little bit of money." *Poquitos dólares.*

He would have liked a guest-worker program that allowed him to come across safely and work in peace until he had enough money to change his family's fortunes. He was not unaware of the dangers of la frontera. That was why he was here without his wife and little boys. "I prefer to do the suffering part on my own."

The armed Douglas ranchers had gotten plenty of publicity in Mexico, but Gabriel only scoffed. "I'm not afraid of anything. I'm going to be the Mexican Rambo." His quiet friend, Juan Antonio, was more matter of fact: "I'm afraid of getting shot."

Unbeknownst to the four of us, at the same time we were dining on tacos that evening, Silverio and Ismael were setting out to cross into Arizona. We had no way of knowing that one of the young Guatemalans would die in the desert the next day. In any case, both Gabriel and Juan Antonio seemed indifferent to warnings about the desert's deadly heat. Their concerns were more immediate. "People don't have fear in them when they try to go across," Gabriel explained. "The deaths happen because the guides lie to them....I don't worry about it. You worry about the basic struggles. What will I eat for breakfast?"

Gabriel knew that the United States had deployed a vast arsenal to catch him when he came. He wasn't worried about that either. He would play David to the Border Patrol's Goliath. "They can send out millions of Border Patrol agents, but Mexicans can still get across. I'm going to break their cameras with my slingshot."

Juan Antonio and Gabriel and all the rest kept the Tucson Sector Border Patrol busy in the coming days. As Héctor and I drove northwest out of town on Route 80, we saw still another roadside arrest: three SUVs idling, one airplane circling, three agents running. The target of this costly military mission was one very sweaty, overweight Mexican man stumbling through a field. We watched for a few minutes, but it was not long before the agents caught him. They cuffed his hands behind his back with plastic tubing and escorted him back to the road. "Buenas tardes," he said to the officer at the vehicle, nodding politely. Thirsty from the chase and his day in the sun, he asked for water: "Agua, por favor." But there was none to be had. Equipped as the agents were with airplanes and guns and sensors of all kinds, they had no water to spare. The thirsty captive would have to wait. Only back at the office, the agent said, would there be water.

North of Tombstone, site of the famous 1881 shootout at the O.K. Corral, the Border Patrol struck migrant gold. A road construction project happened to be stopping traffic in both directions. The coyotes were apparently unaware of this disconcerting development, and the agents were arresting their human cargo by the vanload. By four in the afternoon, two hundred travelers had been pulled out of dangerously overloaded vans, an agent on the road told us. (He wouldn't give his name. "Call me ZZ Top," he said.) We had stopped to look at a van that had disgorged twenty-three people. As vacationers zoomed by on the scenic road, soaking up the Old West vibe, the captured migrants huddled in the van's shadow, trying to stay out of the fierce July sun. They'd been tied together with plastic tubing. The agent had had a little water, but his prisoners were so parched they'd already drunk it all. They'd have to wait to get to headquarters for more.

One of the prisoners had something of the swagger of Gabriel Hernández Cortez. He had a big name, too, and he wrote it in my notebook: Ronal Estuardo Donado. Showing true western grit, he'd walked in the searing desert two days before he picked up his ride near Bisbee, north of Douglas. The van had been en route to Phoenix, and everybody was to pay $800 to the coyote upon arrival. Two hundred more people, he said, were waiting in the hills nearby for rides right now. There would be more the next day, and the next.

Estuardo grinned.

"There's thousands more waiting to come," he said.

———

Until a week after his death, Silverio remained officially unidentified, an anonymous foreigner in cold storage. On the morning of July 26, the Cochise County medical examiner received a notarized letter that had been typed in the office of the mayor of Santa Cruz Cajolá. A local family, the mayor wrote, was certifying that the body being held in faraway Arizona was that of their son, twenty-three-year-old Silverio Huinil Vail, born June 20, 1977. His parents had received the terrible news of his death in a phone call from a cousin traveling with him. They called the Cochise County sheriff to confirm it, and then walked to the office of the mayor—home of the village's only typewriter—to record their relationship to their son in black and white. The mayor enclosed an ID photo of a young man. It matched up with the victim the medical examiner had seen. With Silverio's body having been brought in within an hour of his death, Janice Fields noted, "he was very identifiable."

The grief of Silverio's family was compounded by financial catastrophe. Instead of receiving the young man's wages, his parents had to pay to have his body shipped back to Guatemala for burial. A short time later, after he was sent home, he was laid to rest in Santa Cruz Cajolá, the village of the Children of Water. Dead of exposure and dehydration in the parched desert, Silverio was buried among the rivers that flow down the mountain slopes.

Ismael Vasquez Vasquez was taken to Florence, Arizona, an hour and a half north of Tucson, to a federal detention center that in those pre-9/11 days was still run by the old Immigration and Naturalization Service. Most Mexicans captured trying to come across waive their right to a hearing before an immigration judge, and within twenty-four hours are "voluntarily returned" across the border. Not so for other foreign nationals. The reasoning is that if you drop a Guatemalan or an El Salvadoran across the line in Agua Prieta, he's so far from home that you're almost guaranteeing he'll try again, and hop the fence into the United States. Mexico doesn't want wayfaring foreigners, either.

Ismael was detained in Florence, then deported, flown back home to the extravagantly beautiful, extravagantly poor highlands of Guatemala, his American journey a disastrous failure.

CHAPTER 2

Strangers in Their Own Land

To leave our land is to suffer.

—*Eduardo Perez Verdugo, migrant from Chiapas, Mexico*

Hugo Cifuentes, a baby-faced nineteen-year-old from Chiapas, barely broke a sweat as he leaned over a coffee roaster in Agua Prieta, just across the border from Douglas.

"It's hot but bearable," he said cheerfully in Spanish. Hot was right. He was tipping coffee beans into a roaster that had been heated up to 466 degrees. But the warmth inside the small roasting room felt good on this late December day in 2006. Outside, the sky over the rundown town was overcast and the air was brisk. Hugo was cooking up a forty-pound batch of beans for Café Justo, a co-op owned and run by coffee-growing families from Chiapas, a Mexican state so far south it's practically in Guatemala. Pots of coffee were percolating in the next room, and between the beans and the brew, the rich aroma of joe was everywhere.

Café Justo's roasting and bagging operation is in Agua Prieta, and the other Chiapanecos who work there—Hugo's father, Noë, included—were about to pile into a van and drive some twenty-one hundred miles home to their village of Salvador Urbina for a post-Christmas visit. Somebody had to stay in Agua Prieta and mind the fire, and that some-body was Hugo.

"I hope to go home around Holy Week," he said, shrug-ging.

For twelve minutes, his coffee beans spun slowly—and noisily—around and around inside the *tostadora*. His father got burned once, so Hugo always put on big oven-proof gloves before reaching in to stir the beans. When the green beans had turned a rich brown, he turned the flame down and allowed cool air to blow in.

Once the beans had cooled, Hugo would grind some up, and pour others whole into the shiny gold Café Justo bags, depending on what the business's American customers had ordered. Each of the bags was labeled with the name of the Salvador Urbina grower who'd raised that particular batch of beans. Cifuentes laughed when he looked over the names: Manuel Cifuentes. Hernán Cifuentes. Reinaldo Cifuentes.

"Mis tíos," he said. *My uncles.*

The name Juan Carlos Perez stood out from the sea of Cifuenteses. Perez was a cousin.

"Thirty-five families from Chiapas are in the co-op," Hugo explained. "They're not all my family, but a lot of them are."

With his spiky gelled hair and striped T-shirt, Hugo looked like a typical teenager, but his bio is unlike the aver-age American kid's. He started working in his family's coffee fields as a twelve- or thirteen-year-old, a common age for a Mexican farm boy to take to the family trade. After coffee prices started tumbling, he came up by bus from Chiapas in 2003 at age sixteen, and moved in with a sister who had al-ready come north to work. Until the roasting job came along, he spent his days making blinds in a maquiladora in Agua Prieta.

The *maquilas*—American factories set up south of the border—are a sweet deal for the U.S. companies. They import their raw materials tariff-free into Mexico, pay low wages to the workers who assemble their products, then ship the finished goods duty-free into the United States, right next door. To be sure, the maquila pay is good by Mexican standards. The Mexican minimum wage is 45 pesos a day, about $3.50 in U.S. dollars. But maquila workers regularly earn bonuses, for meeting production goals and so on, that double the minimum, bringing their pay up to about 90 pesos a day, or the equivalent of $7. Wages at Café Justo were a lot better than at the blinds factory: the coffee company paid Hugo three and half times as much, around $25 a day. "It's better," he said. "This is a good job."

Hugo paid a price for those high wages, though. Agua Prieta, a desert city of 120,000, is nothing like his tiny mountain village of 7,000. Hemmed in by the metal border wall on the north and teeming with trapped migrants waiting to cross it, Agua Prieta is crowded and drab. Dirt roads meander up the hills, and in the poorer parts of town—like the barrio where Café Justo is located—the makeshift cinderblock houses seem ready to tumble down into the yards. A.P. is in the Chihuahuan Desert; it's lucky if it gets a foot of rain a year. Back home in Salvador Urbina, the climate is temperate, and twelve feet of rain pours down the lush mountains each and every year. The village nestles into the slopes of Tacaná, a volcano that climbs almost thirteen thousand feet into the clouds. Tacaná is so big and so wide that its eastern side descends into Guatemala, not fifty miles from the village where Silverio Huinil Vail lies buried. "There are lots of trees," Hugo told me wistfully. "I'd rather live in Chiapas, but I like living here."

He missed his mother terribly, he said; he hadn't seen her in the three years since he'd moved north. My own son, Will, a college student the same age as Hugo, was home for Christmas and had come with me on the trip. Hugo eyed the pair of us enviously and asked, "Is that your son?" At least Hugo had *some* family in Agua Prieta. In an apartment adjoining the business, in the hilltop barrio of Pueblo Nuevo, he lived with his dad, who'd come up two years before. His uncle Daniel Cifuentes and aunt Victoria, and their little son, Danielito, crowded into the space with them.

Anyway, roasting coffee in a small business was a lot better than hammering out blinds in a big factory. Plus, Hugo knew that the operation was keeping his extended family and neighbors at home on their own farms, earning a living wage. He was proud of the work they did.

"We're from Chiapas," he said. "We know coffee."

Any day of the week, young men like Hugo Cifuentes come to Agua Prieta. They ride the bus up from Mexico's impoverished southern states—Chiapas, Veracruz, Oaxaca—in hopes of hopping the fence *al Norte,* "to the North." And then there are the migrants going back in the other direction. They're headed, unwillingly, south into Mexico, their northerly journeys cut short by a little Border Patrol intervention.

One Sunday in October 2008, almost two years after I watched Hugo roast the coffee beans, I was back in Agua Prieta. The Border Patrol had just dropped off its latest catch. Summer's heat had eased into autumn balm, but the morning sun was still bright enough to make a stream of migrants blink as they walked back across the border.

About a dozen men, most of them young, trudged along, more than a few of them joking and laughing about their failed attempt to make it into the United States. They walked past the long line of cars waiting at the U.S. port of entry to drive into Douglas, past the trinket sellers offering up plastic Virgins of Guadalupe, past the kids darting around selling Chiclets.

With its brightly painted stores, *panaderías* (bakeries) and *tienditas* (snack shops), lined up in dense rows, the noisy

Mexican streetscape must have felt like home to the travelers. It was a world away from sleepy Douglas on the other side, with its deserted downtown and vast chain-store parking lots.

The men's first stop back in Mexico was the Migrant Resource Center, an aid station run by volunteers in a small storefront just steps from the border. Here migrants can chow down on a free bean burrito, and get directions to a men's shelter in the nearby Catholic church, Sagrada Familia, or to a women and children's shelter run by the government. Volunteers fill them in on ways to get home. They can get half the bus fare home from Grupo Beta de Protección a Migrantes, a federal aid agency. If they're in really bad shape, the Mexican consul over in Douglas might spring for a bus ticket at full fare.

Carlos Ortiz, twenty-seven, a Mexican deportee originally from León, wasn't sure what to do. He was still wearing the Chevron shirt he'd had on when he was arrested on the job in Seattle the week before. As he chomped down on a burrito, he explained that the Americans had flown him to El Paso and dumped him into dangerous Ciudad Juárez. Then he'd made his way west, jumped the wall near Douglas and gotten caught. His disappointed coyote tried to extort money out of the rest of the Ortizes. While Carlos languished in a cell in the Douglas Border Patrol station, the smuggler "called my family and said I was in Phoenix." The ruse failed, but now Carlos was high and dry in Agua Prieta, with no money and no plan.

Outside the center, another coyote lingered, leaning against a railing, looking over Carlos and other likely customers. Dressed in a black cowboy hat and black shirt, he looked every inch the bad guy. None of the newly released migrants stopped to talk to him, at least not yet.

No one else paid much attention to the unkempt returnees. They're a common sight in the border town. Migrant apprehensions were down to 317,696 in the Tucson Sector as a whole in fiscal 2008, but they were inching up again in Douglas–Agua Prieta. The arrests had peaked locally in 2000—the year all hell broke loose in Douglas—then dropped. But in 2008, Rev. Mark Adams, a Presbyterian minister stationed on the border, said, "They've been trending up [again] for the last four years."

And the bodies kept piling up. Eight years after Silverio Huinil Vail died in nearby Douglas, 183 border crossers were found dead in southern Arizona.

There but for the grace of Café Justo went Hugo. "I never wanted to go to the U.S.," he told me in 2006. Thanks to his co-op job, he didn't have to.

Café Justo is a small-scale operation that has helped pull several dozen families up from desperation, keeping multiple Cifuenteses at home on their lands and Hugo out of the maquilas. Its impact on the border crisis may be insignificant in the larger scheme of things, but it has sustained its members for more than six years and continues to grow. And as an economic model that could be replicated, the Mexican-owned co-op just might ease the intractable twin problems of rural poverty in Mexico and illegal immigration to the United States.

"This is the best response to the issues of migration that I've seen," said Adams, the thirtysomething out of South Carolina who's been serving in Douglas and Agua Prieta since 1998. Four years into his mission, horrified by the migrants flooding into Agua Prieta, crossing the border and dying in the countryside, Adams helped found the co-op with Daniel Cifuentes, Hugo's uncle, and others. The group snared a tiny start-up microloan of twenty thousand dollars from the Presbyterian border ministry Frontera de Cristo— Border of Christ—and soon Café Justo was providing its owner families with a good price for their coffee. Two more villages have joined Salvador Urbina in the co-op, and as of 2008 there were two hundred co-op families in Mexico "who don't have a reason to come [across the border]," Adams said. "For the United States, it makes sense on an economic and political level."

Not to mention on a moral level.

"I was tired of the deaths," Tommy Bassett, another co-op founder, declared. A freewheeling American with a gray ponytail, he managed a maquiladora in Agua Prieta until the company shut down the Mexican plant and moved production to Asia. He's lived in the southeastern corner of Arizona for more than twenty years. Like Adams, Bassett is a man of faith, a Catholic, and when "a woman died in the corner of my yard" he felt called to help stop the carnage. "There's only so much you can do by giving out water and blankets," he said. "That's like cold syrup for cancer. We started [Café Justo] to deal with the root problem of migrants into the U.S."—the problem of poverty.

The co-op idea is somewhere between Karl Marx and Adam Smith. The workers control not only their means of production; they control every aspect of their business, from farming the raw materials to processing to distributing—and they bring all the profits back home to Mexico. They can stay in their home country, do the work they know best, and earn a living wage.

By cutting out the middlemen, the farmers have upped their earnings by as much as a factor of 10.

"Regular coffee comes through channels dominated by large coffee companies," explained Chuck Barrett, economic development coordinator for the Catholic Relief Services Mexico program. The large enterprises force prices down, and most growers have no choice but to sell to coyotes for "forty or fifty or sixty cents a pound." (The farmers slur the buyers with the same name they give the despised people-smugglers.)

The Fair Trade coffee movement improved those numbers. Justice-minded "fairer traders" buy the raw beans from the growers for about $1.25 to $1.50 a pound, a good step up from coyote prices. But Café Justo goes Fair Trade one better, calling itself "Fair Trade Plus." The co-op members raise organic, shade-grown coffee on their own mountain plots in Salvador Urbina. Then they send the beans on up to Hugo and company in Agua Prieta. All ten of their full-time staffers, three in Salvador Urbina and seven in Agua Prieta, are Mexicans.

The co-op does the "roasting, packing, and selling—where the profit comes from—and ends up netting five to six dollars a pound, a huge jump over Fair Trade," Barrett said. It's enough money to "enable more people *not* to migrate" and to encourage others to return home.

Within a few years, the extra money coming into Salvador Urbina allowed the community to buy a filtration system to purify the local water supply, and to buy books for schoolchildren. And the co-op members have health insurance for their families for the first time. "That's unheard of in Mexico," Barrett said. "Now they can go to doctors if they're sick." Best of all, by 2009, seventy Salvador Urbina natives who had been working in the United States came home to stay.

Daniel Cifuentes, production manager at Café Justo's Agua Prieta operation, first met Rev. Mark Adams at El Lirio de los Valles—the name means Lily of the Valley—a Presbyterian church that serves the Chiapas natives marooned in town. Set atop one of Agua Prieta's many steep hills, the stucco building is Protestant plain, except for the startling coat of purple paint outside. Inside, the sanctuary is simple and whitewashed, stripped of the ornate statues and painted *retablos* so beloved in Catholic Mexico. Still, cloth banners lovingly embroidered with flowers hang at the back of the low stage that stands in place of the Catholic altar, and plastic lilies of the valley are arranged in vases on pedestals.

On any given Sunday, Daniel, an elder, can be found speaking to the Chiapanecan congregation, in between sets of Spanish Christian rock banged out by a quartet of teens. The week I visited, he lamented the wall that divides Mexico from the United States. In the Holy Land, Daniel told the faithful, the warring Israelis and Palestinians are also separated by a wall. Here on the embattled Mexican border there was at least one thing to be grateful for. The Border Patrol might brag of its "battlefield management" of the borderlands, but "thank God we don't have a war," Cifuentes said, then paused. If it were an all-out war, the Agua Prietans would surely not be winning. "The U.S. is very powerful."

Pastor Rodolfo Navarrete likewise peppered his sermon with references to immigration, couched in biblical metaphors. The Hebrews were lost for forty years in the desert, he reminded the exiles, but they had entered at long last the "house of the Lord." Giving an Amen to that, the faithful sang about arriving in the promised land themselves, then segued into the pointed hymn *"Dios cuidará de ti"—God will take care of you.*

The parishioners were in need of that heavenly TLC. They were cheerful enough, singing out *bienvenidos*—"welcome"—to friends and strangers alike in the church, but their list of troubles was long. Agua Prieta had become a far more dangerous town in the last two years. A cop had been killed a few months before, in July 2008, presumed victim of the escalating drug wars of northern Mexico, and ten of his fellow officers resigned in protest—or in fear. Before that, in February 2007, the town's top public safety officer, Ramón Tacho Verdugo, was shot to death with a submachine gun chillingly called a *matapolicia*—"police killer." Now the U.S. economy was tanking, jeopardizing the livelihoods of the church members' loved ones up North and perhaps threatening their remittances, the money their loved ones sent home.

The separation from families was the worst of it. Many of the parish households had been torn apart—husbands from wives, parents from children—by economic necessity. The family of still another Cifuentes, Carmina Sanchez Cifuentes, twenty-five, is scattered to the four winds. She was fortunate to have her husband and two young children praying alongside her in El Lirio de los Valles, but her father had been working in Atlanta for years. Her mother and brother had gone back home to Salvador Urbina; her sisters married and moved away to Hermosillo, the Sonoran state capital two hundred miles south.

Carmina sat down after church to talk. Her seven-year-old daughter, Daphne, bored after the long service, hung her arms around her mother's neck and pestered her to go home. Her husband, Oscar Gastelum, a Sonorense from Ciudad Obregón in the south, took baby Carlos Eduardo outside to keep him entertained.

Carmina gently shushed her little girl, then began recounting how her family fortunes were tied to the rise and fall of the maquilas. Her father had always been a laborer, not a farmer; he had married into the coffee-growing Cifuentes family, but his wife, Carmina's mother, had not inherited land. He moved north first, and got a job at Allied Signal in Agua Prieta. Carmina followed with her two sisters in 1999, and at age sixteen she was hired on at the same maquila. When the plant closed in 2002, some five thousand employees were thrown out of work. The Allied Signal layoffs demonstrate how the maquiladora system can backfire on the United States. Plenty of workers were stranded a thousand or even two thousand miles from home, and it was easier to try to hop the border than to go all the way back. So they did the logical thing, making what an economist would call a rational choice.

"Many people left for the U.S.," Carmina said.

Her father was one of them. After Allied Signal shuttered its doors in Agua Prieta, he worked in construction locally, but that lasted only six months. Then he decided to hazard a border crossing in hopes of a better job. He paid a coyote to take him, and walked twelve hours through the desert near Douglas to his ride, his daughter said. He had no trouble at all. Ever since, he'd been in Atlanta, tending the greens on a golf course. Migrant workers like her dad used to come home fairly often, maybe even every year for a month at Christmas, a sacrosanct family holiday in Mexico. Now, with the border hardened, it's too difficult, too dangerous, too expensive to come back often.

"He went five years without seeing his family," Carmina said. His granddaughter Daphne was a month old when he left, and by the time he returned in 2007 she was in first grade. He had "gained a lot of pounds," his daughter said, and she teased him that he was as fat as an American. The high-calorie gringo diet might suit him, but he missed his wife, his children, and his grandchildren. Still, after his visit home, he went back to Atlanta. The golf course wages were keeping the family afloat. His wife and daughters worried about the crossing, but he had no trouble this time either. "He just walked a short time," Carmina said. "He paid two thousand dollars to go all the way to Atlanta." Packed in a van with other migrants, he had a couple of close calls with the authorities on the long drive from Arizona to Georgia. They were stopped twice by police, but both times, miraculously, the cops allowed them to proceed. Having cleared all the hurdles a second time, he returned to the job awaiting him at the country club, where he spends his days manicuring the links for the American rich.

Carmina's own young family was split up for a year. Her husband left to work in Atlanta, with his father-in-law footing the bill for the trip. But Oscar was unhappy so far away from his wife and daughter, and doesn't want to leave them again, Carmina said. Now with two young children at home, he would only go back legally, with a visa so he could return easily. "He wants to be with his family."

After more than six years apart, Carmina's parents longed to be together, too. They didn't see how Carmina's mother could go to the United States, though. They're afraid the crossing and the desert passage would be too dangerous for a middle-aged woman. And it would be awkward for her in Atlanta, where her husband bunked in a house full of men, fellow migrants from Mexico. It was difficult for them to be apart; they were lonely, and when they were sick, they had no one to care for them. Her mother was raising their youngest, Carmina's brother, alone, and she'd taken in a niece who has health problems. Her husband faithfully sent her money, but she had to soldier on at home alone. "He wants to return at the end of the year," his daughter said. But it's a wish often heard, and "want" is not the same as "will."

Mark Adams isn't a pastor per se to these suffering souls. Instead of leading a congregation, he labors in border ministry, aiming "to promote justice in all ways of life." He preaches about the travails of his Agua Prieta neighbors to Presbyterian congregations around the United States, and, closer to home, works to alleviate the problems of the borderlands. After cofounding Café Justo in 2002, he helped start up the Migrant Resource Center in downtown Agua Prieta. "Before that, we went out on cold nights," he said, looking for returned migrants with no place to go. Mark wasn't always so attuned to injustice. A self-described recovering racist, he was horrified as a teen that a high school girlfriend planned to go on a mission trip to Mexico. Toward the end of high school, he said, he was moved at last to love his fellow humans, Mexican, black, and white, by that radical bit out of St. Paul's letter to the Galatians: "There is neither Jew nor Greek, there is neither slave nor free man, there is neither male nor female; for you are all one in Christ Jesus." He was called to ministry—and Mexico—after serving on the Texas border in college. He's tall, with the athlete's build of the tennis player he once was, and a surprisingly boyish fringe of bangs; he speaks Spanish with a trace of Carolina drawl.

He regularly worships at El Lirio de los Valles, a church, like the town in which it's located, teeming with émigrés from Chiapas. He married one a few years back. He fell in love with Miriam Maldonado Escobar, a handsome woman with the black hair and striking profile of the Maya. Miriam's father had come from Chiapas to Agua Prieta to work in the maquilas; she followed later, hiring on at a production plant for Shure microphones. The rest of her family eventually turned up, too. Adams wanted to know why so many had landed in this remote northern town.

"Mark was curious about all the people from Chiapas here," Daniel Cifuentes recalled. Cifuentes himself was one of the displaced workers who'd fled north, so the Mexican gave the minister a primer in Chiapanecan economics. Farmers in Chiapas traditionally grew corn, coffee, and peanuts on the moist, shady mountain slopes, but the cash-crop economy in the southern state had bottomed out in the mid-'90s. The North American Free Trade Agreement (NAFTA) of 1994 had allowed cheap American corn to flood Mexico, undercutting small farmers and turning Mexico from a corn-exporting nation into a corn importer almost overnight. (It was NAFTA that triggered the Zapatista uprising that began in Chiapas on January 1, 1994, the day the treaty went into effect.) At the same time, a worldwide coffee glut pushed coffee prices down. On top of this double disaster was the peso crisis of 1994–95; the currency's value plummeted.

"Many of the people in Agua Prieta had worked in coffee production in Chiapas," Daniel said. "But there'd been a drop in coffee prices. People were desperate because of the low prices. Some of them moved to other Mexican states, but mostly to northern Mexico. Others went to the U.S. *como illegales*"—as illegals—"including my own friends and relatives."

Daniel joined the exodus out of Salvador Urbina. He worked a series of jobs in Agua Prieta. The late 1990s and early 2000s were the heyday of the maquilas, and about forty-five factories were churning out goods. By 2008, the number was closer to twenty or twenty-five. Of late, many have been closing.

Daniel made seatbelts for a while, and when that plant shut down, he switched to a factory producing John Deere and Caterpillar farm equipment. Then he worked construction, helping build a hydroelectric plant. During the years he was bouncing around from job to job, Agua Prieta turned into the hot spot for migrants trying to cross into the United States. But Daniel never joined the throngs spilling over the international line into Douglas, Naco, and the surrounding ranch country. He heard too many stories about people's "horrible experiences" in the desert, its "dangers and heat," not to mention the hunts by la migra.

Adams's own father-in-law, Pedro Maldonado Lopez, fifty-seven, had been beached in the dry interior city of Agua Prieta since 1994, the same year Daniel Cifuentes arrived, and for the same reason: *problemas económicos.*

Back home in Frontera Comalapa, Chiapas, "we rented land to grow corn," Maldonado began, speaking after church in the cadences of a minister. He made his life story sound like a fairy tale. "We had a rich family. They had land. They had *ranchos,* raising cattle. They grew *maíz* [corn], *frijol* [beans], *calabaza* [squash], *cacahuetes* [peanuts]. We worked for that family. They were our cousins. They also gave us a piece of land to grow our corn. It was a very good situation"—*una muy buena situación.* "It paid us little, but we had land."

The good times came to an end after a family dispute, and the Maldonados had to start all over. This time they had to pay rent for a patch of ground, and they earned "very little. Our income wasn't enough." By the time the crisis hit in 1994, Pedro and his wife, Florinda Escobar Matias, were the parents of six hungry children, the biblically named Miriam, Levi, and Usiel, and Febe, Eliel, and Gerson. Pedro had some neighbors who had already migrated to Agua Prieta, and they invited him to join them. "I didn't want to leave my family," he said, but he went north, by bus, promising to return in six months. That was fourteen years ago.

"There was work in the maquiladoras. I became a janitor at Allied Signal. The pay wasn't great but it was more than what I was making [back home]. There we were making sixty pesos a week. Here it was four hundred pesos a week. We looked for the lowest rents, eating simply, living together with friends." Every two weeks, he sent money back home. But it wasn't enough. He had to send for Miriam, his eldest, pulling her out of a teacher-training program and putting her to work in a maquila to help support the family. She was nineteen.

At least Pedro wasn't in the United States, where the difficulties of crossing the border would have made it even harder for him to see his family. Still, he missed them, and back in Chiapas, Florinda "was suffering." She and the rest of the children came for a visit, meant to last a month. They never went back.

Daniel Cifuentes and Mark Adams started brainstorming ways to keep agricultural laborers like Pedro on their lands. But it was another parishioner from El Lirio, Eduardo Perez Verdugo, who came up with the idea of a coffee co-op. A native of Buena Vista, Chiapas, on the border with Guatemala, he had hung on in the precarious economy at home until 1998, when Hurricane Mitch struck. He was in his forties, old to be making such a move, but the storm leveled the houses in his village and flattened the local Presbyterian church. He fled to Agua Prieta with a group of friends.

He signed on at Standex Electronics of Mexico, an electrical-components factory run by an American corporation. But some friends had made it to Phoenix, and they pestered him to migrate, extolling the much higher wages he could earn in Arizona. "They asked him three times," Adams related, "'How long will it take you to earn enough to go back home? Three years? In Phoenix you can make ten dollars an hour.' He did the math and decided to try."

In October of 1999, Eduardo slipped over the wall.

"He had a horrible experience," Adams said. "The next Sunday, I saw him at church. He was limping. His face was all scratched up. I asked him what happened."

Eduardo had crossed the border at night. In the darkness, he scraped against the desert's sharp thorns, then fell into an arroyo—a dry wash—and twisted his ankle. Stranded and unable to walk, he was caught by the Border Patrol. The agent threw him down to the ground, he told the minister. "He said to the agent, 'Hey, brother, the same blood flows through our veins.'" But la migra took no pity on him: the agent kicked him in the face and jammed his boot on his neck. After being unceremoniously arrested and dropped over the line, Eduardo hobbled back into Mexico. He told Adams, "To leave our land is to suffer."

But he had a thought. "If we could only control our coffee we could stay on our land, and sell coffee at a fair price." Eduardo ultimately went back to Chiapas, and Adams lost track of him, but his words haunted the minister. By then, the Starbucks phenomenon was going full steam, and caffeine-crazed Americans were demanding boutique coffees. "We realized the high prices people pay for coffee in the U.S.," Daniel recalled. "Mark said, 'Why do the growers get so little for coffee when in the U.S. people pay three dollars a cup?' The Chiapanecos weren't making a profit; the coyotes were. We thought of organizing a co-op in Chiapas. We came up with the idea of creating Café Justo."

For business expertise, the pair roped in Bassett, the old hippie who'd managed a maquila. They started calling the farmers in Daniel's village. Salvador Urbina had a single phone, and whoever answered would say, "'Call back in ten minutes,'" Adams remembered. "Then they would all come to the phone."

In May 2002 Miriam Maldonado Escobar, Mark Adams, Tommy Bassett, and Daniel's brother Isaac Cifuentes crammed into a Saturn and drove the 2,100 miles to Chiapas. "Miriam made sixty-three chimichangas," Adams said, "We had a big old cooler of water, only stopped one time for more than fifteen minutes. It was a forty-three–hour drive."

Religious divisions in the town made the farmers wary of each other. The Cifuentes clan—fourteen siblings in Daniel's generation—was Presbyterian, but plenty of others were Catholics. They wondered whether Catholics and Presbyterians could work together; they were taken aback that the Catholic Bassett was in deep with the Presbyterian minister. And they were leery of the gringos coming to town with big ideas and big promises.

"Some of them had doubts," Daniel remembered. "They didn't believe in the idea, or they were afraid. They knew how to make better beans," but they didn't yet know how to run a business that would stretch from Chiapas to the United States. But twenty-five Salvador Urbina families took the plunge the first year. Ten more would follow later.

An infusion of outside capital was the magic bullet that helped raise the Café Justo members a notch up from the desperate poverty of their coffee-growing neighbors. Frontera de Cristo's "microcredit ministry provided the loan to get the business started," Adams said. The little group had written a five-year business plan that was "a joke, looking back." They sent the proposal anyway to the board, and to their surprise, "The board said, 'Okay, here's twenty thousand dollars.'"

Workers had already begun hand-roasting the beans over open fires in Agua Prieta in November 2002. But once they got the microloan, they invested in their first small roaster, and dedicated it in January 2003. Since then, the business has grown steadily, said Adrián González, the customer relations manager, an Agua Prieta native who's the only non-Chiapanecan in the Café Justo bunch. The co-op bought a second roaster, and together the two roasters can churn out fifty-two pounds of cooked coffee beans in fifteen minutes.

The first year, the new co-op sold thirteen thousand pounds of coffee, Adrián said; the second year, twenty-seven thousand pounds; the third year, thirty-seven thousand. By the fifth year, 2007, sales were up to fifty thousand pounds. At eight dollars a bag retail, "that's four hundred thousand dollars a year in sales right now," he exulted. By fall 2008, business was up 20 percent, with peak Christmastime purchases still to come. "This year has been amazing."

During his years on the job, Adrián has taken to the dark brew himself. "I'm a coffee drinker now," he said with a salesman's smile. "That's one of the benefits of the job."

The co-op makes about 15 percent of its earnings via the Internet, but for now its customers are primarily in the "solidarity market"—justice-minded church congregations. In its early years, sales were concentrated in a couple dozen churches in Tucson, where parishioners bought the coffee on Sundays. By 2008, Adrián counted two hundred and fifty churches around the country as customers, with "at least one church customer in every state." Several colleges and universities, including Vassar, have signed on. It's not only do-gooders who buy the beans, he insisted. Café Justo won the coveted U.S. Department of Agriculture organic certification in April 2008. "It's not just charity. We're selling high-quality coffee at a good price."

Café Justo Center—a nonprofit run by Daniel Cifuentes, Bassett, Adams, University of Arizona planning professor Laura Huntoon, and others—is intent on spinning Salvador Urbina's success out into other villages. Two other villages have joined up. The co-op farmers in El Piñal, Veracruz, near the Gulf of Mexico, send their beans to Agua Prieta. The growers in La Aguila, Chiapas, ship theirs to a second roaster in Tijuana, where two part-time Mexican employees roast the beans and dispatch them to the United States. The plan is to have the Tijuana operation target California, and eventually to have the Veracruz enterprise "create a market in the Chihuahua Texas corridor."

Café Justo has some hurdles yet to leap. For now, the marketing is mostly free, courtesy of churches wanting to do good works. The members are trying to make the jump to regular retail, to grocery stores and restaurants. The trick is in persuading a supermarket chain to go with a still-young business. The co-op had problems with supply in the summer of 2008, when the demand jumped unexpectedly to one thousand pounds a week, double the usual orders of five hundred to six hundred pounds a week. They were puzzled by the rapid rise. Adrián González takes the spike as a good sign.

"We're growing so much faster than expected," he said. "I see a lot of future for this model."

The original twenty-thousand-dollar loan not only got the co-op up and going; it has begun to spread the modest wealth to other Mexican entrepreneurs—and lured at least one stray Mexican home. Adrián had migrated illegally to Phoenix, where he worked at a golf course and perfected his now-excellent English. But his father called him back home to Agua Prieta to join a new family printing business. His father's first and best customer? Café Justo, which contracted with the new enterprise to print up its shiny coffee bags.

"From an international planning standpoint, entrepreneurship and microcredit are the hot issues of today," Professor Huntoon said, so much so that the 2006 Nobel Peace Prize went to a Bangladeshi bank and banker for giving small business loans to the poor. The Nobel committee praised Grameen Bank and Muhammad Yunus for helping the recipients "break out of poverty" and proving "that even the poorest of the poor can work to bring about their own development."

Café Justo's supporters believe it's an example that bears repeating. The small amount of money the Presbyterians lent the co-op pales in comparison to the billions the United States is spending on border enforcement. A lowball estimate of the cost of the 670 miles of wall across the southwest border is $2.6 billion. That's not even counting the $6.7 billion for the virtual fence Homeland Security wants to put in place by 2014.

"It's unbelievable," sputtered Barrett of Catholic Relief Services. "If we spent even 10 percent of what we spend on enforcement on people instead, if the U.S. spent more money on this kind of thing, it would have a bigger impact on migration. The ultimate solution to the problems of the border is economic development in Mexico."

Pedro Maldonado Lopez, former grower of *café* and *cacahuetes,* would agree. Times are as hard as ever in Chiapas, and in Agua Prieta, "the maquilas are firing, not hiring. It's hard at home, hard here."

Mexican labor might be cheap, but the multinationals have discovered that Chinese and Thai labor is even cheaper.

Pedro lost his maquila job, but he was luckier than many of the other displaced workers, luckier for sure than Carmina's lonely dad, tending the turf at a golf course in faraway Atlanta and living in the company of men. Some of Pedro's friends went north, but he has no plans to leap the wall himself.

With his wife, children, and grandchildren nearby, he intended to stay put in Agua Prieta. He had a new job. Homesick, Hugo Cifuentes, the teenager I met in 2006, had abandoned his roaster and returned to his family and their coffee-growing lands in his beloved Chiapas. Adrián grinned. "He went home to be with his mom."

Now it was Pedro Maldonado Lopez who spent his days cranking up the roaster, and he's made it hotter than Hugo ever did. "I took Hugo's position," he said, brightening. "I'm roasting the coffee to four hundred and eighty degrees."

CHAPTER 3

Crossroads *al Norte*

This area from Altar to Sásabe is dominated by a mafia.

—*Father Prisciliano Peraza Garcia, parish priest,*
Altar, Sonora

A wedding party spilled out of Nuestra Señora de Guadalupe church in Altar, a Sonoran town fifty-nine miles south of the border. A *norteño* band played merrily, the musicians scratching their violins and pumping their accordions, as the bride and groom—Nora and Roberto—strode out onto the plaza. Family and friends rushed to embrace them, hugging, kissing, squealing. "¡Felicitaciones!" they called out. "Qué linda la novia." *Congratulations! What a beautiful bride.* The bride in question, in strapless white, and the bridesmaids, in matching strapless red, shivered in the Saturday-evening chill.

The wedding guests were not the only ones looking on as the young couple took their first steps together as wife and husband. Outside the sand-colored Spanish church on this December night in 2003 there were clusters of men with the unmistakable look of migrants *en camino*—en route. Dressed in dark jackets and pants, knit caps, and sneakers, they stood around the edges of the square by the dozens, their hands thrust in their pockets for warmth. Others sat on benches or wandered aimlessly across the plaza's concrete pavers. Never mind that it was just two weeks before Christmas. These men had just left their homes in villages all over Mexico and Central America to try for jobs in the United States.

Martín Ramos, forty-five, had already traveled long days and nights to get to Altar. "I came from Chiapas yesterday," Ramos told me the morning after the wedding. "I spent three nights and two days on the bus." He'd been working in the sewers in Tuxtla Gutiérrez, capital of the poverty-stricken state, making forty-eight pesos a day, hardly enough to support himself, his wife, and their two children, ages six and seven. Ebert, twenty-two, a young friend Martín had made on the journey north, was a campesino, a farmworker who used to grow corn and coffee in Chiapas. He didn't have the advantage of a co-op like Café Justo, and prices had dropped too low. "There's not a market for coffee and corn now," Ebert explained. "I have two children, five and three, and I have to see if I can find a better job."

These two knew that before they could get to the promised land, they first had to go through Altar. A couple of hours south of *la línea,* the international line, the once-sleepy town had become the new jumping-off point for migrants heading to the United States. As promised, the Border Patrol closed in on Douglas, Arizona, with Operation Safeguard, and now the routes had shifted west. Migrants were traveling north up Highway 15 from all points in Mexico, then turning west on Highway 2 and streaming into Altar.

Life went on as usual in the provincial town. Weddings were celebrated, local couples danced in cantinas on Saturday night, kids raced bicycles in the plaza on Sunday afternoon. But the local economy had been caught up in the migrant trade. Businesses catering to travelers were flourishing all around the church plaza, the town's central gathering place. It was here that the migrants arrived by bus and, when they stepped out of the *camión*, where they spotted any number of casas de huéspedes. Colorfully named for exotic places around the globe—El Chino (the Chinese Man), Hotel Lima, Hospedaje Río—these migrant flophouses offered wooden bunks sans mattresses for four dollars a night. "Open 24 hours!" their signs exclaimed. Small eateries called *comedores* advertised *cocina económica*, cheap food, in signs hand-painted across vivid pink and blue stucco walls.

Stores had reoriented their merchandise toward people who planned a dangerous desert trek *al Norte*. In a shop across from Nuestra Señora de Guadalupe, a young clerk named Mercedes Celaya said that the most popular migrant items were bottles of water ("They buy four gallons when it's hot, two gallons now"), rehydrating fluids, telephone cards, canned tuna, and toenail clippers to open the cans. "For the journey, they bring prepared food," Celaya said. She'd seen and heard plenty from her anxious customers. "Some of the migrants are sad."

The prices seemed reasonable to an American—7.5 pesos, or 75 cents, for tuna—but Altar's lone priest, Father René Castañeda Castro, made price-gouging the topic of his sermon the Saturday night of the wedding. After uniting Nora and Roberto in holy matrimony in a nuptial Mass, the padre hurried to a Catholic shelter blocks away to say a less-festive "migrant Mass." The travelers lucky enough to land the free meals and free bunks—with mattresses—prayed side by side with Altar Catholics at an improvised altar in the dining room. Everybody called the place CCAMYN, an acronym for Community Center for Migrants and Those In Need. Father René prayed for the safety of the travelers, but he also chided his parishioners for jacking up prices and taking advantage of the migrants. Slim and dark, with movie-star good looks, Father René was building up a rep on both sides of the border as *el padre del desierto*.

"These are our brothers and sisters," he reproached his flock. *Nuestros hermanos y hermanas.* Show some compassion.

Altar was pricey and difficult for migrants, but worse was yet to come. Martín Ramos and the others biding their time at the shelter and in the *hospedajes* still had to get over the border at Sásabe, a lawless frontier town on the edge of Arizona. Smugglers eager to take them there were easy to find. Coyotes, the head guys, and their pollero underlings were skulking around the church plaza, their white vans parked in long lines on the adjacent streets. The smugglers had retrofitted the vehicles for the migrant trade, removing the seats and replacing them with benches—or nothing at all—the better to cram their customers in. Migrants from the south tend to be small, and for the rough two-hour ride up the dirt road north to Sásabe, coyotes routinely packed in a couple dozen.

Sásabe was a hardscrabble settlement, a place where pickups bounced over rutted dirt streets, swerving to avoid skinny dogs and wandering pigs, and where crumbling adobes were overshadowed by flashy new houses bankrolled by the twin trades of drug and people trafficking. "There is no law," Victor Armendariz, a Grupo Beta agent in Sásabe, told me. He and the ten other Grupo Beta agents in town were paid by the Mexican government "to take care of *migrantes*. We talk to them about the risk of being abandoned in the desert, or problems with the Border Patrol." In wintertime, he advised migrants to bring "plastic bags to cover themselves from the frost. Out here, if you get wet, you're going to die."

In 2008 the Americans built intimidating metal walls for more than seven miles along the border on either side of Sasabe, but in 2003 there was only a barbed-wire fence. Armendariz showed me a place in a mesquite grove west of town where migrants, led by their polleros, could easily slip beneath the wire and into Arizona. He looked over toward the rolling hills across the line; on the far side of a gulch, a Border Patrol officer got out of his SUV and stared right back. The Mexican agent gestured north. The migrants would head through the Buenos Aires National Wildlife

Refuge, a grassland paradise for birds and pronghorn deer, then up through the broad Altar Valley, the long blue line of the Baboquivari Mountains always to their left, on the west. Interrupted only by the occasional ranch house, this Arizona backcountry had become so heavily traveled by crossers that critics had begun to call it the Amnesty Trail. Armendariz had the world-weary look of a man who wasn't bothered by much, and the number of Christmastime crossers didn't really surprise him. "It's odd, because Mexicans are supposedly religious, and December is the month of the Virgin," he said, smiling a little. "But it's *la necesidad,*" necessity.

If the migrants were lucky, and the coyote kept his word, their pollero would travel with them by foot for three days or more to Three Points, sixty miles north. After that, if they didn't get captured or sick or injured or lost, the coyote's network of drivers and vans could take them anywhere they wanted to go in the United States.

"It's possible to go without a coyote, but it's dangerous," said José, a Mexican staying at the Catholic shelter in Altar. "The desert is a big place, and you can get lost." He'd recently been deported from Kentucky, where he had a good job with a good boss on a tobacco plantation, earning ten dollars an hour. Coyotes know the ropes, he said, and he planned to hire one again. The last time he crossed, "we walked three days with the same guide, and he had a guy waiting with a truck."

César, another wayfarer at the hostel, had been making a good living working construction in Chattanooga, Tennessee, when he was picked up by the state highway patrol after a minor traffic accident. Last time he'd crossed, he traveled with a pollero in a group of fifteen. He knew that the going price for coyotes now was $1,500 to $1,700, but to get back to Chattanooga, he had no choice but to pay up.

"We'll trust them again," he said. "God knows we need the work."

—

Esperanza and Belén—Hope and Bethlehem—had spent the last hour cooking up a meal big enough to serve the nine migrants staying at CCAMYN, as well as a group of visitors, including my husband, Kevin, and me. They spooned refried beans and rice onto foam plates, ladled out a ground-beef stew, and filled serving dishes with warm wheat tortillas, a specialty of Sonora. Then they called their guests to table. Xavier, a cheerful Honduran who'd recently been deported from San Francisco, stood up to say grace.

The two women beamed. Despite the human misery they witnessed daily, their faces glowed with kindness, as though the light of the Lord himself shone through them. Each wore a large wooden cross strung on a cord around her neck. Eleven years before, back in 1998, both had joined other women of Altar in bringing food to the travelers who had suddenly alighted in the plaza. Now it was January 2009—more than five years since I had met César and José at the shelter. I had come back to see how Altar was faring. Migrant numbers had shot up in the years since 2003, I was learning, but by 2009 they were dropping again, and the journey had become far more dangerous. In one respect, as far as Esperanza and Belén were concerned, not much had changed. In more than a decade of volunteering, the women had served thousands of hungry travelers, and each had a tragic tale to tell.

"We've heard many sad stories," Belén sighed. "Every migrant has one."

At dinner, a Guatemalan named Mario Alapizco Castro, thirty-one, told a particularly tough one. He'd worked seven years to save up his smuggler's exorbitant fee, at eight thousand dollars the highest I'd heard yet. (The price for travelers from Central America is higher than for Mexicans.) He'd gotten across okay, but just four months after he settled into a restaurant job in San Bernardino, California, he'd been caught by the Border Patrol. Seven years' labor down the drain. Now he was stranded in Altar, and sick. It was no use trying to sneak back. "My heart doesn't permit it," he said, speaking of his *corazón* literally. He had a cardiac condition—an enlarged heart and a damaged valve—and his skin was sallow. He had hoped to earn enough money in the United States to pay for surgery. Now his head was pounding, he was worried about his blood pressure, and he didn't know how he was going to get back to his wife and three little girls in Guatemala City.

"Estoy lejos de mi país," he said sadly. "Tengo ni comida ni dinero." *I'm far from home, and I have neither food nor money.*

Technically Mario was supposed to stay at the shelter only three days, but exceptions were allowed for hard cases, or for refugees awaiting funds from their families. The residents were required to go out in search of work each day. While they were at CCAMYN, they were inundated with information about the dangers of the journey north. White crosses bearing the names of dead desert crossers stood outside beneath a shrine to the Virgin of Guadalupe. Inside, a cross hanging on the wall was collaged out of slips of paper clipped from Kat Rodriguez's lists of Arizona's migrant dead.

Maps of the borderlands with warnings in Spanish hung on the walls. Red dots marked the locations of known migrant deaths, and arcs drawn across the landscape indicated how long it takes to walk the desert. From Sasabe, *un día caminando*—"one day walking"—would get trekkers to Arivaca. Two days would land them in remote desert, and three days would bring them almost to Three Points. Compiled by the Tucson group Humane Borders, the maps put the lie to smugglers' claims of short ambles to Tucson or Phoenix.

Altar's new priest settled in at the table after Mario and the other migrants had wandered off to their beds, their bellies full for once, and Esperanza and Belén had tidied up the kitchen, a spotless domain of white tile. Nearby were some leftover Christmas decorations: two large statues of the biblical migrants Maria and José, Maria on a donkey, searching for shelter in Bethlehem.

"In every migrant we see the face of Christ," Father Prisciliano Peraza Garcia said, gesturing toward the ceramic representation of the Holy Family. "We can't leave them in the street." Father Prisciliano had replaced Father René, who had left the priesthood to marry. The new padre was a convivial fellow with a jolly round face and a thick head of black hair. Instead of a priest's black cassock, he was decked out in a black down vest over jeans and cowboy boots.

"Altar was always a crossing point for migration," he said, and for good reason. "We're ninety-eight kilometers [fifty-nine miles] from Sasabe and we're along the principal highway from Tijuana to Chiapas. We're two and a half hours from the international airport in Hermosillo. We're one and a half hours from Nogales."

Migrants once traveled through Altar in manageable numbers, he recounted. They were almost always men, farmworkers who came and went with the harvests and returned home regularly to their wives and children. Mexico had long been accustomed to the comings and goings of this perennial migrant underclass, and their travels didn't attract much attention. Altar was a small town of six thousand in those days, a hub for the ranches and farms around it. The occasional tourist would come through on the Ruta de las Misiones, a driving tour of the region's charming seventeenth-century churches established by the itinerant Jesuit missionary Father Eusebio Kino. (Kino, like today's migrants, traveled north to where Tucson is now, and eventually on to California, establishing some twenty-four missions along the way.) In a pretty hilltop village a few minutes up the road from Altar, visitors would stop by Kino's San Antonio de

Oquitoa, a small white adobe church, and pause to take in a fine view of the valley below and the mountains in the distance. Altar had just two hotels, "between a half-star and one star," Father Prisciliano joked, to serve these stray tourists. Then, suddenly, in 1998, "Things got crazy in Altar."

Sixteen hundred migrants a day—11,200 a week—began converging on the town. "In a week more people were coming through than there were residents of Altar," the padre said. Like the Reverend Mark Adams, Father Prisciliano blamed NAFTA for pushing the rural poor from their homes. "People started abandoning the countryside because there wasn't enough food." And once the Border Patrol blockaded Nogales, El Paso, and San Diego, "the migrant was obliged to cross through the mountains and desert."

Local residents were overwhelmed. Kindly women like Belén and Esperanza began taking the travelers food, but others raged against the Arizona-bound migrants, vilifying them as *oaxacas,* a racial epithet that conjures up the heavily Indian state of Oaxaca. The charismatic Father René helped people understand their Christian duty, recalled Sister Lil Mattingly, a Maryknoll nun in Tucson who arranges educational trips to the border. "He turned the situation around." Under his guidance, many of the townsfolk began to help out.

"We realized these people were hungry," Padre Prisciliano recounted. "We gave food to three hundred to four hundred a day. They needed clothes, a place to shower and to communicate with their families. We needed a house to do this."

By 2000, the number of arriving migrants shot up to two thousand a day, and the church scrambled to respond. In 2001 the Catholic community built a kitchen and a *comedor,* a rustic dining hall, out of cinderblock, on a dirt street about a mile from the plaza. Eventually, a couple of dorm rooms were added, one for women, one for men, outfitted with bunk beds, complete with mattresses. The tidy rooms were arranged around a pleasant courtyard open to the sky. Iron bars on the gate and barbed wire atop the walls were a reminder that the town could be dangerous. And poor—the municipality sends a truck out occasionally to pour water onto the dirt roads to keep the dust down. The shelter was cleaner and safer than the casas de huéspedes, but no match for the number of migrants who sought refuge there.

By 2005, the peak year, three thousand migrants a day were thronging the streets. (It was also the year border-crosser deaths were highest in southern Arizona.) With the migrant population ballooning, organized crime grabbed the opportunity to make big money, and the mom-and-pop smugglers of old gave way to elaborate trafficking syndicates. By 2009, the dirt road from Altar to Sásabe, which I had traveled safely without incident in 2003, was infested with bandits extorting money from migrants.

"This area from here to Sasabe is dominated by a mafia," Father Prisciliano said. "The mafia who control it charges fifty dollars for every migrant going up the road to Sasabe. That's apart from the three hundred and fifty to four hundred pesos they pay for the van." Sister Lil no longer sent her groups down the bumpy dirt road. "It's too dangerous," she said. "The Mexican government started a clampdown on the drug cartels," and the drug cartels in turn started preying on migrants. "The drug folks burned thirteen vans two years ago as a show of force. They extort money from migrants. Drug smugglers have staked out places in the desert. People in masks demand money. It's been going on for over a year."

The drug crackdown triggered murders across northern Sonora, but it didn't stop drugs from getting over the line. In fiscal 2008, the Tucson Sector Border Patrol seized $650 million worth of marijuana—812,412 pounds—a jump of 8 percent over the previous year's haul, along with 265 pounds of cocaine, 61 ounces of heroin, and 23 pounds of methamphetamine. And 2009 was on track to go even higher. In the first six months of the fiscal year, agents had corralled 600,000 pounds of marijuana. After a bust of a major drug syndicate in December 2008, Arizona's attorney general, Terry Goddard, had gone so far as to declare that "trafficking across our southern border is the organized crime threat of the twenty-first century."

Migrants kept making their way through this volatile territory, controlled by drug and human smugglers alike, but they were vulnerable. More women were on the road than in the past, some traveling with children, and trying to join husbands and fathers. Rapes in the wilderness had become common, Father Prisciliano said. Women confessed to the priest that they "take contraceptives when they know they're going to cross, because they know they will be raped." They knew that birth control was a sin in the eyes of the church, but they were determined not to get pregnant by a coyote or bandit or fellow traveler.

The whole region was on edge. "Nogales is pretty violent right now," the priest said. That was an understatement. The Sonoran state chief of police, Juan Manuel Pavón Félix, had been gunned down in Nogales two months before, in November 2008, succumbing to a "barrage of gunfire as well as grenades," as Tucson's *Arizona Daily Star* reported. It was the most high-profile murder in Sonora since the slaying of Agua Prieta police chief Ramón Tacho Verdugo in February 2007. The day we met with Father Prisciliano, Kevin and I saw *federales* armed with rifles patrolling the highway between Nogales and Altar.

Earlier that afternoon, in hilly Nogales, Sonora, an hour and a half north of Altar, a knot of men were sitting outside a shabby office at the bottom of a potholed road. They had just walked down the slope from the port of entry—or more accurately, in their case, point of exit—and now they were resting in a Grupo Beta parking lot. Next door was a gravestone maker, and across the street was a cemetery full of the stone carver's handiwork, white crosses bedecked in plastic flowers. A few paces farther down the hill was the metal border wall, patched and tarnished and loaded with anti-*yanqui* graffiti. Armed federal troops were loitering nearby on foot or idling in open-air jeeps.

Two of the men sitting on the curb were from Sinaloa, south of Sonora; one was from Durango, east of Sinaloa; and two others were southerners, one a Veracruzano and the other a Chiapaneco. They'd all just been ejected from the United States. They looked weary and dirty, but they still had some spirit. "Do you have some shoes?" one asked me. He laughed when I showed him the only shoes I had—worn sneakers, one of which had a hole. Another related, "I got to Tucson and I got caught." Still another, in a T-shirt on this fifty-degree day, shrugged when I asked where his jacket was.

These travelers were hoping for help from Grupo Beta. Founded in 1994, the agency is the Mexican government's answer to the U.S. Border Patrol and to humanitarian groups, all wrapped into one. Grupo Beta gets migrants coming and going—those trying to sneak into the United States and those who've been kicked out. But when I asked the men what Grupo Beta could do for them, one said disgustedly, "Nada." *Nothing.*

Inside, the agent in charge had a different story. "We offer two forms of help," he said grandly. A man with a fine head of wavy black hair and a well-fed frame, he presided over a large desk. He didn't want his name used. Call him Danilo Gutiérrez. "We're here to orient the migrants to their surroundings. And we're here to do search and rescue in the desert zones. We try to do what we can to get them to return home." But Mexico's a free country, he added. "We can't prevent them from crossing."

He marveled at the sea of humanity relentlessly surging up from the south, impelled by the "necessity" his Sasabe colleague Victor Armendariz had spoken of. "We see old people, women, children," he said, tallying them up. "A little bit ago a woman gave birth in the desert! I met an eighty-two-year-old woman who wanted to cross the mountains."

The Mexican government officially discourages people from hopping the fence and hazarding the dangers of the American desert. The office was filled with posters begging would-be migrants to turn back. One pictured a snowy-haired dad, lonely at home in a Mexican village. "Before you go far away, think of those who are staying behind," the text read.

Grupo Beta has seventeen stations spread in an arc across Mexico's northern border, from Tijuana on the Pacific Coast to Playa Lauro Villar on the Gulf of Mexico. Six are in Sonora, opposite Arizona. Nogales and Agua Prieta are the busiest locations ("We get two hundred to two hundred and fifty migrants a day in the Nogales office," Danilo Gutiérrez said); less active are those at Naco, Sonoyta, San Luis Río Colorado, and Sasabe—where Officer Armendariz plied his trade. Nine agents, clad in the service uniform of bright orange shirts, staff the Nogales station.

Disconsolate travelers whose journeys have been cut short courtesy of the American migra are entitled to one free phone call and a half-price bus ticket home, Danilo said. If they need medical help Grupo Beta can point them in the right direction. Women can stay at a Nogales shelter run by an order of Mexican nuns, and Beta directs the men to other *albergues,* or hostels. For food, the agents send hungry travelers to a *comedor* run by Jesuit priests near the port. But Grupo had plans to add an eatery of its own. "We're constructing a *comedor* this season."

Padre Prisciliano and the Border Patrol both maintained that migration was on a downslide, but Danilo didn't agree.

He'd been seeing higher numbers. He had two explanations: "One, more people are trying to cross. And two, the Border Patrol are getting better at their jobs."

But he concurred with the priest that the travelers are routinely abused. Many are from the rural south, from Oaxaca and Chiapas, with no clue of the northern geography. The coyotes tell them "it's a one-hour walk to Tucson and Phoenix," but Tucson alone would be a walk of four days or more for a hiker in peak condition. "They tell them lies," he said with disgust. "Many people cheat them and take advantage. There's much suffering. In the desert, people die. Women are raped."

Coyotes' fees vary, he said, but whatever they charge they make good money. Large groups are more readily detected and caught, but profits are higher the more migrants the polleros guide. "So they take thirty migrants and they charge two thousand dollars; that's *muchísimo*"—a lot of money: sixty thousand dollars total. "From Central America they charge five thousand to six thousand dollars." With all the money to be made, there's *una mafia muy grande*, "a very big mafia." Mario Alapizco Castro's story bore him out. The man stranded at that very moment in the Catholic shelter in Altar had paid a staggering eight thousand dollars upfront to a coyote in his hometown of Guatemala City and then set out on an epic journey to California, by bus, by train, by foot, and by van. Every step of the way he met up with different coyotes and polleros in the smuggling syndicate, each one handing him off to the next.

Naive travelers are often cheated, Danilo continued. "In some cases, migrants, through ignorance, give the money before crossing. The coyote takes them a couple of kilometers across the line and abandons them. In other cases, they sequester migrants in 'stash houses' until the family sends more money, two to three times what was agreed." The migrant is in effect held for ransom.

Nogales has a neighborhood that looks like the United States, lined with American chain stores from Subway to Applebee's, from Carl's Jr. to Chevrolet. Sometimes "the migrant pays and the coyote drives him around," then stops at the all-American strip and announces, "'Here you are in the United States,'" Danilo said. The hapless migrant is left to discover on his own that he's still in Mexico, without his money.

The Border Patrol can prosecute a coyote for human smuggling, but only if the migrants in tow are willing to rat him out. Same goes for Grupo Beta. "If migrants don't denounce the pollero, my hands are tied," Gomez said. Coyotes have been known to turn up at the Grupo Beta office in search of new customers. "We kick them out," he said. "We can arrest them but they spend only two or four days in jail.

"There are bad coyotes and good coyotes. Some migrants speak well of them. But there are a lot of bad ones." Still, coyotes are a "necessary evil," Danilo lamented. "A person from Oaxaca doesn't know where to cross."

The Border Patrol was no better, he said. Migrants are often dumped back into Mexico stripped of their IDs, their money, their cell phones, and their wallets, which often have their contact phone numbers tucked inside. "The Border Patrol takes all this," he said. The policy of returning migrants far from where they were picked up is a deliberate disorientation strategy, Danilo argued. The Border Patrol says they do it to break migrants' connection to their coyotes, but "it's to confuse them mentally," the Grupo Beta agent said. "If they cross at Tijuana, then send them back to Matamoros [near Texas], they make you impotent, they hurt you psychologically." He had seen cases of families separated, with "one brother in Tijuana, another brother in Matamoros." And even a case of a "lady with a baby or child. They will separate them and the minor goes to separate deportation. I don't know if it's a policy but for sure it's not in accord with international law. They don't respect that."

The agency drops migrants, including young women, over the border at night, at three or four in the morning, releasing them into sketchy downtown Nogales. At least they don't drop off minors after dark. "They respect that rule," Danilo conceded. The Border Patrol had one policy he approved of: agents separate children from adults who are not relatives. "Children will say they're with a cousin or a brother, but it's actually a pollero. They separate the child from the pollero. The minor is given to the Mexican consul and handed over" to child protective services in Mexico.

During the hour that Gutiérrez was speaking to us, a whole new wave of migrants flowed into his parking lot, among them several women. They were *indígenas*, with the angular faces, brown skin, and jet-black hair of the native peoples of southern Mexico. A couple dozen came into the office to get help, while twenty more waited outside. The agent looked up at the arrivals. They were never ending.

"We Mexicans are ingenious," he concluded. "We are always crossing. We have always crossed. Whatever solutions you can come up with, we will always migrate."

Down in Altar, the entrepreneurs were ready for them. "Altar depends almost completely on migration," Padre Prisciliano declared. The town's population had ballooned up to twenty thousand, and elaborate two-story houses—paid for with smuggling money—were lording it over modest traditional homes. There were more stores in 2009 than in 2003, and a veritable explosion of migrant merchandise in every direction around the church plaza. Shops open to the street were wholly given over to migrant wear: black winter jackets (twenty-five dollars); black-and-silver backpacks (a pricey ten dollars apiece); and plenty of bras for the escalating number of wayfaring women. T-shirts were printed with the image of the Virgin of Guadalupe, patron saint of the Altar church and protectress of all Mexico. Talcum powder for the feet, to ward off the blisters that can cripple in the outback; socks for the same reason; ditto for thick insoles; and lighters, to ignite cigarettes in good times and rescue flares in bad. One black knit cap was stamped with a wish: the word LUCKY in big yellow letters.

Sonora has its own *cocina,* a cuisine anchored by pinto beans, beef, and huge flour tortillas, which women often make in open kitchens in full view of their customers. But in deference to the preponderance of southern travelers, many *comedore*s now were specializing in the food of Chiapas. El Chiapaneco, a blue-and-white stuccoed eatery, sold the black beans, pork, and corn tortillas favored in the south.

Casetas telefónicas—"telephone stores" (advertising "$3 a minute")—and *casas de cambio*—"currency exchanges"— were tucked in between dozens of *hospedajes,* the fleabag guesthouses that took up the considerable slack left by the Catholic shelter. According to Padre Prisciliano, there were now more than fifteen hotels ("from one star to four star") and "more than ninety casas de huéspedes."

On Sunday morning, at Hospedaje Hidalgo, a woman, Graciela, was cooking breakfast, her face drawn and anxious. The dimly lit front room had what could be called bunk beds only by the kindest of euphemisms. They were wide, bare plywood shelves, built for stacking humans, flesh against wood. Jammed together, with no spaces in between, the bunks forced bedmates to crawl over each other to get to their assigned slot. Beyond the beds was a dark alcove outfitted as a bare-bones kitchen, with a stove, refrigerator, and sink.

Graciela was disinclined to speak with me, but her husband, another Mario, twenty-three, said they were traveling with his two *primos,* his cousins, from their village of Tapalapa in Chiapas. They had left their little girl, three-year-old

Marielisa, at home with her grandmother. He told the same old story. In Chiapas, "no hay ni dinero ni trabajo." *No money and no work.* When he did manage to find a job, he labored in the fields for a big grower from seven in the morning until four in the afternoon, earning fifty to sixty pesos a day, equivalent to $4 or $4.50. In their minds they were going to North Carolina, where they had friends "working in the pine forest." But Mario and company weren't making much progress. They had just been sent back to Mexico a third time by the Border Patrol. Now they had used up their "three chances for one price" with the coyote, he said. They had paid twelve hundred dollars apiece in advance in Chiapas, with a guarantee of a trio of tries over the border. The third and final time they were traveling in a group of nine and got caught in the desert outside Phoenix. "The Border Patrol treated us okay," Mario said. Now the familial quartet was spending forty pesos a person a night for accommodations in the dicey Hidalgo, and debating what to do next.

Mario had a hopeful question for me, about Barack Obama. "Will the new president change things?"

Migrants like this Chiapas family were getting rarer, according to Padre Prisciliano. The Altar numbers had dropped dramatically, to seven hundred a day. The U.S. economy was in free fall—"Word is getting around that jobs are scarce," Sister Lil said—and then there was that new border wall wrapped around Sasabe. The Mexican government was reporting that declining remittances—money sent back home from migrant family members abroad—was causing a slump in the macroeconomy. But Altar's migrant microeconomy was nosediving too. As the migrant business went, so went the local economy.

A young Nogales woman with a booth set up near the plaza was feeling the pain. She had a van parked beside the curb, and sidewalk racks festooned with winter jackets and backpacks. Every day, she drove the one-and-a-half hours from Nogales, where there was "no work at all," toting not only her cut-rate travel merchandise but her two-year-old son. Once in Altar, the boy rolled around inside the van, bored to distraction, while his mother tried to sell her wares. Sales were way down. "There are hardly any migrants now, not like before," she said anxiously.

Elsewhere, *comedores* tried to lure us in to eat, in lieu of the missing Chiapanecans, and shopkeepers stood idle. We saw only three travelers making a transaction at a store. But others were standing around the plaza as usual, and several drifted toward Nuestra Señora de Guadalupe.

A funeral was under way. A hearse had driven right into the plaza and backed up to the church door, where it was met by the grieving family and by Father Prisciliano, his cowboy boots and jeans now peeking out beneath bright-green vestments. The undertaker, a dapper young man with a wave of black hair, and his older assistant slid the copper-colored coffin out of the hearse, then pushed it up the aisle on wheels. Priest and mourners followed in somber procession. The deceased was not a desert tragedy, the assistant assured me, but a *viejicita de ochenta y tres años*, "a little old lady, eighty-three years old." Francisca was a woman from the town, whose long life had been a blessing to her large family of daughters and sons and grandchildren. She had lived just a few blocks from the church all her life, he said, and now she would be buried in her own parish, and laid to rest among her forebears.

Like those who had watched Nora and Roberto's wedding five years before, the migrants now wandering the plaza stepped into the church to witness Francisca's funeral. Her settled life among family and neighbors was the polar opposite of their unstill lives, marked as they were by departures and distance and danger. I noticed Mario Alapizco Castro, the sick Guatemalan from the shelter, standing in the back. He gazed up at the painted Virgin of Guadalupe over the altar and recited the responses to the priest along with the rest of the congregation. "Señor, escucha nuestra oración," the group intoned again and again. *Lord, hear our prayer.* When the Mass was ended, and the church emptied, Mario stayed behind. He took a seat all alone in the last pew and bowed his head.

CHAPTER 4

Desert Rescue

They left me all alone in the desert. I lost hope that I
would survive.

—*Marta Gomez Garcia, migrant from Honduras*

On a blistering day in late September 2005, a party of some
fifty undocumented migrants slowly made their way through
the dangerous desert country southwest of Tucson.

The rough terrain they were crossing is part of the Buenos Aires National Wildlife Refuge, just north of Sasabe.
The preserve's yellow grasslands roll across 118,000 acres east
of the Baboquivaris. Birders flock to this avian haven, home
to the tiny pygmy owl and hundreds of other species. Hunt-
ers prowl the refuge, too, tracking mule deer and javelina.
In earlier generations, the remote valley was the domain of
cowboys, and of easterners playing cowboy at dude ranches.
Today it has thousands of miles of bushwhacked trails—and
thousands of migrants.

Buenos Aires rangers fret over the damage the foot traffic
wreaks on fragile desert soils, and over the trash that migrants
drop in the once-pristine preserve. They alert visitors to be-
ware of border crossers and to report suspicious activity to
the Border Patrol. So the walkers that September day slipped

through the eastern edges of the preserve, the better to avoid detection. They walked single file over rocky hills studded with shindagger agaves and thorny mesquites. Thousands of footsteps had pounded out primitive trails through the desert tangle, but they were nothing like the carefully tended paths in national parks. If a walker concentrated on stepping around the rocks that litter the path, she ran the risk of hitting her head on a spiky branch overhead. Sometimes the injuries were far worse than a bump on the head or a pricker in the skin. Twenty migrants are known to have died in the refuge since 2002.

Marta Gomez Garcia, then twenty-seven, a mother of two from a village in Honduras, was in the large group of strangers crossing. She'd left her two small boys at home in the care of her husband's father, and made her way alone to the Arizona border in hopes of joining her sister Irma in North Carolina. She hadn't seen her sister in the four years since Irma went north, and she hadn't seen her husband in almost as long. He'd left her in the village with a toddler to care for and a baby on the way.

Once he arrived at the Arizona border, Marta never heard from him again. She believed he was dead.

"I think he died in the desert," she would say later, from a hospital bed in Tucson.

But her husband's possible death and the manifest dangers of the southern Arizona desert didn't stop her from making the same journey. Honduras, she explained, is *bonito pero pobre*—"pretty, but poor." In the United States, she hoped to earn decent money and send some back home to her boys. They might not have a mother or a father to raise them, but they would have enough to eat.

Marta traveled alone across Guatemala, by bus, and north through Mexico to Arizona. At Sasabe, she found a coyote. The village is full of open-air cantinas, with norteño music—the trademark accordion music of Mexico's northern borderlands—spilling out into the dirt lanes. It's not hard to track down a guide lounging at one of the tables, or loitering close to the international line. They're on the lookout for people like Marta, migrants in jeans and sneakers, carrying a telltale backpack. Once she found a coyote, she pulled out the cash she had gotten from her sister and paid him five hundred dollars to take her into Arizona.

She wasn't in great shape for the desert hike ahead. She was wearing a decent pair of gray running shoes, but she had some extra weight on her five-foot-three-inch frame. The coyote assured her that the walk would take just four hours, and that there'd be water stations conveniently placed along the way. So she started out with the others. For fourteen hot miles, she managed to keep up with the group, but the hike took at least twice as long as the coyote had promised. And still they had not arrived at their destination along Arivaca Road, east of the refuge, where the smuggler had arranged a pickup. Just a mile and a half south of the road, and rescue, Marta tripped and fell, smashing her left leg against the rocks.

The fall was catastrophic. As she would learn later, she had broken her femur, the long thighbone that connects hip to knee. It's an injury that can be fatal; if the jagged edge of the bone slashes the femoral artery, death from bleeding can come quickly. Marta knew only that the pain was excruciating. Walking was out of the question. Her pollero wasn't about to carry her, and neither was anyone else. And with temperatures topping one hundred degrees, the guide knew that if he left her behind, she was likely to die a slow and painful death from dehydration and exposure.

So he took a page straight out of the Old West, where cowboys shot horses that go lame. He pulled out a gun and said he would shoot her to put her out of her misery.

"He was going to kill me," Gomez remembered later, her eyes widening in horror at the memory. "I cried and told him about my two children."

Her pleas apparently worked. The coyote put the gun away. Still, he and the rest of the group abandoned her in the wilderness, which was about as close to a death sentence as a shot through the skull.

"They left me all alone in the desert," Marta said. "They left me all alone."

The young woman spent the night huddled up on a low hill overlooking a wash, in agony from the pain in her leg. She was terrified. She thought she was going to die in this strange, dangerous country, as her husband had before her. With two parents lost to the desert, her little boys would be orphans.

"It was so cold," she remembered. At least she had water— no thanks to the smuggler. She'd carried the water in herself.

Her luck changed with the sunrise. Early in the morning, a small band of Mexican migrants happened to come along the same trail. They were an extended family group from the village of Tecozautla, in the mountainous central Mexican state of Hidalgo. Among them were Maria and Isaac Cruz Olguín, a young married couple, and their two-and-a-half-year-old son, Isaiah; the little boy's young uncle; and their cousin Raúl Cruz Uribe, a curly haired young man with a genial smile.

The Cruz family was shocked to find the injured woman stranded on the trail. Curled up on the ground, her misshapen leg thrust out among the weeds, Marta told them what had happened. The Cruzes talked the matter over. They were already worried about little Isaiah, his uncle would later explain. The boy seemed to think he was on some kind of adventure, but the trip had already been long, hard, and hot. Back home, in the Hidalgo highlands, temperatures rarely hit eighty degrees, even in the summer. They had never experienced anything like this Sonoran Desert heat.

The Cruzes decided to go for help. Raúl would stay behind to care for Marta while the others went to find the Border Patrol. The family knew full well that helping this Honduran stranger would cost them their own hopes of slipping undetected into America.

"What could we do?" Raúl Cruz Uribe would ask later. "We had to save her life."

Around the time the Cruz group, minus Raúl, made it out safely to Arivaca Road and planted themselves under the thick mesquites to await a passing Border Patrol vehicle, Vince Hampel was starting his shift in Tucson.

A former Navy man, Hampel used to be a regular Border Patrol agent, patrolling Nogales on horseback and mountain bike. Nearly five years before, he'd moved up to the elite Border Patrol Search, Trauma, and Rescue unit. BORSTAR, as it's called, was founded in 1998, the same year the feds initiated Operation Safeguard in Arizona. With migrants pushed farther out into dangerous country like the Buenos Aires wilderness, the deaths and injuries were starting to mount. The new search-and-rescue group was organized specifically to save crossers in distress.

"We find people looking like *Dawn of the Dead,*" said Vince, who'd worked his way up to deputy commander in charge of forty-eight rescue agents. "They're glad to see you at that point. For that moment in their life, I was not the bad guy. I watch them come back to life before my eyes on a good day." He paused. "That isn't always the case, though."

Sometimes, the case is, they die. Deaths were up all along the Arizona border. The broiling year of 2005 was one of the worst in memory for heat and injuries and death. On fifty-two days that summer, the temperature spiked over one hundred degrees.

In that fiscal year, which ended on September 30 just after Marta took her near-fatal fall, the Tucson Sector tallied

216 migrant fatalities, up 75 over the previous year, when 141 perished. The numbers of migrant dead are always a matter of grim dispute, and Kat Rodriguez's Coalición de Derechos Humanos had an even higher tally. Gleaning her figures from the medical examiners in all four border counties, she counted 279 recovered bodies in all of southern Arizona that year. Her body count made a sharp jump up from the 234 dead on her list for 2004. The 2005 deaths set a record that still stood in 2009.

Twenty-one died in September, the same month Marta found herself dangerously injured in Buenos Aires. Among the dead were two young people almost her age. Maria de la Cruz Ramirez Garcia, twenty-six, died on September 7 in Bisbee. Marco Hugo Hernandez Tellez, also twenty-six, fell victim on September 28, in Sierra Vista. Exposure to hot weather killed them both.

But BORSTAR also saves lives. In fiscal 2005, the Tucson Sector made 980 rescues, a big increase over the 653 migrants agents helped in 2004.

"This was a tough summer for the heat," Vince said. "Our rescues went up significantly from last year." The increase, he believed, indicated "we're getting better at what we're doing."

The two women and forty-six men regularly under Vince's command—a dozen more agents were rotated in just for the summer—worked ten-hour shifts, six days a week during the high emergency days of summer, when desert temps can easily reach 110 or 115 degrees. BORSTAR agents are all emergency medical technicians who've passed a rigorous physical fitness test that they must repeat quarterly. In an hour and a half, they must be able to do forty push-ups, seven pull-ups, sixty sit-ups in under two minutes, run a mile and a half in under twelve minutes, and swim two hundred and fifty yards in under six minutes. Then they have to carry an adult five miles. If they get through the test, they're sent to Fort

Huachuca to a special BORSTAR boot camp, which has a graduation rate of just 33 percent.

"We put ourselves in the desert. We don't want to become a detriment because we're out of shape," Vince told me as he steered his SUV west toward Three Points.

I'd come along with Hampel for the day, along with photographer Jay Rochlin. The issue of providing medical care to migrants in peril had come to a head that hot summer. Two young activists with the humanitarian group No More Deaths had been arrested for transporting migrants they said were ill. Shanti Sellz and Daniel Strauss, both twenty-three, had encountered a trio of migrants in distress in the desert near the town of Arivaca. After getting the go-ahead by phone from their medical advisers in Tucson, the young volunteers loaded the migrants into a car for a trip to the hospital. The Border Patrol arrested the pair almost immediately and jailed them on federal charges of aiding and abetting illegal immigration. Sellz and Strauss maintained that they had a humanitarian right to help people in trouble, but they were facing a felony trial and the possibility of fifteen years in prison. (A federal judge dismissed the charges in 2006.) The Border Patrol disputed that the migrants were in danger. In any case, authorities insisted, the activists should have notified the Border Patrol. After all, agents had the medical know-how and manpower to handle emergencies.

So Jay and I were riding along, to see BORSTAR in action.

After the hectic summer, "it's been quiet the last month," Vince said. Early September was rainy and overcast, but with the fading of the monsoons—Arizona's dramatic summer thunderstorms—temperatures were rising again. When the weather was cool, migrants who were healthy could make the walk from Sasabe to Tucson in about six days, Hampel said. But "if it's consistently over a hundred degrees for days, we see lots of problems with heatstroke and exhaustion."

About 8:50 a.m., Vince's radio and cell phone crackled to life in tandem. Two regular Border Patrol agents down in Arivaca had found the Cruz family at the side of the road. Somebody was injured out in the desert.

"It looks like we're going to have a rescue right away," Hampel said, and turned his vehicle south.

At Milepost 7 on Arivaca Road, the Cruz Olguín family sat in the shade under the mesquites, surprisingly cheerful, considering where they'd been and where they were going. Little Isaiah shyly gave me his name, and his mom proudly said he'd turn three in December. But they were surrounded by Border Patrol vehicles and agents. They were about to be loaded into a van and returned to Mexico.

Isaiah's uncle had already left with two BORSTAR agents to find Marta Gomez Garcia. He was the "witness" in the rescue operation, Vince explained. A witness—the person who's reported that someone lies injured in the desert—first gets interviewed for all pertinent information and then, if he's able, leads the rescue workers back to the victim. Occasionally the effort is all for naught. Sometimes the injured migrant rests and then, feeling better, sets out again and vanishes into the brush.

Not this time. Marta was too badly hurt to go anywhere. Led by the young man from Hidalgo, the two rescue agents, Dan McClafferty, a young husband and father, and Julie Gallagher, a former gymnast at Philadelphia's Temple University, trekked quickly the rough mile and a half back to where she was lying on the ground. They found her in a mere twenty-six minutes, Raúl still by her side. First the agents strung a Mylar cloth overhead, giving her a bit of shade in the midmorning heat. The shiny cloth would also signal their location to a Border Patrol plane that was buzzing overhead looking for them. Then they got to work stabilizing their patient.

Radioing back to their boss out on the road, they reported, "She cannot walk. She can't bend her knee. She's a large person."

Armed with this bad news, Hampel ordered the rest of the rescue team to drive into the desert in two vehicles, to get as close to the injured migrant as they could. They couldn't go by helicopter. The heavy Stokes rescue basket they would use to carry her out was too big to fit inside the only copter close enough to help, so small it's called a mosquito. So the agents planned to haul the basket in by Hummer as far as they could go, and carry it in the rest of the way.

But the effort to reach Marta by car was a failure, the first of many setbacks in her rescue. Vince's SUV and the Hummer easily hammered through fragile desert paths, bounced into dry rocky washes, brushed past mesquites. They had the guidance of the Border Patrol plane overhead, coordinates from their Global Positioning Systems, and radio transmissions from Gallagher and McClafferty at the scene. Yet the longer they drove, the more lost they got.

"Maybe we should head back where we came in," the agent in the Hummer radioed to Vince. "I'm getting close to the border."

Hampel stopped his SUV in a remote clearing and looked around. A yellow butterfly wafting by was the only sign of life. He gave a new order: drive back to the road and go in on foot.

By the time we drove back to Arivaca Road and began our desert hike at Milepost 7, it was 10:20 a.m. An hour and a half had already elapsed since the first call for help was radioed in. Five agents—three BORSTARs and two regular Border Patrol—a rescue dog, and Jay Rochlin and I set out southward on the trail at a good clip. The agents shared the burden of the Stokes basket, awkwardly carrying it on the bumpy path. By now it was one hundred degrees. And despite those overhanging mesquite branches, there was little shade.

The foot search proved to be as tricky as the drive. At a wide, rocky wash, the rescue canine, accompanied by its BORSTAR trainer, Paul Du Bois, urged the team to turn left. The dog stopped and whined and pointed its head leftward, but its pleas went unheeded. The agent in the plane circling overhead disagreed with the dog. He thought the group should turn right, and he directed us across the wash and up a steep hill. Following his command, the agents hiked farther and farther from the injured woman, using up precious time and water.

If a dedicated search-and-rescue team can get so turned around, it's easy to see how migrants unfamiliar with the territory—and not in the agents' prime physical condition—run into trouble. I had trouble myself. Circling up and down hills under the blazing sun, I got winded and flushed and had to stop and rest periodically in the sparse shade.

It should have been a twenty-minute walk to Marta, but by the time the hikers finally reset their course and reached the injured migrant, an hour and ten minutes had gone by. It was 11:30 a.m., more than two and a half hours after the initial radio call. Luckily, under Raúl's care, Marta had stayed adequately hydrated. Now McClafferty and Gallagher had things under control. Marta's left thigh was badly swollen, but the EMTs had managed to splint the leg. All Border Patrol agents are required to know Spanish, and Gallagher asked her if she was pregnant. The question is standard when the patient is a young woman, but Marta was stung. "I don't have a husband," she said.

The agents had also listened to Marta's story. "She heard from the guide that it would be a four-hour walk with water stations," McClafferty said. When she broke her leg, "the smuggler left her behind." He gestured to Cruz Uribe and

Isaiah's uncle, who declined to give his name. "These two guys got help for her."

Now that the full team had finally arrived, the crew loaded Gomez into the Stokes basket and strapped her in. They cooled her down with packs of chilled water in plastic bags, and draped a cloth over her face to keep out the sun. They didn't know it yet, but the grueling mile-and-a-half trip to the road would take them an hour and forty-five minutes. And before long, they would run out of water themselves.

At 11:45 a.m., the seven agents began hiking back out with their heavy burden. McClafferty alone was carrying about forty pounds of medical equipment, and the Stokes basket weighed at least twenty pounds. He estimated that his patient weighed one hundred eighty pounds, though a nurse would later say she was closer to one hundred thirty. It took six adults to carry Marta, each grasping the basket's metal bars with one hand and tilting away from the litter for balance.

Every few minutes, they put the basket down and rested, then traded sides, switching from left to right. It was an awkward job, hard on the shoulders and back, like carrying a baby in a car seat, only ten times heavier.

At first the agents were wary of the two captured Mexicans. Would they try to escape when the Border Patrol's attention was diverted? But their worries were baseless. The two men readily took their turns carrying the heavy litter and struggling along with the others. When McClafferty gave his patient an IV to boost her fluids, Raúl carefully carried the bag of fluids aloft, walking close to Marta's head. For a little while, at least, the agents and migrants didn't have to play the parts of migra and UDAs. For a little while, they were simply human beings, working together to save a life.

Progress was agonizingly slow. The rescuers couldn't easily see where they were going. Whoever was in the lead at a given time called out warnings: "Big boulder on left!" "Tree branch!" They took the low, winding road through the wash instead of the high, direct route through the hills, thinking it would be easier to hike, but the wash was problematic. It was loaded with big rocks and occasionally it dropped off steeply into small cliffs. One such promontory was five feet high. Tilting the basket almost vertically, the agents cautiously slid down the rocks, trying not to jostle the patient.

But Marta was in pain, and tears were running down her cheeks.

"Es que me duele mucho," she cried out. *It's just that it hurts so much.*

After noon, clouds blocked the sun, mercifully pushing the temperature down a few degrees, but Vince kept an anxious watch on his troops, and on me and Jay. He insisted that we all keep drinking. Worried about my flushed face, he squirted cold water into my mouth from the pack strapped to his back. All of the agents had similar hydration packs, but they'd been out so long that their water was running out. Vince ordered two of the hardiest agents to forge ahead, to another Humvee another agent had parked somewhere in the creek bed, to fetch more water. After a long time, they returned with gallon jugs of water and small foil packs of a grape-flavored electrolyte drink. Everyone swigged it greedily.

At long last, about 1:15 p.m., after an hour and a half of walking, the ragtag group made it to the Humvee in the wash. The agents hoisted up the heavy basket shoulder-high and loaded Marta inside through a wide back door. Three agents, the dog, and I climbed up front into the blessed air-conditioning; four other agents, two migrants, and one photographer hopped onto the roof, fenced in by handrails.

We were still in hardscrabble desert, another ten- or fifteen-minute drive from Arivaca Road. Agent Juan Delgadillo maneuvered the bulky Humvee up impossibly steep hills and through thick stands of trees, driving right into the branches. They bent and snapped under the onslaught.

Up on the roof, everybody was jubilant, Jay later reported. Migrants and agents alike were slapping high-fives, congratulating each other on a job well done. But inside, strapped to her litter, still in agony, Marta Gomez Garcia had not yet moved on to joy. She began to sob.

"No esperaba seguir viviendo," she suddenly cried out. *I lost hope that I would survive.*

Arivaca Road was blocked by at least a half-dozen law-enforcement vehicles, courtesy of the Border Patrol and Arivaca Fire. A yellow Air Evac helicopter out of Tucson had alighted in the middle of the road. The copter paramedic asked the patient to rate her level of pain, on a scale of 1 to 10. Marta didn't hesitate.

"Diez," she said—*10.*

The paramedic checked McClafferty and Gallagher's handiwork. "This is the best job for traction I've seen," she congratulated them. The two gave each other a look, then slapped another high-five.

"Score one for the Irish," Gallagher whooped.

"We got the job done," McClafferty said more sedately. "It's all human life."

Marta was loaded aboard the helicopter for the short ride to St. Mary's, a Catholic hospital in Tucson. As she sailed up into the sky, headed north away from the border, the two strangers who took pity on her, Raúl Cruz Uribe and his cousin, were being led toward a van for "voluntary return." There would be no reward for their selflessness.

Would he try crossing again?

Raúl flashed his warm smile. No, he said. Not after this. He was going back to Hidalgo, *permanentemente.* Permanently.

Three days later, thanks in large part to Raúl and the rest of the Cruzes, Marta was resting comfortably in her hospital bed. Apart from the enormous cast on her leg, a great, strappy Velcro affair that went from hip to ankle, she looked healthy and pink-cheeked, light-years from the desperate woman I'd met in the desert. She had nothing but kind things to say about the Border Patrol agents who saved her.

Everyone at the hospital had been kind, too, she told me. Many of the staff speak Spanish (she herself knows no English at all, she said with a grin: "Nada, nada"). Hospital surgeons had reset her leg the day after her airborne arrival, and the day after that, the nurses and physical therapists had gotten her up and walking.

The hospital allowed her to call her sister, and Irma in turn called their mother in Honduras to report the good news that Marta was alive, if not entirely well. Now Irma was en route with her husband from North Carolina. Marta, fresh from her village in Honduras, seemed to have no idea how big the United States is. The couple had left by car only the day before, and she thought they'd be arriving momentarily. She'd been officially discharged, her nurse said, but the hospital would let her stay until her family arrived to fetch her.

"The doctors said I have to go to a doctor in North Carolina," she reported. She didn't say what kind of work she was looking for, or what Irma does, but the doctors had given her one piece of problematic news. "They say I can't work for three months."

Still, compared to dying, a three-month wait for a paycheck was not too bad. She smiled at the memory of the kindly Raúl—"He's a nice man"—but she was dismayed to hear that he and his group had been repatriated to Mexico. She caught her breath a moment when I told her why: he thought it was more important to save a stranger's life than it was for him to get into the United States.

Marta herself had nothing more to fear from the Border Patrol. No agents would be turning up at her hospital room, nor waiting for her in the parking lot when she left with her sister.

"We don't go to the hospital," explained Gustavo Soto, a Border Patrol spokesman. "We focus on the border."

In one of the many ironies of U.S. border policy, as a seriously injured person, Marta was free and clear. BORSTAR rescuers don't inquire about the legal status of their patients if they're in shock or in danger of death.

"Our policy is not to determine the 'alienage' of the person who is injured," Soto said. "We switch roles from Border Patrol to rescuer." In the field, one of the regular agents had put it succinctly: "As far as we're concerned, she's a bird-watcher who's been injured."

Marta literally flew away from Border Patrol custody, but patients with lesser medical conditions don't get the same pass. Agents accompany them to emergency rooms, or even guard them in hospital rooms if they're admitted. Once they've recovered and a doctor gives the okay to travel, they're arrested and taken down to headquarters, then sent out of the country.

Critics maintain that the real reason BORSTAR releases the dangerously ill to hospitals is to shield the Border Patrol from migrants' medical bills.

"If the patient is in their custody, then the Border Patrol would have to pay," said Margo Cowan, a Tucson lawyer active with No More Deaths.

Instead, St. Mary's Hospital footed the large bill for Gomez's stay, which lasted four nights and included a major surgery. Curiously, because she was uninsured, the hospital wouldn't supply the crutches she needed; nor would it provide her with clothes. I ended up zipping out to the thrift shop across the street to get her some half-price crutches and stretchy pants that would slip over the cast.

Between St. Mary's in Tucson and Holy Cross Hospital in Nogales, parent company Carondelet Health Network regularly spent about $1.5 million a year on care for injured migrants, said Tom Pepping in 2005, when he was Carondelet's chief financial officer. Tucson's University Medical Center (UMC) spent millions more, he added; as the only trauma hospital in southern Arizona, UMC cares for migrants critically injured in car accidents.

Hospitals are legally bound to treat any of the sick or injured who turn up at their doors, documented or not. In 2005, thanks to a new federal program, hospitals became eligible to get back at least some of the money they spent on migrant care. Section 1011 of the Medicare Modernization Act was supposed to compensate hospitals around the country for the skyrocketing costs of treating illegal immigrants. The feds were to dole out $250 million a year, from 2005 through 2008, with the funds weighted somewhat toward border states. The fund never came close to reimbursing hospitals fully. The money paid only for emergency care; once the patient was out of danger, nothing at all was covered. By the time the program ended in 2008, some hospitals were so frustrated by the burden they'd been forced to assume that they took the legally questionable tactic of deporting patients who would need months of care. (In one notorious case, Tucson's UMC was accused of trying to fly a U.S.-born baby out of the country without the migrant parents' permission.)

But in 2005, Carondelet's Tom Pepping was optimistic that the Medicare money would help. "A pot of money is coming from the federal government to help with the care," he told me. Arizona alone was expected to get $40 million a year.

Even without the money in hand, the Carondelet hospitals willingly shouldered the burden of caring for injured migrants, Pepping said. "Serving those in need is part of our Catholic mission."

Sister Kathleen Mary McCarthy, CSJ, then Carondelet's senior vice president for sponsorship and mission, added that St. Mary's offers compassionate care to all, rich or poor, gay or straight, old or young, legal or illegal.

"Our mission is to treat everybody with great respect, without exception," she said. "As a Catholic hospital, we take it as a serious responsibility to care for the poor. We believe in a God who has his arms around everybody."

BORSTAR's critics in Derechos Humanos and No More Deaths contend that the agency doesn't always respond in a timely fashion to migrants in distress. They can cite any number of cases where troubled travelers were ignored and left by the side of the road. But on this particular day, in this particular case, almost everything went right. God may have had his arms around Marta Gomez Garcia, as Sister Kathleen believes. But the Cruz family and Raúl Cruz Uribe did, too, and so did the copter crew, the St. Mary's doctors and nurses, and the BORSTAR agents.

After the rescue, Vince Hampel was in high spirits, even though his back was "smoked." The airplane pilot had apologized for sending the agents on the ground in the wrong direction, adding at least an hour to the rescue. "Next time, we'll listen to the dog," Vince joked, then turned serious.

He went into law enforcement to help people, he said, and in BORSTAR, "I know deep in my heart, I'm able to participate in saving lives."

Four days after he helped save Marta, St. Mary's delivered her into the arms of her sister, and she headed east, across America, to a new life in North Carolina.

CHAPTER 5

Aurora Morning

I prayed God would send an angel and he sent three.

—*Aurora Lara Flores, migrant from Mexico City*

Annie Swanson, a college student and No More Deaths volunteer, was out patrolling in the Tumacacori Highlands for the second day in a row, walking downhill toward Mexico.

She and a quintet of companions had set out from their camp east of Arivaca in the cool of the early morning, but now, at 9 a.m., the sun was already blazing. By afternoon the thermometer would hit 103.

It was the first day of July 2008, following a particularly hot and lethal June, and the heat was the main reason Annie and the others were out here. Border crossers traveling this popular route in summer were in desperate need of water, and the volunteers were lugging heavy jugs of H2O. They planned to set them out along the trail.

The Border Patrol had been saying that migrant numbers were dropping, but that wasn't what the No More Deaths folks were finding. More miles of border wall, more agents, and more Big Brother snooping technology notwithstanding, this summer the activists had met more migrants than in any of the four previous summers they'd worked this prickly outback. The travelers were abandoning the fortified Altar Valley and taking their chances in the Tumacacori Highlands. Each day, the volunteers could almost count on finding migrants in need of food or water or first aid or serious medical care. Just two weeks before, in the worst of the June heat, they had found a whole family stranded on this same trail: mom, dad, toddler, and sick baby.

Annie was going down the slope at a fast clip through a sycamore grove. Suddenly she saw a child's backpack lying on the ground, its Day-Glo pink unnaturally bright against the desert's sages and buffs. It was a schoolbag, the frilly kind a little girl would be proud to carry to first grade, but it was nowhere near a school. Far from it. It lay abandoned in country that even the Tucson Audubon Society warned was "difficult and strenuous." The sight of the child's bag in the desert was every bit as alarming to Annie as Josseline's green sneakers had been to Dan Millis the previous winter; Dan had found the shoes, and a body, one canyon over from here.

Annie had been trained to observe her surroundings, and she knew that the bag had not been there when she'd coursed through here the day before. Some little girl had dropped it in the last twenty-four hours. Maybe the child was still close by. Annie stopped and looked around at the trees shimmering in the sun, at the hills rising up to the east. Almost before she could begin the usual No More Deaths chant, "Hola, somos amigos"—*Hello, we're friends*—she heard a rustling. She turned. There right in front of her was a young woman limping out of the brush, clutching two little girls by the hands.

The summer had been shaping up to be a bad one. June had been so hot that the heat was like a biblical scourge, and it unleashed a plague of deaths from hyperthermia and exposure. Tucson burned under temperatures as high as 111 and 112 degrees, and the deserts south and west of town were even hotter. Derechos Humanos counted forty migrant bodies recovered in southern Arizona in June, an extraordinary seventeen in the week of June 15 alone.

"Three dead in three days and it's not getting any cooler over the next ten days," Border Patrol agent Patti Fitzsimmons wrote in frustration in her report on the June 16 death of Rosalba Hernandez Dorantes, a young woman from Veracruz. "Within the last three days we've rescued ten groups who were suffering from dehydration."

Arizona's long deadly summer is split into three distinct seasons. In May and June, the sun is white-hot and the air bone-dry, and the temperature spirals up to oven levels. (Tucson's record high is 117, set on June 26, 1990.) The monsoon rains arrive in late June, bringing in a cooler second summer of humid mornings and afternoon thunderstorms. Traditionally, the longed-for rains begin on June 24, the feast of John the Baptist, the patron saint of the holy baptismal waters, and in the Mexican barrios of Tucson, people once celebrated his fiesta by splashing each other with water and, if they were lucky, dancing in the rain. The air dries out by September, ushering in two more months of 90-degree days.

After the terrible week of June 15, the Border Patrol was alarmed enough by the migrant deaths to stage a press conference, outside, in the sweltering heat of Montosa Canyon. Cutting into the western slope of the Santa Rita Mountains, Montosa is one dry river valley and one sky island over from the Tumacacori Highlands, where, a week later, Annie Swanson would find the woman and two children stranded in the desert.

Agents set the date for June 25, the day after the feast of John the Baptist, but they didn't gather to pray for rain. Press officer Mike Scioli and other Border Patrol officials wanted to encourage the media to publicize the dangers of crossing in the summer heat and to boast a little about their rescue operations.

"We've had a number of rescues here," Scioli told the fourteen reporters dutifully assembled, gesturing to the cacti and scrub on the hills. "This is rugged terrain."

Like most of the border highlands, Montosa is known for its rich bird life. In 2004 the Tucson Audubon Society exulted that some black-capped gnatcatchers had settled into the canyon, joining their more abundant cousins, the black-*tailed* gnatcatchers. And the famous dark night skies of southern Arizona had prompted the Smithsonian to build the Fred Lawrence Whipple Observatory on Mount Hopkins just up the road. But these days, the mountains and canyons were becoming better known for migrant trails and deaths than for stars and birds.

"We did 573 rescues in the last fiscal year," Mike said, speaking of the Tucson Sector. "This year we've done 190 rescues since the end of May, a huge rash of rescues. What would have happened to them if we hadn't been there?" Still, he acknowledged, in the past month, from late May to late June, "we've had 29 deaths." He didn't know it then, but two men died the day of the press conference, one of them nearby on the I-19 frontage road. In the remaining days of June, more would follow.

Rosalba Hernandez Dorantes' death was one of the most brutal. She was a twenty-year-old bride from Mexico's southeast coast, a tiny woman just four feet ten, with long black hair and brown eyes. She was traveling north with her husband, Gilberto Ortiz-Ortega, also twenty. The young couple was from Chiconquiaco, a mountain town sixty-seven hundred feet up in the cool green forests of the Sierra Madre Oriental. The village, a state Web site proudly boasts, is "watered by small streams."

On Monday, June 16, a day of blinding sun and intense heat, husband and wife were tramping across the Tohono O'odham Reservation, a flat, waterless desert where the only green in the landscape was from the intermittent cacti and acacias. The mercury hit 112 by midday. Another young married couple was with them, Agustín Mena-Manzano and Rosio Mejia-Munoz, from Mazatecochio, in Tlaxcala, Mexico, two states over from Veracruz. The four were on their second day of walking in temps over 100; their first day out, Sunday, it had been 110.

They ran out of water by Monday, and Rosalba and Rosio started getting sick. In the evening, both young women collapsed four miles south of the hamlet of Vamori. For all practical purposes, they were in the middle of nowhere. Sells—the small town that serves as the Reservation's capital—was another half day's walk away. A panicked Agustín used his cell phone to call the Border Patrol. As their wives lay ill nearby, the two young husbands hurriedly gathered up some dry twigs and lit a signal fire. Two helicopters managed to track them down.

One agent "determined that the two females were suffering extreme dehydration," Agent Fitzsimmons later wrote in her report, describing the tragedy in the spare language of cops everywhere. "Due to the remoteness of the location and the extreme condition of the females," the agents loaded all four travelers into a copter and at 9:45 p.m. took off for the Indian Health Service Hospital at Sells. The ER doc did an emergency tracheotomy on Rosalba, frantically cutting open her neck and jamming in a tube to help her breathe. Then he shocked her failing heart with a defibrillator, sending jolts of electricity into her chest. She died anyway, within minutes of arrival. She was "pronounced," the report said, at 10:08 p.m.

Rosio still had a chance. An air ambulance flew her to the better-equipped St. Mary's Hospital in Tucson. The two young husbands, one grieving for his wife, the other terrified for his, were arrested and led away in handcuffs. While Rosalba was taken to the morgue and Rosio to another hospital, Gilberto and Agustín were driven under guard to the Border Patrol holding pen in Casa Grande.

—

Exactly two weeks to the day that Rosalba died and forty-two miles to the east, Aurora Lara Flores and her two little girls were perched in a tree. Aurora, a city girl born and bred, was bewildered by the wilderness.

In this place, hilly and surreal, strangely shaped cacti jutted out into the rocky path. Prickers pierced her skin and branches banged her forehead. She'd been walking it two days already and her feet had sprouted enormous blisters, great festering circles the size of silver dollars. She could barely take baby steps anymore, let alone hike.

She was on one of the toughest trails in southern Arizona. Coyotes liked it because it was a hop-step from the border and headed almost straight north, bypassing the tallest mountains thereabouts. In the summertime, it was a migrant expressway, thronged with travelers. Job seekers were not the only ones on the path. The Audubon Society warned birders that "it can be a route for illegal drug trafficking."

Josseline had suffered in the winter cold out here, but Aurora was sweltering in the summer heat, of a magnitude unimaginable in her native Mexico City, where the seventy-three-hundred-foot elevation makes for a temperate climate. The sun here was fierce, so hot it felt like fire on top of her head. And where Josseline was a young girl trying to get to her mother, Aurora was a mother herself, trying her damndest to keep her two little girls alive. The three of them, twenty-seven-year-old Aurora, seven-year-old Cynthia, and four-year-old Vanessa, had been stranded out here since the night before.

Back in Agua Caliente, in Mexico City, Aurora worked as a cashier in a *tienda,* selling soda and gum and *pan dulce,* the popular Mexican sweet bread. The store was not exactly a high-profit enterprise, and for a hired cashier, "it doesn't pay much." Aurora and her husband were separated, and he did nothing for their girls, bought them nothing, "nada, nada," she would tell me later, anger in her voice.

So she hatched a plan to join her sister in Sacramento. Go to Altar, her friends advised, find a coyote. "Everybody knows that's what you do to get into America," Aurora said. So she packed up the little girls and headed north by bus with a cousin. In the Sonoran town, she settled on a coyote and a price: two thousand dollars apiece. Her sister would pick up the tab, six thousand dollars, payable on delivery in Sacramento.

"Eight people in all were in the group," she said: a Salvadoran headed for New Jersey, a Chiapaneco en route to Kansas, a deported Tucsonan trying to get back home.

The guide had guaranteed them a walk of *un día y una noche, no más*—"one day and one night, that's it"—but after two days they were nowhere near their destination, the Arizona town of Amado, on Interstate 19. Aurora was plump, and her only exercise back home had been punching keys on the *tienda* cash register. She had trouble with the hills and the heat, and after two days of up-and-down hiking she began to falter.

The pollero was young, about twenty, and *muy amable*, "very kind," she would say later. Unlike Marta Gomez's gunslinger, "he behaved very well." He had crossed la frontera with his dad as a child, and he tried to help the young mother by carrying her girls. When Aurora grew weary, he insisted that the others stop while she rested. "They waited and waited for me," she said. And they shared water on the hike; when it ran low, "they reserved it first for the women and children, and then the children."

Their kindness did her little good. Aurora's blisters grew until finally her shredded feet could carry her no farther. She sat down in the dirt in despair, and declared that she simply couldn't walk another step.

The guide took precautions to keep the little family safe.

He got them as far as a regular No More Deaths route, and he pointed out the water jugs left in the shade by the activists. Aurora and her kids would have plenty to drink. The young man assured her that some of the American humanitarians would be back in the morning. He and the other travelers picked up some water for themselves, then turned and hurried north, scrambling up the slope.

Now Aurora and the girls were alone. The noises of the desert night—the snapping of tree branches, the calling of birds, the lowing of wandering cows—seemed louder than the car horns and street music back home in Mexico City. And scarier. Ranchers here let their cattle loose to fend for themselves, and the Floreses were terrified of the big *vacas* wandering in and out of the glen. Though they were in every possible peril—from hyperthermia, from dehydration, from rapists, from bandits, from arrest by the Border Patrol—it was the cows Aurora focused on. When one ambled close, mom and girls scrambled up a spiky mesquite. There was not much she could do about all the other dangers of the desert, but in the tree at least Aurora knew that her kids were out of bovine reach. They spent the night up there in the branches.

Cynthia's pink schoolbag—she had just finished first grade in Mexico City—dropped unnoticed to the ground.

Annie Swanson was spending her summer vacation roughing it in Arizona precisely because of Aurora, Cynthia, and Vanessa, and other migrants like them. No More Deaths volunteers came from all over the country—Annie was going to college in Washington, D.C.—to spend a week or two or more camping in primitive conditions and traipsing on arduous trails looking for border crossers in need. Often they hiked morning and afternoon, racking up twelve miles and more in one day. Despite the hope expressed in the group's name—"No Más Muertes," in Spanish—they knew they couldn't save every migrant from dying. But they could save a few. "We're doing Band-Aid work," sighed Rev. Gene Lefebvre, seventy-four, a retired Presbyterian minister from Tucson who was on patrol with Annie when she found the Flores family. "We call it civil initiative, not civil disobedience."

The No More Deathers were inspired by the Sanctuary Movement of the 1980s. Back then, Tucson activists had helped smuggle Central American refugees into the United States and then spirited them to safety—to sanctuary—in churches. What they were doing was against the law. Leaders Jim Corbett and John Fife and fourteen others were arrested for smuggling aliens, and Fife and seven others were convicted. The sanctuary workers believed they were answering a higher moral calling. U.S. dollars had paid for the death squads that the Salvadoran and Guatemalan refugees were fleeing, and the sanctuary folks felt duty-bound to save the people U.S. policy had put in jeopardy.

No More Deaths was taking a similar stand, in their case against a U.S. border policy that the activists believed was killing poor workers whose only crime was trying to make a living. (Fife, then pastor of Tucson's Southside Presbyterian Church, was a cofounder of No More Deaths in 2004.) The activists blamed the migrant deaths on NAFTA, which had pushed border crossers deeper into poverty at home, and on Operation Gatekeeper, which had funneled them into perilous Arizona.

"It's hard to *not* feel it's a conscious choice" to tolerate a certain number of migrant deaths, Oona, a young volunteer from California, told me. "It's violent."

No More Deaths asserted that humanitarian aid was never a crime, and the volunteers followed a number of basic tenets, inspired by the "civil initiatives" formulated by Corbett, a Quaker. Gene Lefebvre explained the rules: "Be directly involved with victims. Get the stories out. Do it openly. We apprise the government [of] what we're doing, why we're doing it. We work toward a time when we don't need to do this work, when the policy will change."

The group got its start out of frustration. In 2002, when fatalities along the border were starting to mount, a humanitarian group calling itself the Samaritan Patrol began roaming the deserts southwest of Tucson, looking for migrants in need. In 2002 I went out on a Samaritan run with Rick Ufford-Chase, a Presbyterian minister who at the time headed BorderLinks, a group that organizes educational trips to the border. We left Tucson at 5 a.m. on a summer morning and stayed out all day, driving the back roads around Arivaca and traipsing through the Buenos Aires National Wildlife Refuge, where Marta Gomez Garcia would later break her leg. Rick had a booming pastoral voice, and as we hiked the backcountry he did his best to summon migrants out of hiding, calling "Hola, amigos!" We had plenty of water and food to give, but all day long we never found a single soul to give them to.

Rick pondered the problem as we walked. A fixed camp deep in the desert, along the most-traveled migrant routes, he said, would make more sense than all this wandering. Activists were already starting to plan for it. Two summers later, in 2004, multiple migrant-aid groups in Tucson came together and founded No More Deaths. Camp Byrd unfurled its flag, a green cross on a white background—counterpoint to the green and white of the Border Patrol SUVs—in the wilds near Arivaca.

Author Byrd Baylor owns a ranch out here, a wide-open spread south of Twin Peaks, a matched set of shapely mountains. Byrd is well known for her lyrical children's books about the Southwest, and a novel of O'odham life, *Yes Is Better Than No.* Living just six or seven miles north of the border, Byrd has seen more than her share of desperate migrants. She makes a point of getting up every morning to see the sun rise—one of her books, *The Way to Start a Day,* is about greeting the dawn—and she's used to sharing her breakfast with the half-starved travelers who regularly knock at her door.

"Today I started my day when two migrants came to the door at four thirty a.m.," she said during a talk in Tucson in October 2008. "By the time we figured out what they needed, it was getting on toward ten or eleven."

Unlike many of the "faith-based" No More Deaths volunteers, Byrd said she is "not in the least religious, which frees me from a lot of things. But I'm devoted to the saints, Jude, Martin, El Niño de Atocha, the Virgin of Guadalupe. All the people who come to my house want to light a candle [to the saints] before they continue their journey."

Beginning in 2004, and every year since, Byrd has allowed the activists to set up their camp on her land all summer long. Short and skinny, with a face deeply creviced by years outdoors, Baylor was already eighty by the time Camp Byrd rolled out. A feisty sort, she took the risk of alienating her neighbors when she okayed the camp.

Some of the Arivaca ranchers hated that the migrants were streaming through, hated that Byrd was letting do-gooder outsiders in. The first summer that college kids and lefties and religious types from around the country came down to southern Arizona to save the migrants, merchant Jack Baker was apoplectic. Baker ran the feed shop in town, and whenever he saw a No More Deaths vehicle cruise by on Arivaca Road, he would run outside past the bales of hay and shake his fists. Then he'd give the driver the finger. When I went to interview him, he turned to me with such anger I thought he might hit me. He loathed the migrants.

"They leave behind millions of water bottles," he snarled. "Cowboys are fixing their fences all day. Calves get shredded going through the holes in the barbed wire" cut by migrants.

"It should be legal to shoot them. Illegal is illegal." He didn't much care for the volunteers either. "These assholes are making it tougher on us. If those kids had a job they wouldn't have time to do this."

Then he hesitated. "Byrd is a customer of mine," he said. He didn't like to speak ill of a local.

Arivaca, population one thousand, is a rugged individualist kind of place, part ranch town, part hippie haven. Longtime ranchers mix with the artists and New Agers who started moving here in the 1980s when land was cheap. Some of the neighbors thought that Byrd was doing a fine thing, and others hewed to the western axiom of live and let live. Certainly it was true that many were troubled about the migrants crossing their land.

Sundog, the solo-named caretaker of Ruby, a historic ghost town between Arivaca and the border, told me in 2007 that he was exhausted by the needs of the migrants who paraded nightly through nearby Chimney Canyon. He was "supportive" of them, he explained, and he often fed them and gave them clothes. "A guy doesn't leave his wife, travel one thousand miles, doesn't see his wife and kids, unless he's desperate. If I'm down there by myself, and one or two show up, I do what I can to help. But when a hundred or a thousand go by…" He sighed. "It's an emergency for them when they come to my door. To me, it's another wetback, somebody else who needs help. It's wearing me down."

No More Deaths, he added, "take[s] the pressure off us. They're doing good work. I'm grateful to have them around."

Most of Arivaca's rural libertarians, even if they despise the volunteers, are none too keen on the Border Patrol's virtual occupation of the town. When Homeland Security built a tower almost one hundred feet tall on a hill overlooking the town, Arivacans reacted in fury. The tower was part of a prototype "virtual fence," just one in a chain of high-tech surveillance towers outfitted with cameras, radar, motion detectors, thermal imaging, and the like. Called Project 28 for the twenty-eight miles it covered along the border around Sasabe, the system was phase one of the Secure Border Initiative, or SBI-net, a projected network of virtual fences all along the southwest line. But Project 28 never worked right. Built at a cost of $20 million by Boeing, the faulty towers became a major embarrassment for Homeland Security. The feds handed Boeing another $65 million to fix them.

By 2009, the towers were taken down. Homeland Security again hired Boeing, this time to build fifty-three miles of a new and improved SBI-net fence around Sasabe and Ajo. Boeing's new paycheck: $100 million. If that worked right, the Border Patrol was dreaming of erecting a virtual fence from the Pacific to the Gulf of Mexico, to the tune of $6.7 billion.

The Arivaca locals didn't much like the low-tech enforcement either. They hated having to go through the checkpoint at Amado to reach the highway, and the checkpoint's generators and radios blasted noise at all hours. At a fund-raiser for Byrd Baylor in September 2007—she'd been diagnosed with cancer—neighbors were inflamed with talk of the Black Hawk helicopter that had buzzed several of their homesteads two nights before. A woman who lived alone said the copter had hovered over her house for an hour, its bright lights turning night to day. Six armed officers turned up at her door and tromped around her outbuildings, but refused to say why. "The helicopter saw a bunch of wets on your property," a local cop told her the next day. "But they only caught one."

A man who gave his name only as Kyle was disgusted. "Six times it shone its light on my house," he said. "It was Homeland Security. It was sixty to seventy decibels. It rattled. The walls shook. Around here it's *1984*."

———

No More Deaths had its own uneasy relationship with the Border Patrol and the other law enforcement agents who worked the public lands around Arivaca, as the 2005 arrests of Shanti Sellz and Daniel Strauss demonstrated. As of 2009 Sellz and Strauss had faced the most serious charges, for transporting migrants; their case eventually was dropped, but only on a technicality. Other cases followed.

The day after Dan Millis found Josseline in February 2008, he mourned at home, shaken by the girl's death and the harsh reality of her corpse. "It was hard," he said later. "It was a haunting image. It was horribly draining." But the second day he set out again with new purpose, so as "not to feel helpless," and began leaving water jugs near Brown Canyon on the Buenos Aires refuge. Although he regularly picked up migrant trash in his forays into the wilderness, this time, two U.S. Fish and Wildlife Service officers arrested him for littering. They made him go back and fetch the water bottles he had left for thirsty migrants. Instead of paying the fine, Dan insisted on a trial, prompting the *Tucson Citizen* to editorialize against the government for literally making a federal case out of littering, in a case where the "litter" was bottles of water intended to save lives. He was found guilty but sentencing was suspended, hence no punishment.

"To have my hands slapped by the same government that caused the problem [of migrant deaths] in the first place!" Dan exclaimed. "It was absurd."

In December the same year, Fish and Wildlife went after No More Death's Walt Staton, in the same place, and for the same reason: littering the refuge with water bottles. The Border Patrol sent three agents and one helicopter to help track him down. Staton was convicted in June 2009. The judge ordered him to perform community service—picking up trash on public lands.

In another incident, one August afternoon in 2008, the Border Patrol horse team surrounded the No More Deaths camp. Agents and equines blockaded the shelter. A dozen seminary students were there, volunteering along with some of the Tucson regulars. (The seminarians were in for a tough week. A few days later they were banished from the Tohono O'odham Reservation for accompanying a tribal activist who was filling tanks with water for migrants, an activity banned on the Rez.)

I happened to be riding to a hearing in Nogales with Margo Cowan, the indefatigable pro bono attorney for No More Deaths, when the "situation," as she called it, erupted.

Three migrants resting at the camp had been arrested, two young volunteers had been read their Miranda rights, and everybody else was ordered to stay put. Gene Lefebvre arrived back from patrol to find the young workers encircled by law enforcement officers on horses. He insisted that as camp leader he and only he should be arrested. Margo went into high gear. As she maneuvered her yellow truck down the highway, she worked her phone nonstop, calling the U.S. Attorney, the agents in the field, the volunteers.

"I said we would voluntarily present anyone they want to talk to," she explained to me. "We wanted no field arrests." Eventually she got the callback she was hoping for. The agents had left, taking only the three migrants with them, leaving even Gene behind. "Hey brother, good work," she exulted to the minister over the phone, then turned to me. "The Border Patrol has agreed to continue the discussion later."

The threatened arrests were the first by the Border Patrol since Daniel Strauss and Shanti Sellz were picked up in 2005, Margo said: the group had learned its lesson from that incident. "We were naive at first. We thought we should put the ill migrants in a car" and drive them to a hospital. "We realized they should be in an ambulance. We call 911 now. Our sophistication evolved.

"Everything we do is transparent. We're just a group of people who think migrants shouldn't die in the desert on their way to clean toilets."

If the Border Patrol thought the No More Deaths volunteers were skating on thin legal ice, the volunteers threw the same charge right back at them. They were regulars at the two second-degree murder trials of Agent Nicholas Corbett in Tucson in 2008. Corbett had fatally shot an undocumented migrant on June 12, 2007, in the desert near Douglas. The six-feet-four-inch Border Patrol agent claimed self-defense, saying he had fired on Francisco Javier Domínguez Rivera when the much smaller man threatened him with a rock. Francisco's companions, including his two brothers, contradicted the agent, saying Domínguez had been kneeling to surrender when Corbett shot him.

At an early hearing, Cochise County medical examiner Guery Flores, the same doctor who had examined the body of Silverio Huinil Vail, presented evidence that went against Corbett's story. Two separate juries failed to arrive at a verdict, and after two mistrials, Cochise County declined to go for a third trial. Corbett was a free man. Border Patrol supporters applauded the ruling, saying that a law enforcement officer should not be prosecuted for doing his job. Migrant supporters decried the result as evidence that the agency was above the law.

No More Deaths volunteers and other activists were also regular witnesses at the daily Operation Arizona Denial trials in the federal courthouse in downtown Tucson. Starting in January 2008, every weekday, sixty hapless migrants were paraded in chains into the courtroom for a mass trial the likes of which has rarely or ever been seen in the United States. They were still dressed in their dirty traveling clothes, muddy jeans and sweaty shirts. Eight or ten lawyers congregated in front of the judge, each having had the opportunity to spend just a few minutes with his or her clients before the hearing. On the day I attended, in April 2008, every single migrant pleaded guilty, calling out in Spanish one by one, *"culpable, culpable, culpable."* Those getting caught for the first time were sentenced to time served—a period of several days—but repeat offenders were remanded to jail for up to 180 days in a for-profit Corrections Corporation of America prison.

The new convicts were the unfortunate guinea pigs in a new program. Most of those caught by Border Patrol were still part of "catch and release"—they'd get processed at a station, then quickly shipped back over the line through "voluntary return." But now, under Operation Arizona Denial, sixty a day were arrested near Sasabe, randomly skimmed from the rest, and slapped with criminal charges. With the criminal conviction for illegal entry, none of them would ever be permitted to apply to come to the United States legally.

"Our goal is to eliminate voluntary return," Tucson Sector Border Patrol chief Robert Gilbert explained at a news conference in October 2008. The message Denial sent was, "If you come into this country illegally you will be prosecuted. Ninety percent are coming up here for economic reasons. But they've violated the law."

Critics argued that the trials themselves violated the law. "This has come at great cost to human rights and due process of law," Thomas W. Hillier II, a federal public defender, wrote in a letter dated April 22, 2008, to the U.S. Senate Judiciary Committee. "Arrestees are detained in overcrowded facilities....There is no time or space for defense counsel to consult privately or individually with clients, and insufficient time to investigate legal or factual defenses. In *en masse* assembly line proceedings, 30, 80, 100 people who do not speak English and are not familiar with the American legal system are asked to waive their constitutional rights and are convicted and sentenced on the spot."

If the Denial program was denying due process to its

detainees, it also sought to control the citizen observers in the courtroom. The atmosphere was harsh. When I stood up during a break to count the lawyers in attendance, a federal marshal rushed over and curtly ordered me to sit down. The same marshal enforced another courtroom rule: no eye contact with the prisoners. At the end of the hearing, when the No More Deaths observers smiled at the migrants marching past in their chains, he yelled at the women to stop. No smiling, either.

"You treat these people like fucking criminals," one young woman screamed back. "Now you think you can treat me like a criminal."

In September 2008 No More Deaths issued *Crossing the Line,* a formal report documenting human rights abuses of migrants in short-term custody on the Arizona/Sonora border. The volunteers had compiled two years' worth of data, gleaned from interviews of returned migrants who'd turned up at their aid stations in Agua Prieta and Nogales, Sonora.

"With every bus load of repatriated migrants, we hear testimonies that they weren't given enough to eat, they had little access to water after being in the desert for days, and were denied needed medical attention," Maryada Vallet, an emergency medical technician who was a mainstay of the Nogales aid station, said at a press conference at the Unitarian Universalist church in Tucson. (No More Deaths had recently become a ministry of the church.) "Even more distressing, we regularly have people coming to us still crying, bleeding, or wincing in pain from abuse suffered while in U.S. custody."

Crossing the Line assembled a litany of complaints from four hundred individual migrants: "A young woman, age 17, reported being touched inappropriately while in Border Patrol custody." "34 men, one woman, and two youth, both age 17, reported being held for about 8 hours and only receiving a little cup of water and crackers. When they asked for food, they were told, 'We're not a *fucking* restaurant.'" "Alejandra, a woman who was four months pregnant, reported being denied food and water while in Border Patrol custody." "Jacobo was held by the Border Patrol for 36 hours before being repatriated in the middle of the night. He was not given 'real food,' only crackers...he also was not released with the rest of his family members."

I'd heard similar stories from migrants myself. Carlos Ortiz, the deported Chevron worker I met in Agua Prieta, had spent a night at the Douglas Border Patrol station in October 2008. "It was dirty. Forty or fifty people in one cell," he said, and "one toilet." He was given only juice and peanut butter crackers. In June 2008 I met Raymundo Ahuatl Martinez, twenty-four, at the Migrant Resource Center in Naco, Sonora. A deportee originally from Puebla, lately a cook at Olive Garden in Dayton, Ohio, he had been held in the Naco, Arizona, Border Patrol station three days, he said. "I slept on the floor, no blanket. They gave us just water and crackers."

Long-term detention facilities must abide by certain legal standards, providing food, water, medical care, and sanitation facilities. The Border Patrol processing stations, meant to hold migrants for only twenty-four hours, fall between the legal cracks. The No More Deaths authors demanded new standards that would guarantee appropriate treatment for migrants in the Border Patrol's short-term custody. Maryada Vallet was carrying the report to Washington, in hopes of persuading elected officials to take action.

Tucson Sector chief Gilbert was angry about the report, and denied its charges out of hand. "I've seen the allegations," he said a month after the press conference. "If medical attention is needed, it gets provided. We're not mind readers. How do we know if someone has family traveling with them unless they tell us? When we make an arrest in the field you go through a whole process. You see the fear in their eyes. By the time we get them to the station their fears are dispelled."

He also blamed the activists for not bringing the complaints directly to him at the time they were made. "I have heartburn with No More Deaths," he said. Some of the accusations were two years old, and the Border Patrol had no means of investigating them. "These allegations of abuse— it's grandstanding."

I told him I had seen two young women and a four-year-old girl dropped off in the evening, in Nogales, Sonora, in the sketchy downtown neighborhood of bars and brothels. They were from faraway Puebla, and they were wandering the streets when a couple of No More Deaths volunteers happened upon them and offered to take them to a shelter. Why leave them so vulnerable? Why not at least return them in the daytime?

The Border Patrol is "between a rock and a hard place," Gilbert insisted. "We can't keep them too long. And Nogales has hotels."

Camp Byrd is a primitive affair with an outdoor kitchen under a ramada—an open-air shelter—and a single latrine out behind the creosote bushes. Campers were free to put their cots anywhere under the stars.

I camped out with six No More Deaths volunteers the night before the Aurora morning. While Aurora Lara Flores and her girls dozed fitfully in their tree, I slept in a comfortable cot in the cool open air, with a fine view of Twin Peaks and an inky sky sprinkled with stars. I heard migrants walking past in the night, their soft footsteps crackling twigs, their metal food cans faintly clanging. Following Byrd Baylor's example, the campers rose with the sun at five. By 6:30 a.m., just before the heat started stoking up, a four-woman search team ventured out with the septuagenarian Rev. Gene, with me in tow.

Two of the volunteers were college students—Annie, from American University, and Jennifer, from Berkeley—and two were young working women, a couple named Oona and Kate. Hadley from Boston stayed behind to mind the camp and help any travelers who might turn up.

Gene was proud of his Toyota FJ Cruiser, a sturdy vehicle that managed to stay grounded on the tilting ranch roads. Even some Border Patrol agents had admired it, he said. Swerving and shimmying up the hilly dirt tracks, he could go only a few miles an hour. He traveled south, crossing a patchwork of public lands and private ranches leased from the state. Metal gates slung across the roads at irregular intervals kept the cows from wandering too far, and we had to stop at each one. I was riding shotgun, so I had to get out, swing the gates open wide, and then close them again once Gene chugged through.

First stop was the "bonsai tree," a twisted mesquite growing in fantastic shapes. It cast some nice shade, making it a popular migrant resting spot. Border crossers had recently been by. A plastic food bin was empty, and the jugs of water the activists had placed in the shade a few days earlier were gone. The travelers had left behind bottles of green "cow tank" water, drawn from the artificial ponds dug by ranchers. Cattle can drink the bacteria-infested water safely; humans can't. The team dumped it out—to keep any future travelers from vomiting it up—then set out fresh gallons of clean water, along with a supply of applesauce and granola bars.

We split into two hiking groups, each armed with trail maps created by volunteer Ed McCullough, a retired geoscientist. Oona, Kate, and I headed north on the easier path to a cow tank; Annie, Jennifer, and Gene picked the more arduous route south toward Mexico—and toward the Flores family, anxiously awaiting help. Everyone lugged the eight-pound water jugs, in packs on their back and in their arms. Our walk was tough going at first, between the extreme heat and the uphill path and the overhanging branches. Our clothes quickly soaked through with sweat. Soon enough, though, the path eased into a flat wash at the bottom of the shady canyon.

Sneaker footprints in the dirt signaled that the trail was live. Just like their opposite numbers in the Border Patrol, the activists were adept at tracking.

"Tracks when they are new are very precise," Kate said authoritatively. This was her third July as a No More Deaths volunteer. "People would have been walking here about an hour before." The walkers had left trash behind too, a fresh trail of empty tuna and meat cans, and plenty of Red Bulls, the high-caffeine drink that's a migrant favorite.

Oona had worked with migrants in the Pacific Northwest, and she spoke empathetically of what would push workers to take a trek like this in order to get a job. "In the work I've done organizing day laborers, what I hear is, 'I'm willing to take a risk, to do something dangerous, to be looked down on, so I can take care of me and my family.' I've met so many people who say, 'I'd go back tomorrow.' But the reality is that people migrate to where the work is."

We dropped off the water jugs at designated spots, labeling them in black marker with the date and location, to keep track of where migrants were drinking water and where they were traveling. Sometimes the No More Deathers left a friendly note on the bottles. "Buena suerte," they'd write. *Good luck.* Once we got rid of the heavy jugs, the hike turned into a pleasant ramble, and we ate a snack at a cow pond under the shade of some dewy trees, sunlight slanting in on the water, mountains rising up above the canyon. Only the clattering of a Border Patrol helicopter overhead interrupted the peace and quiet. "It's so beautiful here," Oona said.

The mood turned urgent a couple of hours later, when we got news of Aurora and her daughters. Jennifer and Gene turned up late at our meeting point on the ridge. They climbed up to the dirt road after a round-trip hike of six miles in the heat, and reported they'd found a migrant family. It was a mother and two little girls. The mom couldn't walk because of her blisters, and Annie had already bandaged up her feet. She was staying with them in the desert until Gene could come back around with the SUV.

If the roads we'd traveled earlier hardly deserved the name, the ones closer to Mexico were like wilderness trails, only slightly wider, marginally able to support a vehicle. Gene grappled with the wheel, trying to keep his Toyota from tipping, while Jennifer, trained in GPS technology just the day before by geoscientist McCullough, directed him through the backcountry's twists and turns. Cows wandered lonely over all these parts, standing in the trench that passed for a road, peering out from behind the trees, looking with mild-eyed surprise at our noisy intrusion. Rain clouds were starting to gather, blocking out the sun but raising fears of lightning and flash flooding.

The car engine announced our presence in advance in this quiet place. When Gene finally got to the bottom of the hill where the Floreses were stranded, they were already walking—make that mincing, in the case of Aurora— emerging out of the shady glen. Cynthia held her mother's hand as they descended the slope, and Vanessa was on Annie's hip.

They were beautiful little girls, each with wide brown eyes and a single black braid dangling down her back. Cynthia, the first grader, was missing her front teeth. They were wearing jeans and tiny pink-and-white sneakers eminently unsuited to the strenuous trails they'd been hiking. They made for an amazing sight, sweet and lovely and incongruous in this dangerous place. Their mother had wept while they waited on the ridge for rescue, Annie said, and praised the volunteers, crying out, "I prayed God would send an angel and he sent three."

But the girls were happy. They were enchanted by the butterflies darting about, and they careened around the scrub, their arms flapping, chasing the butterflies, playing at being *mariposas.* Now as they came down the hill, they smiled shyly at the first Americans they had ever met.

CHAPTER 6

Ambos Nogales

They found two bodies floating.

—Mike Scioli, U.S. Border Patrol agent

Mike Scioli stood along a concrete drainage ditch on a street in Nogales, Arizona, and peered down at the water rushing north. The stream was at least three feet deep, and pouring out of a tunnel. We bent over and squinted. We couldn't see very far up the pipe, but Scioli said it went clear to the other side of the border, deep into Nogales, Sonora.

On the morning of July 15, 2008, Scioli, a public information officer for the Tucson Sector, had driven me down to Nogales, a straight shot to the border sixty-four miles south of Tucson, to get a look at the operations in the busiest Border Patrol station in the nation. Mike was a cheerful sort, a gregarious Italian American from Buffalo, but he began our day on a grim note. The first thing he said to me was "we found two dead bodies last night."

Four migrants had slipped into the pipe on the Mexican side, on Monday evening, July 14. To get to the United States, they were willing to brave the filthy sewer water but they hadn't counted on a flood underground. A fierce storm had deluged the pipes a few days earlier. "The water was rising,"

Mike said, making the always treacherous passage even riskier. Almost as soon as the men plunged into the whirlpool, they realized the danger, but only two were able to slosh their way back to Sonora.

Once on dry land, they ran to the port of entry to raise the alarm. The U.S. Border and Customs agents, absorbed in the tedium of checking passports and poking through car trunks, looked up in surprise. Two men, the migrants frantically told them, were still below ground, in the water.

"We got a call from Customs," Mike said. "They said two people took off north. We did a search but we couldn't find anything. The water was so high." Cops from the Nogales, Arizona, Police Department joined the hunt, too, and they located the pair. But by that time the men had drowned. Mike said, "They found two bodies floating."

Both men ended their journeys *al Norte* in an American ditch. The bloated corpse of Oscar Montoya Nava, forty, surfaced on Monte Vista Drive, and Ventura Portillo Torres, twenty-four, came to rest at North Grand Avenue, Nogales, Arizona, U.S.A.

The hills of southern Arizona slope downward toward Mexico, dipping at the border into a deep wash at the twin towns of Nogales. On the far side of the international divide, the land rises up again, cascading into the hills of Sonora.

The border fence—built in the 1990s and rusted and graffitied like crazy by 2008—runs through the ravines and snakes up the canyons in between the two Nogaleses. Nicknamed Nogy (rhymes with "bogie"), the two hill towns also answer to Ambos Nogales, meaning "both Nogales." *Nogales* is the Spanish word for "walnuts," and the name is a tribute to the nut trees that once grew abundantly in the mountain passes in this high desert.

Today, straddling the international line, the towns are

hard urban places, stripped of almost all vegetation, not to mention walnut trees. Cramped storefronts line the sidewalks, and walkers and cars throng the streets.

Tucson painter Paco Velez grew up in Sonoran Nogales, and he crowds his crayon-bright canvases with the pungently colored walls and lettered signs of the Mexican streetscape of his childhood. Born in 1975, he used to walk over the border daily to go to a Catholic elementary school in the other Nogales, in Arizona.

"It was never a big deal," he said. "In first and second grade, I would see the same officers every day. They would know, 'He's going to school.' It was easy."

But the border turned into a menacing place of barriers and turnstiles and concrete, and customs agents demanding identification and explanations for his trip. Paco was legal, but he began to dread crossing.

"You feel guilty, powerless. The way you're approached, you get that guilty feeling. They interrogate you. I have a right to cross the border, but you have to be submissive. I hate crossing. It's intimidating."

Border Patrol vehicles race up and down the American cliffs and summits, and their observation towers and cameras keep an eye on whole populations. Thirty thousand people live on the Arizona side, Mike Scioli said, and ten times that number on the Mexican, making Ambos Nogales the biggest city on the Arizona-Sonora border.

"Nogales is the largest station in the Tucson Sector," Mike boasted as we walked into the station. "Forty-six percent of all [migrant] trips in the sector" take place in the territory patrolled by the Nogales agents.

"We have a big rush after Three Kings Day," January 6, the customary close of the Mexican Christmas season. "We can't fit them all in here." The giant holding pens that handle the holiday hordes were empty on this July day; only about thirty prisoners were in the regular cells. Three women were lying down in the "female" cell; two were stretched out on benches, one on a bare mattress on the floor. They looked exhausted. Mike shrugged off the allegations of abuse made by No More Deaths and others. There's no bedding, he agreed, but that's because "by law, we can't keep them longer than twenty-four hours." The menu is not extensive but it's adequate, he said. "We give them crackers, chili, water, juice."

Outside, horses from the patrol's equine division whinnied in their corrals. "Our Tucson Sector Horse Patrol has just three percent of our manpower, nine percent of our apprehensions. It's a tradition since the 1920s."

Migrants had long traveled here north up Mexican Highway 15, and easily slipped through the twin towns to Arizona's northbound I-19. During the first clampdown of the 1990s, the feds patched together a three-mile metal fence from military surplus, just like the one in Douglas.

Now in 2008, the rusty walls had been fortified with concrete. Outside the city, new eighteen-foot bollard fences, metal poles filled with concrete, stretched for miles into the hills. The bigger, longer wall drove down the numbers of migrants making it through the city, though they still tried. Rudy Garza-Salas, thirty-eight, a Puebla native who got picked up in a workplace raid at a Panda Express restaurant in Tucson in 2008, told me he had sauntered through the pedestrian port of entry in 2004 in a driving rain. No one noticed.

The Nogy security situation is complicated by a labyrinth of tunnels below ground. The network of pumps and drains and culverts is designed to control the water that flows downhill between the two towns. The underground Arroyo Nogales diverts floodwaters from the city streets, and each day sewage pipes pump eighteen million gallons of raw waste northward to a plant on the American side. And then there are the outlaw drug tunnels, surreptitiously dug by smugglers—and routinely discovered by the Border Patrol.

"We found ten tunnels between October [2007] and July [2008]," Mike noted. "They dip off the main tunnels."

Migrants regularly try their luck in these holes in the ground. If they can make it through safely, they emerge quickly in Arizona, well beyond the fortified fence. But it's not a sure thing. Besides unexpected floods and sewage, they have to contend with robbers underground. "Bandits jump the groups," Mike said.

Sorties through the pipes are frequent enough that the Border Patrol has a "tunnel team." The sewage channels are so foul that agents have to be decontaminated when they come out. They're sprayed with disinfectant, and they toss out their clothes. The filth doesn't deter determined migrants. One time, Mike said, "I saw nine guys walk out of the canal in the rain."

When the monsoons come, the dangers escalate. On Saturday, July 12, two days before the deaths by drowning of Oscar Montoya and Ventura Portillo, an apocalyptic storm broke over Ambos Nogales, a squall so ferocious that a funnel cloud, rare in this part of the world, hissed and twisted overhead. The rains dropped in torrents, and the border wall turned into a dam. It didn't help that in February the Border Patrol had sealed up one of the tunnels with concrete to keep smugglers out.

The destruction was mostly on the Mexican side, where water pooled up six feet high against the border wall. The surge picked up cars by the dozens and floated them down to the barricade. Buildings on Calle Internacional, the Sonoran street that hugs the line, were badly damaged. Some were destroyed. Old-timers said they had never seen anything like it. The U.S. side, protected by the impromptu dam, was mostly spared; rainwater puddled up only a few inches. The Mexicans were furious. They blamed the flood on the new American barriers, and demanded restitution to the tune of $8 million.

The migrants who'd ventured underground before the

cloudburst fared even worse than the inundated towns above. Rainwater raced through the tunnels, and by late afternoon trapped migrants were screaming for help. The Customs agents working the port of entry heard their cries, according to the *Nogales International,* and ran to the grates and peered down into the tunnels. They saw a young Mexican man, twenty-seven, beneath the streets, pressed against a wall, struggling to keep his head above water. The frantic agents pried open the metal bars and dropped a rope down, then hauled him up to safety. Later, a couple of teenage boys, ages fifteen and seventeen, were saved when agents lowered a ladder down into the swirling hellhole.

Two nights later, Oscar Montoya and Ventura Portillo weren't so lucky. They drowned in the darkness.

The Nogalenses—the people of Nogales—kept up daily life amid these agonies. A Mexican American waitress in a burger joint told me she wished the migrants would just stop coming, stop causing so many problems. But family ties and economics still link the two towns, and there's plenty of perfectly legal foot traffic back and forth. Mexicans with shopping passes walk over to Arizona to browse the shops along Morley Avenue, where the decades-old Bracker's sells Wrangler jeans and men's dress suits alike. American tourists park their cars at McDonald's, then stroll south through the turnstiles. They eat tamales and tostadas at La Roca, a restaurant carved into a rock cliff. At the trinket shops, they stock up on striped blankets in polyester and pottery in terra-cotta clay. "Pase adelante," the shopkeepers call from the doorways. *Come inside.* "I'll give you a bargain."

Five-year-old vendors sell candy on every corner, their dirty faces all business, and migrants wander the streets. If tourists are of a mind to get an up-close look at the famous border wall, they can amble west past the port of entry. White crosses memorializing the migrant dead are nailed to its corrugated metal. Nearby, flat aluminum sculptures warn travelers of the desert's dangers: a green-faced metal migra chases a migrant; skulls cluster around an Arizona saguaro.

Tourists can stomach poverty, and even border politics, but violence is another matter. By 2009, the Sonoran drug wars were beginning to scare the visitors off. The souvenir shops were barely holding on.

Nogales, Sonora, has one rich neighborhood, Barrio Kennedy, with Spanish-style *casas* and modernist palaces in concrete and glass, hidden behind protective walls. More visible are the *colonias*, the shantytowns on the hillsides. The shacks are made of trash, hammered together from wooden flats and sheets of tin scavenged from the maquilas. The streets are dirt lanes; there's no plumbing to speak of. The huts cling to the slopes above the highway border crossing at the western outskirts of town. Arizonans can see them readily rising up over the international line, a startling sign of third world poverty adjoining first world prosperity.

The people who live here clamber down to the road below, where Americans coming back from Mexican beaches are idling in their cars, waiting to get through security. Darting in and out of the line of traffic, the locals sell maps and sodas and sad little doll dresses. "Candy? You want candy?" they call out, thrusting their wares at the car windows. If they don't make the sale, sometimes they ask for food.

Incongruously named Mariposa—butterfly—the port of entry is surrounded by a no-man's-land of overpasses going every which way. It's mostly geared toward the tourists, and the truckers bringing up produce from Mexico—and toward drug interdiction. Dogs sniff out the bales of marijuana not infrequently tucked among squashes and melons. It's here that the Border Patrol releases its returnees. Passing the curious sunburned vacationers in their cars, the migrants go on foot over the bridge, over the ravine, back to Mexico.

———

On a sunny Sonora morning, Alicia de la Paz sat in a broiling white tent just a few feet from the border. She was hot
and exhausted, but at least she was better off than she'd been
the day before, when she was wandering by herself in the
desert. She had just been sent back from the United States,
one of two hundred Mexicans who had streamed out of four
Homeland Security buses and trudged across the bridge. She
and the others arrived in their homeland on foot, to the casual scrutiny of a couple of uniformed guards.

Mostly men that day, the returnees were dressed in grimy
jeans, plaid shirts, and sneakers. Some were still carrying the
ubiquitous migrant backpack, but others, empty-handed,
had lost everything. One man, a scar etched into his face,
crossed himself as he stepped back onto Mexican soil. With
no *tiendas* or vendors to welcome them home in this barren
part of town, most of them headed to the migrant aid station
at the end of a ramp. Alicia had limped over with them on
her torn-up feet.

It was summer 2006, two years before Oscar Montoya
and Ventura Portillo drowned in a ditch nearby. No More
Deaths had been operating its desert camp for two years,
trying, in vain, it seemed, to stem the tide of migrant deaths.
Now the activists were trying a new tactic. In cooperation
with the state of Sonora, they had established an aid station
on the Mexican side of the border to minister to the "voluntarily returned" migrants freshly disgorged from the buses.

In subsequent years, the aid station endured some shut-
downs, partly because coyotes were preying on the travelers.
On an August day in 2007, I saw a people smuggler loitering
nearby, accosting a contingent of young mothers with kids
who'd been dumped back over the line. But the station was
needed, and it was ceremonially reopened in February 2009.

Alicia de la Paz was one of the first customers in 2006.
I found her inside the aid station tent. She was perplexed,
if not a little amused, by the scene unfolding before her.

The American border agents had picked her up and ejected her in short order, but here in Mexico an American woman knelt reverentially in front of her. In a gesture that echoed the biblical Jesus washing the feet of the downtrodden, the American bathed the Mexican's blistered feet in a basin of cool water.

"They need help," Maryada Vallet, the young woman doing the washing, said of the travelers. Twenty-three years old, Maryada was an EMT and a devoted volunteer, a regular at the desert camp. It was she who delivered the abuse report to Washington, D.C. in 2008. "The reality is most will try crossing the border again. They'll do whatever it takes. If they try immediately, with blisters and dehydration, they'll be more at risk."

A platoon of American volunteers, including a high school student from Philadelphia and her mother, were ministering to the tempest-tossed travelers. Dan Millis, the young man who would later find Josseline's body, sat on a curb nearby, speaking gently in his flawless Spanish to some weary men. A couple of Mexican helpers—themselves deportees with no home to go back to—were busily passing out bottles of water and bean burritos wrapped in foil.

"We want everyone to have a liter of water and a little bag of two burritos," Maryada said. "We do a lot of first aid, checking vitals. We call an ambulance if necessary."

Alicia de la Paz (her last name means "peace") smiled at Maryada. She didn't need an ambulance, but she appreciated the careful attention to her battered feet. Once they'd been thoroughly soaked, Maryada patted them dry and wrapped them in bandages.

A forty-year-old mother of three and native of Chiapas, Alicia had gotten herself to Altar. In the town plaza, "a coyote recruited me," she said in Spanish. She managed to make a decent deal. She paid no money up front, and the guide agreed to accept $1,700 from her nephew in Tennessee only after she'd safely arrived. She had no complaints about the smugglers. "The coyotes treated me well."

The group of fourteen migrants and two guides crossed the border near Sasabe in the cool of a Sunday evening and walked north all night, east of the Baboquivari Mountains. They hiked all day Monday, and through the next night, taking occasional rests. "My shoes were too small," she said, and all those downhills soon bruised her toenails and blistered her feet. Still, she kept up with her fellow travelers until Tuesday morning, when they were spooked by a Border Patrol helicopter hovering overhead. Dusting, the activists call it.

Everyone scattered. Most of her fellow travelers were men, Alicia said, and "they ran so fast, I couldn't keep up." She was left behind. Hobbled by her inflamed feet, she managed to get out to Route 286, the northbound road that goes from Sasabe to Three Points. She hoped for help from drivers zipping by. "Only one stopped," she said. The driver gave her some water, then sped away.

"People are afraid," Maryada told her in Spanish. They didn't want to be like the two No More Deaths volunteers who'd been arrested when they put border crossers into their car.

Alicia nodded. She was familiar with border politics and border fears. Back home in the coastal town of Tapachula, Chiapas, clear at the other end of Mexico, she lived close to the Guatemalan line, where hordes of desperate Central Americans played cat and mouse with Mexican agents, in a mirror image of the American border chaos.

In Tapachula, "the men have left," she said. "The women clean houses and work in kitchens." For half the year, her husband, José Antonio, and their seventeen-year-old son, Didier, went north to pick grapes in a vineyard outside Hermosillo, in Sonora. Alicia used to stay back in Tapachula to do laundry for hire, but lately she'd been joining the grape migration herself, moving for six months at a time to the workers' barracks at the vineyard. She entrusted her younger children, eleven-year-old Lester and ten-year-old Emili, to the care of her sister in Tapachula.

This year, though, she'd formed a new plan. She'd go farther north, to the United States, to join her nephew in Tennessee, where she would do *cualquier trabajo,* "whatever work she could find." She'd stay just two years, long enough to earn enough money to build a house of her own. But the mortgage for this dream house—the perilous journey—could have cost her her life.

Now, marooned in Nogales, she had no money and no way she knew of to get back home. But she had no intention of returning to the desert.

"Nunca," she said, shaking her head. *Never.* "No vale mi vida." *It's not worth my life.*

No More Deaths didn't give out money to travelers, but Maryada told Alicia that the Sonoran State Commission for the Care of Migrants sometimes bought them tickets back home. It was the best news Alicia had gotten in days. She and Maryada climbed into the rickety No More Deaths SUV to drive to the commission office, the high school student and I tagging along. We inched our way through the teeming Nogales streets, past pastel-painted *farmacias* and *carnicerías,* past women doing their marketing and schoolkids running home. Cheered up now, Alicia looked on with interest. "This is a pretty town," she declared.

The commission office was in a red-and-white stucco building in the red-light district on the east end of town, near the pedestrian border crossing. Its front door faced the border wall. The American volunteers used the office as a base all summer, storing up the mountains of water bottles there, and even sleeping in cots in one of its rooms. The plumbing functioned only sporadically.

Xochitl Barreras, a law student in Nogales, was energetically running the place, making phone call after phone call, tapping away on the computer. "Our mission," she said in Spanish, "is to help immigrants, to give them care, to help them return to their families and places of origin."

The city of Nogales and the state of Sonora joined forces to buy the bus tickets, she said, but they would pay for travel only as far as Mexico City. Southerners had to find their own way from there. And to avoid the appearance of helping their countrymen enter the United States, they refused to pay the fare to towns along the international line.

"We can't help people cross," Barreras said firmly. "We won't send them to places along the border. People who live close to the border, we can't help."

They could stay for free in the city's migrant shelters for three days. The commission workers made a stab at finding them jobs, but with so many desperate people streaming into town, competition was fierce. Homeless and jobless—and hundreds or even a thousand miles from home—not a few migrants tried to cross again, as Barreras readily acknowledged.

Border communities in the United States were burdened by the migrant onslaught, but so were their counterparts in Mexico. "It's a problem for Nogales," Barreras said. "So many migrants arrive here. Many stay here, become hobos or bums and cause problems, even rob people."

The tickets out of town helped Nogales ease a spiraling social problem, but they were a lifesaver for stranded travelers like Alicia de la Paz.

Barreras beamed at the Chiapaneca and invited her to sit down. She busied herself entering Alicia's name, age, and hometown into her computer. Alicia didn't mind that the commission couldn't buy her a ticket all the way to Tapachula. She just needed to get to Hermosillo and the grape vineyard, where José Antonio and Didier no doubt were worrying over what had become of her.

While Barreras worked the phone to inform the bus company another passenger was on the way, Maryada told Alicia she could wash up in the bathroom. The volunteer issued her a brand-new tube of toothpaste, a toothbrush, deodorant, and a clean T-shirt. But when Alicia went into the dingy bathroom, she faced still another setback: no water. Maryada apologized. Often, in late morning, the water in Nogales simply stopped running. Instead of taking a shower, or even a sponge bath in the sink, Alicia would have to make do with one of the all-purpose liter bottles of water. Her face fell.

When she emerged from the bathroom, though, she was all smiles. She felt *mucho mejor*, "much better." Then it was back to the office to sit and wait for the Mexican bureaucracy to play out. Barreras had a million things to do before she could send Alicia on her way: type up an official letter authorizing the ticket; print it out for Alicia to present at the bus station; make multiple phone calls to find someone to drive her there.

Maryada had work to do, too, back at the tent, so the high school girl volunteered to stay with Alicia until a driver turned up. The woman from Chiapas doled out hugs all around.

"Muchas gracias," she said with a smile. *Thanks for helping me.*

Back at the border, the volunteers were busy taking care of a fifty-five-year-old guitarist from Veracruz with high blood pressure, and a twenty-two-year-old adventurer from Guerrero who had hurt his hand riding the rails. They were debating whether to drive the guitarist to the commission office and the train jumper to the hospital when they heard a rumbling noise to the north. Everyone looked up.

Another Homeland Security bus had just pulled up on the other side of the wash, and dozens more migrants were beginning the slow walk over the border, back to Mexico.

——

Mike Scioli knew more than a little bit about tragedy along the line. He played a mean jazz trumpet—his native Buffalo has a big music scene—and one of his sidelines was blowing the horn for the Border Patrol's dead.

"I used to be in a funk band," he said. "Now I'm in an Honor Guard for the Border Patrol. I play trumpet for funerals."

He flew all over the country to play mournful tunes over the flag-draped coffins of Border Patrol agents. He'd played in San Diego, El Paso, even Pennsylvania, but his most recent gig had been a few months earlier right here in Arizona. On January 19, 2008, Agent Luis Aguilar, working out of Yuma, had been run down on the highway near the border crossing at Andrade, California. Aguilar, thirty-two, and his partner were trying to close in on a couple of guys they suspected of smuggling drugs, and Aguilar stepped out onto the blacktop to lay out stop sticks. The spikes were supposed to deflate the suspects' tires, but the vehicle didn't even slow down. It slammed into the agent and sped south. Aguilar died out there on the road.

"The guy escaped into Mexico," Mike fumed. The suspect, Jesús Navarro-Montes, was arrested and then set free, because "Mexico won't extradite to a death penalty sentence." So the American authorities reduced the charge to second-degree murder, and Navarro-Montes was rearrested. In 2009 he was awaiting extradition.

Aguilar had been the middle of three Luises, grandfather, father, and son, and the other two, his dad and his little boy, were graveside at his burial. His wife, Erica, and daughter, Arianna, were there, too, and so was his brother, Marcos, a Border Patrol agent in the Nogales station. The funeral was one of Mike's toughest.

Given where he'd grown up, it was a little strange that

Mike now found himself roving the dry desert Southwest. Buffalo is on Lake Erie, upstream from Niagara Falls. Ontario, Canada, is just across the Niagara River, making Buffalo, improbably, a border town. But with its cool waters and snowy winters, Buffalo is as far away and as different from the Arizona border as it's possible to get and still be in the United States.

Mike had maybe eight relatives in law enforcement; his father was a policeman in the juvenile bureau. "I wanted something different," he said. So he bided his time working for the Internal Revenue Service, until one day an application for the Border Patrol landed on his desk. Before long he shipped out to Arizona.

"It's an exciting time to be on the border," he said as he drove his SUV up and down the roads around Nogales. "We're starting to get control."

He'd been out in Arizona five years now, and he'd worked Casa Grande, Nogales, Tucson. With his outgoing nature and boyish good looks, he'd been bumped upstairs to PIO—public information officer—but what he'd really loved was his early assignment tracking in the west desert, out of Casa Grande. Patrolling the Tohono O'odham Reservation and lands to the north, "we did cool stuff—tracking sign, making arrests. We were a team. We'd be tracking smugglers north of the reservation, we'd get five guys."

Like Edmundo Erik Moncayo in Douglas, he learned to detect footprints that were nearly invisible, to "read" the bend of a twig or the twist of a cactus pad. It was something the cops up in Buffalo couldn't do at all.

"In New York State, a guy killed two troopers. The Border Patrol was out there tracking. Tracking is our thing. It's not that we're more manly. It's that we're used to terrain. It's two different jobs, but the Border Patrol doesn't get much law enforcement respect." Even the cops in his family didn't think much of Mike's job at first. "But my parents started seeing all that's going on in Tucson"—the giant drug busts, the huge numbers of migrant arrests—"and my dad wrote me a letter. He's proud of me now."

For a while, Mike worked the airport and bus stations in Phoenix. "No one liked us up there 'tearing families apart.' If you see a mother and child, you're gonna feel bad, but it's the law. It's like if you see a woman selling drugs, you have to arrest her. Is it fair to let the mother go and arrest two guys? I feel worse for the kids." The tales of mothers or children lost or dead in the desert struck him as the predictable result of irresponsible choices. "You find mothers breastfeeding babies. You think, 'Can't you wait until the child is old enough to make the trip?'"

In the heat of July 2005, he'd been tracking a group of twelve through the desert when he came upon a four-year-old boy sitting by himself. He thought it might be a trap at first—that migrants might throw rocks at him as he approached the child. But nothing happened. Nobody else was around. "The kid was happy, sweet. He tells me his mom left him. His dad is on his way. I waited twenty minutes with him and called for backup. I went after the group and caught eight people, a couple of females."

For several hours, none of the women mentioned a missing child. Finally, one told Scioli, "I left my son out there." He didn't tell her right away that the boy was safe. Instead, "I played around with her." Then he reproached her. "'Why would you leave your son out there?' She claimed his father was on the way." He shook his head.

"A lot of the stories are the same. They're coached though. They all say, 'I came over for a better life. I'm coming across to make money for my family in Mexico.'"

He did feel sorry that the migrants were exploited. The coyotes were "ruthless," he said. "We would check a vehicle" and it would be so jam-packed, "people fell out of the back of the vehicle. We see it time and time again. It's sad." And the journey was more dangerous than people realized. "Horrible stuff happens. Women get raped a lot. You have a twelve- or thirteen-year-old, say, with an eight-year-old brother. She's in the desert with all adult males. They rape her and they leave her."

He'd even seen trophy "rape trees"—a "bush with women's undergarments dangling. Smugglers take the groups and take women to a spot and rape them. They hang the undergarments as a trophy." One woman he arrested had condoms in her bag. "She told me, 'I've been on this trip before.'"

Still, Mike relished the drama of the chase. "I loved the midnight shift. There was lots of action." He learned to make big group arrests even when he was alone. "I get everybody on the ground right away. I see their hands. I don't let them talk. I have them sit in a row and take their shoes off. No one's gonna run without shoes.

"One time I arrested guys three miles from the border, ten guys. It was nighttime. I was by myself. They were running everywhere. I got them on the ground. One guy pushed me, one guy took a swing at me. I have pepper spray and I sprayed one. You've got to handcuff them."

Another time he stopped a runaway vehicle on I-10. A truck packed with border crossers was lurching along the highway, and when Mike gave chase, the driver jumped out. The vehicle sped on. "I jumped in, grabbed the wheel, and slowed it down. People were screaming." Down on the side of the road the wayward driver fought Mike's partner. He got slapped with charges of assaulting an officer and endangering his passengers, but "it never made it to the courts. They're so overloaded. It's frustrating. They were booked but let go back to Mexico.

"Now we're getting more resources. It's a great time now."

———

Even city patrolling had its adrenaline moments. The day I rode with Mike, his radio announced an impending arrest. "They've seen two guys jumping a fence in Nogales," he said excitedly.

The pair of migrants thought they had the border all figured out. They walked up the steep slope east of the pedestrian port of entry, climbed over the wall, and slipped down to the other side. Easy as pie. What they didn't know was that a camera was transmitting their every move to a computer screen at headquarters. The news squawked over Mike's radio. "Two bodies, back of a warehouse," the dispatcher reported. "They're by the stairs, dropping down. They're getting on the roof of a warehouse. Now they're back down the stairs."

As the men tiptoed down one of the staircases that climb Nogales's steep hills, three musclemen on bikes were on their way to meet them at the bottom. Seventy-five, maybe one hundred steps into the United States, the would-be entrants walked right into the bulked-up arms of the U.S. Border Patrol Bike Unit.

Mike hurtled through the zigzagging streets of downtown, but by the time he arrived at the scene of the crime, the three bike agents were filling out paperwork and the two migrants sat nonplussed on the curb. They were from Tlaxcala, the same state as Rosio Mejia-Munoz, the woman who'd barely escaped death on the Tohom O'odham reservation the month before. Their American sojourn had been even briefer than hers.

"In the city, people can disappear into a store," Mike said. "They'll jump from the fence at the end of the street and run into the back of the store. They'll wear two shirts, take one off, and try to blend in with shoppers."

Coyotes regularly burn holes in the metal fence with blowtorches and have their clients shimmy right through. And the Border Patrol routinely seals up the gaps. "We have a crew every twenty-four to forty-eight hours and they patch up the fence."

Mike drove up one of the new roads that line the border wall west of town. Travel along here was far better than it used to be, he said, thanks to members of the National Guard who built the streets, concrete in town, gravel outside. To my eye, the wide new roads were still another scar scraped into the landscape, extending the ugliness of the border wall. But to Agent Scioli, the roads were a sign that the border was getting safer and better.

"We never had a road along the border until the National Guard came out." In the midnight hours of June 3, 1998, Alexander Kirpnick, a twenty-six-year-old agent, was shot to death in an isolated canyon nearby. Police blamed the murder on drug mules, the underlings who go through the desert on foot, carrying bales of marijuana on their backs. If medical help had gotten to Kirpnick more quickly, he might have been saved. "We only had bad track roads to reach him," Mike said. "National Guard built a nice gravel road. It's awesome out here now."

The soldiers, 600 strong, were deployed to the Arizona borderlands in June 2007, and stayed until July 2008. Their mission was to support the Border Patrol, building roads, for one, not to catch migrants. But death did not spare the National Guard. The same summer day in 2006 that Alicia de la Paz plunged her feet into Maryada's healing waters in Nogales, Kirsten Fike, a National Guardswoman from Pennsylvania, collapsed in Yuma, a couple of hours to the west. Fike, a thirty-six-year-old single mother, had spent just two hours in the 104-degree heat, stretching some netting along the international line. She died the next day, leaving behind a thirteen-year-old son.

From the Nogy hilltop, across the border ravine, Mike spotted a coyote sitting in the shade of a Mexican mesquite. He was coolly watching Mike's vehicle on the other side, ready to report to his cronies via cell phone. Agent and smuggler traded stares. "It's like that book, *Where's Waldo?*" Mike said. "You're trying to see people in the landscape, hiding in plain sight. You see something move and it turns out to be five guys. Your eye gets trained."

Low-ranking agents were parked here and there in canyons and on hills, junior officers who had the stultifying job of sitting in their SUVs in one spot, keeping eyes peeled on the line day and night. They were easy targets for kids on the other side who didn't mind showing their disdain for the United States by pitching the occasional stone. The Border Patrol has suffered so many cracked windshields that rock-resistant chicken-wire screens now cover the windows. The stones were no joke. "One agent lost his eye, cracked his skull," Mike said. Attacks of all kinds on agents were up. "We had two hundred sixteen assaults last year. Now this year we're already at two hundred six. We'll go way over."

Unlike the grunt agents trapped in the ditches, Scioli was free to bounce up and down the hills at will, starting and stopping each time he thought he saw somebody move in the brush. Pausing on a summit to look at the highway far below, we saw a man emerge from a ravine only to stumble into the sharp-eyed agent who was waiting for him. Back downtown, at the McDonald's, we watched another migrant being loaded off the back of a Jeep and into a Border Patrol SUV.

The crackdown, Mike said, was working, so much so that some agents were getting bored. "A lot of guys were built for the job. They were making arrests every five minutes. To these agents now, it's 'Jeez. It's getting a little dull.'"

In 2008 the Tucson Sector had thirty-three hundred agents, six hundred more than two years before, and migrant arrests were dropping. By the end of fiscal 2008, apprehensions had dipped to 317,696, a decline of 16 percent over the previous year. In the Border Patrol's distinctive arithmetic, often lampooned by critics, fewer arrests added up to greater success. It meant that the agents and hardware aligned along the border were stopping crossers in their tracks.

"We have towers all over," Mike said. "We have eighty cameras all over the sector. The Sky Watch towers have heat and AC. Guy sits in there with a camera. We have the BORTAC, Border [Patrol] Tactical Unit, our SWAT team." Agents went out on ATVs on land and in Black Hawk helicopters in the air. A mobile surveillance system—"one of the greatest tools"—installed on the back of a truck, "picks up heat movements. It has a camera on it and gives GPS coordinates.

"The fences are just speed bumps in the desert. They're going to slow groups down. They have a fourteen-foot fence to climb over. By then I can get out there."

Operation Arizona Denial, the program that randomly prosecuted 60 migrants a day, was scaring would-be crossers away.

"You'll see a judge, get prosecuted, you might get jail time. When people get voluntarily returned, the smuggler meets them over there. The cycle continues. Now it's a huge deterrent effect. Now they know they'll get jail time. It's having an effect, absolutely."

Mike was an enthusiastic advocate for all the enforcement measures that civil libertarians and many border residents opposed, from the mass trials of Arizona Denial to the towers snooping in people's backyards. At the checkpoint on I-19, where agents stop any and all vehicles and question any and all drivers, "some people say, 'I don't have to tell you my citizenship.' I say, 'Why not? Aren't you proud to be an American?'"

One man, a professor type, often drives through the checkpoint, Mike related. And every time, he gives the agents the same lecture, declaring that the interrogation violated his rights. Mike rolled his eyes. "You've got to be tough-skinned, have a sense of humor."

The checkpoint was just a couple of trailers at the side of the highway in the Santa Cruz Valley, but the Border Patrol was pushing for a permanent building. So far, they'd been losing the argument against the many neighbors and government officials who thought it would be an eyesore in the rolling valley, where birds are a tourist draw. Cynics thought smugglers would simply go around it.

"We made sixty-seven thousand arrests at the checkpoint in fiscal 2007," Mike argued. "This is a major route north-south from Mexico to Tucson." It was a heavily traveled corridor for cocaine and marijuana, as well as migrants. "We need a permanent checkpoint."

By now, Mike had steered around to the ditch where the two men had drowned the night before. We got out and looked down at the dark water. Just then, a trio of Mexican officials jumped out of their car to inspect the scene. They razzed Scioli in Spanish about the damage his wall had done to their town. Mike grimaced, but he took the ribbing stoically. No one mentioned the deaths.

Each year Mike saw thousands of farmers and would-be factory workers like Oscar Montoya Nava and Ventura Portillo Torres go through the Tucson Sector's revolving doors—and he knew that hundreds died in its ditches and deserts. But criminals and gang members hide among these economic refugees, he said. The Border Patrol estimates that 10 percent of migrants surging over the border have criminal records in the United States "What bothers me are the sex offenders who come across. If he's an illegal alien, he's not reporting in."

September 11 had upped the ante. Homeland Security had redefined illegal immigration as a security threat, and now every migrant was seen as a potential terrorist.

"It took one terrorist act to make people realize we have borders that need to be protected," he said. "What's been done so far is the greatest thing that could have been done for our country. We haven't gotten any terrorists here that I can talk about," he acknowledged, "but Texas has. A very sensitive, touchy situation.

"You're doing a job to protect the country. I'm proud of what I do."

Mike Scioli still missed Buffalo. At Christmastime 2008 he was lonely, and sorry to be missing the record snowfall back home, not to mention his big extended family. But he was adapting a little to life in the borderlands. He was jamming with a mariachi band, a traditional Mexican ensemble of marimbas and strings and horns, learning to trill Latin melodies. And he'd even brought his music to the local community. At a civilian funeral, he wailed taps on his trumpet "for a boy who died who wanted to be a Border Patrol agent."

CHAPTER 7

Bones in the Rain

No one deserves to die in the desert for lack of a cup
of water.

—Mike Wilson, Tohono O'odham tribal member

It was a monsoon morning on the Rez, thick with humidity and the promise of rain. The sky was still mostly blue
at midmorning, but stray clouds were starting to gather at
the edges of Baboquivari. Mike Wilson could see the jagged
peak to the east, over his right shoulder. I'itoi, creator god of
the Tohono O'odham people, is said to live in a cave below
its sacred summit.

"This is K-O-H-N, the voice of the Tohono O'odham
Nation," the deejay called out on the radio in Mike's truck.
"It's nintey-eight degrees on this Saturday morning."

After alerting his listeners to what they already knew—it
was hot but not hellish for southwestern Arizona in early
August—the deejay told them about a new show that would
help reservation kids learn the O'odham language. Then he
launched into a little norteño music, the sprightly soundtrack
of the borderlands, a musical mix that patches together eastern European accordion and fiddles with Mexican guitars
and Spanish lyrics. Freddy Fender's polka rhythms spilled
out cheerfully over the airwaves.

Mike cranked up the music. It was only ten thirty, but he had already had a long morning of talking and driving and hauling water for migrants to drink. He'd been up since five, checking on his four water tanks on the Rez—the evangelically named Matthew, Mark, Luke, and John—and a fifth one, San Miguel, just across the line in Mexico. Now he was heading north back from the border along Topawa Road, passing hamlets with names like South Komelik and Supi Oidak.

"The only livelihood out here is ranching," he said, nodding to the flat grasslands dotted with cacti. Mostly the land was empty, interrupted by the occasional lone house and widely spaced villages, each with a tiny church and cemetery and a few horses ambling around. Roadside crosses, ringed with plastic flowers, marked the sites of fatal car accidents. Mike was in a hurry to get off the low-lying road before the monsoon storm struck. When the desert's violent summer storms hit, an inch of rain, or even two, can drop in half an hour, turning the dry arroyos into raging rivers. "I've gotten stuck out here a couple of times," he said, keeping an eye on the darkening clouds. "I couldn't get across the wash after the rain. Through trial and error I learned. Bring tools and planks. Also bring a set of chains."

Mike was also worried about his buddy David Garcia, a fellow member of the Nation, who was out here somewhere looking for a corpse. A twenty-four-year-old Guatemalan migrant, Felix Matias Bautista, was believed to have died two months before, in June 2008, in the foothills of the Baboquivaris, and today a crew of nine from Tucson was tramping around in the heat searching for his remains. Oscar Padilla, the Guatemalan consul, Sebastian Quinac, a Guatemalan staffer with the American Friends Service Committee, a couple of Samaritans, and other volunteers were picking their way on foot through the dense stands of cactus in the southeast corner of the Rez. Outsiders aren't allowed off road in tribal land unless they're accompanied by a mem-

ber, so Garcia had gone along. It was a kindness he regularly provided to strangers, but their hunts rarely turned up
a body.

Searchers would set out armed with only the vaguest of
tips, gleaned by grieving family members from their loved
one's fellow migrants or coyote. "We had walked a few hours
north of the border," they might say, or "The mountains were
in the east." Josseline's smuggler, for instance, had confused
everyone with the clue about the mysterious *pistas*. Felix
Matias had paid his coyote three thousand dollars up front—
another three thousand dollars would have come due on safe
arrival at his destination in California—and his brother
had insisted that the pollero help the distraught family find
him. So the smuggler went back in July to the general area
where he'd left the ailing young man on June 8—or so he
claimed. He hadn't found Felix, but he told the family that
he'd spread a yellow curtain in the brush as a signal of where
to look. Now it was August 9. Two months in, there was no
guarantee, what with the heat and the animals doing their
separate work of destruction, that there would be any body
left to find. But Felix's mother back in Huehuetenango was
insistent. Even if only a single fragment of her son's bones
remained, she wanted it.

"These searches are emotion-driven," Mike sighed. "It
will be the blind leading the blind. David would have liked
me to come with my truck, but it's more critical for me to
maintain water stations than look for someone who's been
dead for two months."

Anyway, the Nation is a big place to search. The only
Indian reservation in Arizona along the border, its forty-
five-hundred square miles sprawl from the Ironwood Forest National Monument northwest of Tucson clear down to
Mexico, sixty miles away, and west about seventy-five miles.
It's the second-largest reservation in the United States, almost the size of Connecticut. (The Navajo Nation is number

one, so big at twenty-six-thousand square miles that it spills out of northeastern Arizona and into Utah and New Mexico.) But traditional O'odham land also sweeps down into Mexico. The international line slices right through it, cutting the Nation off from its members south of the border.

Except for the forested mountains that break up its flatlands here and there, O'odham territory is pure Sonoran Desert, dense with saguaro, cholla, and prickly pear cacti. ("Tohono O'odham" means Desert People.) Palo verde, ironwood, acacia, and mesquite trees supply scant shade. In a good year, the desert gets only fourteen or fifteen inches of rain. Summer temperatures out here can easily top 110 degrees, particularly in June, the hottest, driest, and deadliest month of the year. Sixteen migrants had died on the reservation in the brutal heat of June 2008, including the young bride Rosalba Hernandez Dorantes, on June 16. Twenty-two-year-old José Juan Lopez Gonzalez lost his life near Hickiwan Village on June 8, the same day Felix was abandoned by his coyote. The temperature was at least one hundred. (Because Felix's body had not been found, he didn't appear on any of the official lists of the dead.)

Migrants by the thousands cross this harsh country. At the peak of migration, 1,500 a day were slogging through. In April 2008 tribal chairman Ned Norris Jr. told a congressional subcommittee that 15,500 were still crossing every month, or 500 a day. On a now-legendary day, the cold and snowy sixth of March in 2000, precisely 336 ailing migrants came out onto the road seeking medical help, overwhelming both the Nation and the Border Patrol.

In the years since, between 2001 and 2007, at least 460 had died out here, with the worst year, 2007, yielding 83 bodies. In 2008, by August, when I went out to the Nation with Mike Wilson, at least 50 had perished. The Baboquivari District, where Felix was left behind, has for years been the deadliest of all the deadly migrant corridors in southern Arizona.

"Historically, this is the most traveled migrant trail," Mike explained. Lately, though, his water tanks had been telling him that the route was shifting away: fewer people had been around to drink the water. "Now they're coming through east of Sasabe, through Arivaca," as the No More Deaths people had discovered. "Or they're going farther west, to the westernmost part of the Tohono O'odham Nation"—where young Lopez Gonzalez had died.

It was easy to see why coyotes long favored this route. The district lies west of the Baboquivaris, a heartbreakingly beautiful series of blue peaks running thirty-five miles north from the border, but the mountains slope down and flatten out into walkable desert. South of the border, a rural Mexican route angles over from Sásabe and leads right up to the traditional border crossing of San Miguel Gate. The trekkers enter near San Miguel, cross a narrow slice of the Chukut Chuk District, and hike north into the Baboquivari District. The trails meander through the desert and up into the foothills, where mountain canyons provide hiding places when Border Patrol copters hover overhead. Not too many people live out here, just 1,650 in the Baboquivari District, and the roads are unpaved. When Border Patrol agents venture out this way, they're usually on horseback. But it's a long walk, thirty-five miles, easily three days, to the nearest road, State Highway 86, running east toward Tucson. And for every mile of that long walk, the risk of death multiplies.

A little past six on a Saturday morning, Mike Wilson sat at a McDonald's on Tucson's west side, drinking coffee at an outdoor table in the early morning light. He's an imposing figure, a big man with a luxuriant head of gray hair pulled back in a ponytail. He radiates calm, and speaks methodically. During the week, he works at a charter high school in Tucson, downtown's City High. He used to teach Spanish but switched to janitorial duty—less stress. Winter or summer, working or not, he rises early on Saturdays to tend to his tanks. Normally his friend David Garcia goes with him, but on this day, with Garcia otherwise engaged with the Guatemalans, he had lined up a couple of newbies to help him, me and my son Will, home from college on summer break.

Mike led us back to his house in Diablo—Spanish for "devil"—a modest community on Tucson's southwest side, and set us to work lugging all twenty-nine of his five-gallon empties out of the garage, where he keeps them neatly arrayed on shelves. We put the jugs in the back of his green truck, and Will filled each one with water from the household hose. A little after seven, all three of us were on the road headed west, hauling a cargo of 145 gallons of H2O.

The Tohono O'odham have some 28,000 tribal members; Mike is one of 14,600 who live off-Rez. He was born in 1949, he told us, the son of a World War II vet, an O'odham who lived on the reservation only intermittently. "My dad went to work in the mines at Ajo," a small town west of the Nation. Its Spanish name means "garlic," but the original Tohono name, *o'ohon*, refers to the region's colorful minerals. The Ajo mines have been closed now for a quarter-century, but in those days, "copper was king. A lot of Tohono O'odham worked there. He had a good job." But he was an alcoholic and got fired. Ajo being a "one-industry town"—Phelps Dodge *owned* the place—the family moved into Tucson. Mike was about eleven.

He doesn't speak O'odham. Scholars estimate that fewer than ten thousand tribal members do, and the language is being lost among children. His Spanish, however, is impeccable. "I went to language school in the army for six months," he said, and paused. "I have a checkered past." Mike had been in Special Forces, the controversial U.S. Army division that conducts unconventional operations abroad, including counterterrorism. He served in Latin America during multiple conflagrations in which the United States played an unseemly part. "I was a military adviser in El Salvador from November 1988 to December 1989. I was there for the final offensive in December 1989. I also was in Bolivia. I was scheduled to go to Guatemala but that got canceled. When the Contra story erupted, they canceled our mission."

By 2001, Mike had retired from the military and embarked on a new kind of mission. He studied in a seminary, intending to be ordained as a Presbyterian minister. But he left early and returned to the reservation, where he became a lay minister in Sells, the Nation's small capital. (He still wears a turquoise and silver cross on a chain around his neck.) Immigration—and migrant deaths—had become big news in Arizona, and one morning he picked up his *Arizona Daily Star* to find a map pinpointing the locations of migrant deaths all over the Tucson Sector. He was horrified to see the toll on tribal lands, particularly in the Baboquivari District.

"When I looked at the death map, I saw a disproportionate number of deaths east of Sells. Nobody was doing anything. I said to myself, 'Okay, a pastor should be doing something.' I was self-appointed."

The newspaper had gotten the map from Humane Borders, a good-hearted group operating out of First Christian Church in Tucson. Founded by Rev. Robin Hoover, a brash minister from Texas, the nondenominational group had taken what members saw as the simplest solution to the problem of the deaths by dehydration. They would give drink to the thirsty. Early in 2001 they began driving out into the parched deserts and setting up water stations—barrels with spigots—in locations where travelers were most likely to be in peril. As of 2009, Humane Borders was operating ninety stations on public and private lands with permission from the respective government agencies and private landowners; a not-so-small army of volunteers regularly made driving runs to refill the barrels. Hoover's team compiled migrant death stats and plotted them on maps. Early on, seeing so many deaths on the reservation, they'd come out asking permission to put their tanks on Tohono O'odham lands.

Tribal elders took a dim view of the request. They were already dealing with a dramatic spike in drug trafficking. Drug smugglers liked the Nation's remoteness as much as human smugglers did, and with jobs scarce, too many O'odham youth had been lured into working for traffickers in both trades. And like the ranchers in Arivaca and residents everywhere along the border, tribal members were complaining of the double invasion of migrants and Border Patrol agents. Traditional O'odham ways, *himdag,* required kindness to strangers, and in the old days O'odham were only too happy to offer water or food to the occasional border crosser. Five hundred travelers a day was something else entirely. People were tired of the trash and the vandalism—one reporter uncovered a rash of bicycle thefts—and they were just as sick of the Border Patrol vehicles racing down their roads and helicopters clattering in their skies. The Nation's own police ended up rescuing many of the migrants who fell ill in the desert, and the strapped U.S. Indian Health Service hospital in Sells wasn't being adequately reimbursed for their care.

"The O'odham suffer from break-ins and other crimes committed by undocumented aliens and drug traffickers," Ned Norris said in his congressional testimony. Despite the money brought in by the O'odhams' casinos, two near Tucson, one out west by Why, the tribe is still desperately poor, with low rates of education and an annual per capita income of well under eight thousand dollars. "Third-world poverty" is how one tribal spokesman described it. And the border disorder was costing the tribe plenty; law enforcement alone had an annual price tag of $3 million. The Indians had taken on an "unfunded mandate to secure the border, which we all know is a federal, not a tribal, obligation," Norris scolded. Some estimates of total costs of illegal immigration to the tribe, counting rescues, hospital care, and enforcement, ran as high as $7 million a year. Rosalba Hernandez Dorantes' autopsy, for one, cost the tribe $1,730, payable to the Pima County Medical Examiner's Office.

The last thing they needed, some of the leaders argued, were water stations that would encourage even more people to cross by misleading them into thinking that the dangerous reservation was safe. Others suspected that it was the despised drug dealers who'd be drinking from the tanks. Tribal government said it was a matter for the eleven districts—the equivalent of states—to decide. The Humane Borders folks made their pitch to the districts, and the districts said no. David Garcia, then serving as a district legislator in Gu Vo, voted yes.

"David was the only one who voted for allowing Humane Borders on tribal lands," Mike said admiringly. "Like me, he's a troublemaker."

The way Mike Wilson saw it, tribal land belongs to everyone in the tribe, and as a member he had a right to put water out on that land, council votes notwithstanding. He contacted Humane Borders. "'You guys can't go on tribal lands,'" he told Hoover. "'But I can.'" He worked out a deal. Humane Borders would provide the tanks and frames, and Wilson would haul them out to tribal lands and keep them filled. "I get reimbursed by Humane Borders, but I need to make it clear. I do it on my own."

Mike selected the dangerous Baboquivari corridor. By early 2002 he had begun putting water out, defying both the tribe and the Baboquivari District. On June 15, the district issued a resolution specifically banning water stations, noting that "this method would encourage illegal entry through the District." On June 21, Ronald C. Ventura, the district's then-chair, sent a letter to Mike's church, Papago United Presbyterian, informing the church clerk that "Baboquivari District Council disapproves of Mr. Mike Wilson, a member of your church, placing plastic water jugs in desert locations where illegal immigrants travel." The church members disapproved, too, Mike said. So he quit. "I couldn't stay. Migrants were dying over here. Now my ministry is putting out water."

He'd been tangling with the leaders of Baboquivari on and off ever since. On more than one occasion they had hauled his water away, and each time, he had returned the next week to replace it. It particularly pained him that the tribe did not make common cause with the large numbers of Indians arriving from south of the border. Felix Matias Bautista, for instance—the man who was lying dead somewhere on the reservation—was a Q'anjob'al Maya from the heavily Indian Guatemalan north.

"To add insult to injury, migrants are not seen as indigenous brothers and sisters." Wilson sighed. "The Tohono O'odham Nation refuses to acknowledge moral responsibility. Part of it is cultural. I respect their sensitivities. Their worldview is only as wide as the Nation. Any incursion of outsiders is seen as a threat, whether it's migrants or bleeding-heart liberals coming out of Tucson to try to provide humanitarian aid. The perception is it's trespassing, not just physical trespassing, but cultural. I honor those feelings. But they do not trump moral responsibility when human beings are dying."

At Topawa village, where his father was born, Mike Wilson turned the truck east onto Fresnal Canyon Road, passing the brand-new Tohono O'odham Nation Cultural Center and Museum, built with gambling dollars. Straight ahead in the distance was sacred Baboquivari, angling its irregular trapezoid peak 7,700 feet into the sky. In the flat desert below, a two-days' walk from the border, were the four tanks that Mike had named after the evangelists. Despite the rupture with his church, Mike still considers himself a "card-carrying

Presbyterian," and following one of the episodes of tribal tank confiscation he renamed the water stations after the saints.

Occasionally he runs into a border crosser. Once, when he had brought along filmmakers making the documentary *Crossing Arizona,* Wilson encountered a migrant right here on Fresnal Canyon Road. The man broke down weeping for the cameras. Just four months ago, Mike said, he'd seen a man hitchhiking on Ajo Road, hoping to make it to Tucson. A ride is what many migrants want most, but it's illegal to drive them anywhere and "further their entry" into the country. "I stay within the law. All you can do is give them food, water, and advice."

What he mostly gives is water. South of the road, the first tank, St. Matthew, was standing peacefully among the desert plants, palo verdes, prickly pear, mesquites, cholla. In the morning light, a butterfly was flitting by and birds chirped overhead. "Coyotes, roadrunners, snakes are all out here," Wilson said appreciatively. The desert floor was soft underfoot and flat, a good place to walk. If it hadn't been so hot—at 8:30 a.m. the sun was beating down mercilessly—it would have been positively idyllic. The saint's two barrels were full to the brim; not a soul had taken a sip in the last week. He'd noticed migrant visits starting to decline about two years before, in 2006. "In years past I couldn't keep up with these stations," he recounted. They'd be completely empty each Saturday when he returned, thirsty migrants having quaffed all fifty-five gallons in each drum. Mike also kept a barrel nearby filled with empty gallon jugs with lids, for migrants to fill up and carry along with them. None of those had been taken, either. Still, he tested the water and added a chlorine tablet to keep it pure. He got out his Humane Borders chart (the group is scrupulous about collecting data) and noted his findings: no water consumption, no footprints, no tracks, no Mexican water bottles discarded on the ground.

St. Mark, a short drive away, had been vandalized. Someone had stomped on the faucets. O'odham who oppose Mike's water ministry have occasionally shot up the tanks too. "If that's not bad enough," he said with a slight smile, "horses or cows come and chew on the faucet." He'd discovered the damage the week before and given it a temporary fix, propping one of the barrels up. Most of the water drained out anyway. He had to add ninety-five gallons to the two barrels. Mike had brought along replacement spigots and screwed them in. Driving a short distance east, he found St. Luke and St. John both full of water. With no work to be done here, it was time to go to Mexico.

Back on Fresnal Canyon Road, a Border Patrol SUV hauling a horse trailer hurried east past Mike's truck. He peered into his rearview mirror; a migrant, he supposed, had tripped a ground sensor in the open desert. The agents would be trotting out on horseback into the wilderness to catch him—or her. Remote it might be, but "the whole area was seeded with sensors," he said. Technology was helping the agents defeat geography.

In fact, the Border Patrol was all over the Rez. On our long drive out to Sells, and then south to the border and back, one agency vehicle after another zoomed along, each one immediately recognizable by its green-on-white color scheme. This might be a sovereign Indian nation, but that doesn't mean the Tohono O'odham can keep the federal government out. Far from it. "The Border Patrol is a federal police agency," Mike explained. "Native American reservations are part of the federal management system. They're federal lands. Any federal agency can have unrestricted access."

And the Border Patrol "has tremendous access. I call it an occupying army, especially around San Miguel," close to the border. "You see helicopters, even Black Hawk helicopters."

In fact, the fallout from the federal border crackdown is one thing the Tohono O'odham Nation and its dissident member Mike Wilson can agree on.

"We are older than the international boundary with Mexico and had no role in creating the border," tribal chair Norris told the congressional committee at the 2008 hearing. "We did not cross the seventy-five miles of border within our reservation lands. The border crossed us."

Before the Gadsden Purchase of 1854, Tohono O'odham territory lay entirely in Mexico. The treaty split the traditional lands in two, one side becoming American, the other remaining Mexican. But the boundary was fluid.

"There was an honorary agreement between the Nation and the federal government," David Garcia told me later. "We could travel freely."

Members could and did go north and south with impunity, visiting friends and relations on the other side, and families frequently straddled the border. Mike's father was born in the United States, he served in the U.S. Army, and he lies buried in Topawa, his grave facing Baboquivari. But his name was José and he lived in Sonora for thirty years. The family still has a home there.

Joe Garcia—no relation to David—is a Tohono O'odham who owns Tucson's popular La Indita Restaurant—the name means "little Indian woman." He goes by Joseph, José, and Joe, and he speaks O'odham, Spanish, and English. A traditional leader who holds the title of lieutenant governor of the Sonoran branch, he grew up near Casa Grande in Arizona, but only partly.

"We'd go back to Sonora. My dad was from Poso Verde, Sonora, thirty-five miles south of Sells, where there was a natural spring. We had a base camp there and another camp for the vegetables. The O'odham back then were still kind of seminomadic."

American O'odham traveled south to harvest the red fruit of the saguaro cactus in family camps, a time-honored ritual each June. In October, they went to the annual gathering in Magdalena, Sonora, to honor St. Francis. (In 2008 the San

Francisco celebration was marred by fears of shootouts in the intensifying drug wars of northern Sonora, and the tribe sent a flotilla of buses to fetch its members safely home.)

Once the feds tried to seal the Arizona border, these fluid traditional patterns were disrupted. They shut down most of the old informal crossings that once gave members easy access to the other side all along the Rez's border; the one at San Miguel, where Mike had a water tank, was one of the few still open. If American Indians wanted to go to Mexico, the U.S. government reasoned, they should go back and forth through official ports of entry like anybody else. The detours could add hundreds of miles to a trip, and members might not have the right paperwork to show the customs agents when they got there. In his congressional testimony, Norris, the tribal chair, complained that families were being prevented from observing their traditional practices, both O'odham and Christian. "Our land is now cut in half, with O'odham communities, sacred sites, salt pilgrimage routes, and families divided."

About fourteen hundred Mexican O'odham were scattered in villages south of the border. They suffered under the same new rules. Their tribal affiliation allowed them to get health care at the hospital in Sells, and until the crackdown they simply passed through the old informal crossings. Many of them didn't have official proof of tribal membership.

"Tribal members must be card-carrying members: Border Patrol only accepts that," Mike said. "Elderly people born in Sonora never had the privilege of being born in a hospital. They have no documents, no birth certificates." The tribe might recognize them as members, but the Border Patrol doesn't always. Agents have even stopped the van that the tribal health service sends to Sonora to pick up the elderly and the ill, he said. "It adds to the tension. The Border Patrol is exercising extra police powers. Border Patrol wants proof of citizenship."

The Nation had cooperated with the Border Patrol and allowed all its security paraphernalia—towers, checkpoints, and cameras. And while Norris has said he will allow a full-fledged wall only "over my dead body," the tribe had permitted vehicle barriers all along its border. But the Nation had been poorly rewarded for that cooperation, Norris complained. Agents were running roughshod over the sacred landscape. The feds had fast-tracked a construction project "within a known jaguar habitat near the reservation's eastern boundary."

Worst of all, in 2007 Department of Homeland Security secretary Michael Chertoff had used his REAL ID waiver power to override archaeological protections on the Rez. The ensuing federal project damaged a resting place of O'odham ancestors. "A Boeing Company subcontractor widened fifteen miles of the El Camino del Diablo, a desert crossing route listed on the National Register of Historic Places, without first performing an archaeological clearance," Norris said. Two archaeological sites dating back to the Hohokam people, who lived here a thousand years ago, were bladed.

"Imagine a bulldozer parking in your family graveyard, turning up bones," Norris demanded. "This is our reality."

Near San Miguel Gate, one of the few traditional crossings that remain, the Border Patrol had planted a substation, pale and prefab and purely ugly. A tangle of trailers and ramps baking in the sun, it occupied a couple of dirt acres, scraped bare of any living thing. It looked like a military outpost in the Sahara. Mike Wilson intended to pay a visit to its occupants before he crossed the border to attend to his fifth tank, San Miguel, on the other side of the line, in Mexico. He didn't want any trouble.

"They rotate the agents in and out," he explained. "Someone who doesn't know me might stop me."

He marched up the ramp and straight through the front door, my son and me bobbing along in his wake. The agent at the desk looked up, startled. He was African American, the first black agent I'd seen; over his dark green uniform he was wearing a bulletproof vest.

"I'm Mike Wilson. I'm a member of the Nation and these are my guests," Mike announced, gesturing to Will and me. The agent listened in surprise as Mike detailed his plans. He'd be going to Mexico briefly, he said, and as a card-carrying member of the Nation he was entitled to travel back and forth through San Miguel Gate. His guests, as nontribal members, couldn't go with him—or couldn't get back in—so they'd stay on U.S. soil. And by the way, he added politely, he'd be filling up his bottles with water from the Border Patrol faucet. After all, this was O'odham water, pumped out of O'odham ground. The agent responded mildly to this speech, asking only the color of Mike's truck so he could alert his men down on the line.

The spigot was out back. Mike pulled the truck over, and Will got the hose going, to fill up the bottles we'd emptied back at St. Mark. All well and good, but right next to the faucet was an outdoor cage, with human beings imprisoned inside.

It was a summer desert day, close to one hundred degrees, and nearly a dozen migrants were being held in a dirt-floored chain-link cage no better than a dog run. To be sure, it had a roof, but it was facing south, directly in the path of the scorching summer sun. Inside the station, where agents were doing paperwork and monitoring camera images, the AC was on full blast. Out here the migrants were left to the elements.

Enclosed by two layers of chain link, the cage was about six feet long and twenty feet wide. Three sides were open-air; the station formed a solid fourth wall on the north. Lying around in the dirt were plastic slabs, meant to be cots, labeled with their brand name, Stack and Bunk. Backpacks, duffels, and water bottles that had been taken from the prisoners were piled on shelves nearby. I busied myself with the faucet, the better to gaze into the cage; an agent took note and positioned himself in front of me to block my line of vision. But I could still see a few things. Another officer frisked one migrant, and then cut the cord on the hood of somebody else's sweatshirt. A third prisoner pointed to his own wrist, as though to ask, "Where is my watch?" and looked up questioningly. The only answer he got was a shrug.

The migrants were being readied for transfer to Border Patrol headquarters in Tucson in a Wackenhut bus. Unfortunately named, considering the business it's in, Wackenhut is a private company contracted to transfer prisoners for the Border Patrol. One agent opened the door of the cage and the migrants trooped out single file to the bus, minus their possessions. There were eleven prisoners in all, six women, five men. The travelers had apparently weathered a monsoon storm or two in the outback. They were covered with mud, from the tops of their T-shirts to the bottom of their jeans. The women were at the back of the line, and several of them turned and smiled at me. One even waved. So I called out, "¡Buena suerte!" *Good luck!* Then they broke out in grins and waved. "Gracias," they said. "Adios."

Later, back in Tucson, I asked Robert Gilbert, chief of the Tucson Sector, how it was possible that the United States of America was keeping prisoners in an outdoor cage in the desert in the August heat. He countered with a question of his own: isn't the holding pen better than the open desert, where they were captured? Gilbert insisted there was a swamp cooler inside, but I went back a few months later and saw no evidence of any cooling system. In any case, he claimed, the Border Patrol couldn't do much with the building, because the Tohono O'odham controlled its footprint. But that provoked another question: why couldn't the pen be enclosed and air-conditioned, as the rest of the building was? It would be a trivial expense, given the billions the United States was spending on everything else related to border security.

A short two miles away, we saw some of the goodies the DHS dollars have bought. Metal vehicle barriers, filled with concrete, were planted along the line, four feet apart; we could see them stretching out a mile or two, but they cover the whole Tohono O'odham border. At $1.25 million per mile, that added up to $93.7 million. Four or five agency SUVs were parked nearby, each with a watching agent inside. Somebody had constructed a man-made mountain of gravel, maybe fifty feet high. One agent was parked on the mound slantwise, the better to spy migrants slipping through the flat creosote desert hereabouts. If there was no mountain to be had, Homeland Security could make one.

Twenty feet north of the new vehicle barriers was the old fence, useless barbed wire sagging between posts. Stray dogs roamed the space between old and new, navigating between broken beer bottles and dried-up palo verdes. The San Miguel Gate is an old-fashioned affair, too, a swinging metal ranch gate. A truckload of Tohono O'odham bounced right through it, five or six in the bed of the pickup, heading to Mexico for an afternoon in the village of S'gogs'igik, O'odham for "many dogs." Mike drove through it to tend to his tanks. The migrant numbers were down here too. Normally he adds fifty gallons, but the tanks only needed ten.

The skies were seriously clouding up, and Mike decided his day was done. He aborted a plan to drive way out west to his sixth tank, at Maneger's Dam, south of the line on the western reservation. The Guatemalan search party had started their hike somewhere near here, but we saw no sign of their vehicles. Mike was not inclined to wait. We got back in the truck and he heavy-leaded it north. By the time we reached Kitt Peak on the eastern edge of the Rez, the sacred mountains were shrouded in gray clouds. Raindrops were spattering off the hardtop on State Highway 86. Within minutes, the rain was falling in sheets; torrents streamed down the dry arroyos, turning them into instant creeks. The trees bent sideways in the wind. At the Border Patrol checkpoint, just east of the Nation, a young agent by the side of the road looked miserable, his hands jammed in his pockets and rain tumbling down his poncho. He waved Mike on. Too wet for questions.

By the time Mike steered his truck into his driveway, Tucson's streets had become rivers and lakes. It was all Will and I could do to get to our house on the other side of town. Cops were putting up road barriers as fast as they could, and we detoured around one flooded street after another.

Later I learned from Sebastian Quinac that the rain had washed out the search. The group had hiked from the road three and a half hours, making it as far as the Baboquivari foothills. Following the usual protocol, the nine searchers spread out in a horizontal straight line, each walker hundreds of yards from the next. Every five minutes they called out one by one—playing a real-life game of whisper-down-the-lane—to make sure no one had faltered or fallen. All the while, each one gazed at the ground, looking for a telltale human limb.

By late morning the rain forced them to turn back. Halfway to Sells, south of Topawa, the water flooded across the road, just as Mike had predicted. Their cars were trapped for hours. They didn't reach Tucson until nightfall, and they came empty-handed. They never found the yellow curtain the coyote had said he left behind, and they never found the body of the missing Guatemalan. Felix Matias Bautista, Maya of Huehuetenango, was still out there in the American desert, the rain pouring down on his bones.

Three weeks later, an O'odham policewoman confronted Mike Wilson at the St. Matthew station and ordered him to take his barrels away. "I respectfully decline," he told her, but he left the reservation with his guests, Gene Lefebvre, John Fife, and the seminarians who'd been detained at the No More Deaths camp earlier in the week by the Border Patrol. (The officer told the students they were banned from the Rez for life.) When Mike and David Garcia went back the next week, Matthew, Mark, and Luke were gone. By the following week John, too, had disappeared.

Mike is a stubborn man, and he returned in October, and again in December, and every month after that. With the tanks gone, he laid out water jugs on the ground at each station, arranging them among the grasses in the shape of a cross.

"No one deserves to die in the desert for lack of a cup of water," he said.

CHAPTER 8

The Science of Death

What makes me mad is you've got a problem, and
nobody is addressing the causes.

—*Ed McCullough, Arizona scientist*

Ed McCullough retired as a geosciences professor at the
University of Arizona in 1997, after stepping down as dean
of science way back in 1992. Ten years later, he still enjoyed
a certain mythic status on campus as the prof who'd won a
bundle in the Arizona lottery. His winnings and his pen-
sion gave him a comfortable life, with a nice foothills house
in Tucson complete with pool and views of the Catalinas.
But neither his riches nor his retirement kept him out of the
field.

On a scalding morning at the end of August 2007, he was
bouncing north along Old Ruggles Road just west of Arivaca, some ten miles north of the Mexican border. The dirt
road might as well have been called Old Rutted—it was that
rough—but McCullough didn't seem to mind. At seventy-
five, the snowy-haired scientist still loved driving his giant
four-by-four into the wilderness—the "tulies," as he called
it—and getting out to hike through the spiny desert.

"I was a field geologist for years," he said, explaining away his impressive fitness. Some days, he admitted cheerfully, he trekked for up to twelve hours, drinking water as he went from the hydration pack strapped to his back.

During his university days, Ed studied geologic hazards in the desert—what happens when rainwater floods the land or, conversely, when too much groundwater has been pumped out underneath. Now, when he strode out into the brush on his long legs, he wasn't looking for landslides or cracks in the earth or other signs of subsidence. Instead, he was searching for trash and clothes and footprints, the traces of human beings.

"There's the trail over there," he said, easing his huge truck to a stop in one of Old Ruggles's deepest ruts. To our right, up a hill on the east, he'd spotted a path winding through the cacti and mesquites.

When he climbed out, he saw two pairs of men's pants and two water bottles lying at the bottom of the hill. And farther up the slope, he found a couple of bottle caps and a mud-caked backpack, sure signs that this prickly path had been trod by undocumented migrants.

What Ed wanted to know was this: How recently did the owners of these pants and this pack pass by? And how far did they continue along this trail? He intended to find out by walking it himself, for miles, calculating the age of its trash and using GPS technology to map its every twist and turn.

He'd been doing this for three years, marshaling his science skills to mitigate the humanitarian crisis of migrant deaths in the desert. If he could get accurate maps into the hands of volunteers, and tell them where the migrants were walking, maybe, just maybe, the activists could find travelers in trouble and help them before they died.

"The deaths are taking place all along these corridors," Ed said. "What I'm doing is a teeny, tiny Band-Aid on the whole thing"—echoing Gene Lefebvre. "We're looking at eighteen hundred square miles, and five thousand miles of trails. We think we know where the trails are, but we've only mapped about 20 to 30 percent of them."

He'd driven down early that morning from his home in Tucson, stopping only long enough to pick up me and my photographer friend Jay Rochlin. McCullough's truck was so big it was like a boat, and it was tough to climb aboard. He'd bought it on purpose, he said, to drive safely over the tippy back roads in the borderlands. (In the summer of 2008 it did roll over south of Arivaca, but he and his passengers weren't hurt.) Before we set sail down the highway, he spread his map out on my dining-room table.

"There are three main corridors from the border," he said, pointing out the region he typically patrolled. It stretched thirty miles along the border, from Nogales west to Sasabe, and north about fifty miles, from the Tumacacori Mountains on the east to the Baboquivaris on the west. Each of the three corridors through here had three or four major trails, all of them heading northeast toward the freeway. They converged north of Arivaca Junction, thirty-five miles and a three-day walk from Sasabe.

If the migrants could get to Interstate 19, they had a shot of getting to Tucson, Phoenix, and other points north. The Border Patrol had a checkpoint on the highway, but the trails, by design, ended a few miles to the north. "The Border Patrol," Ed said, "knows all about it."

For this day's mapmaking expedition, McCullough had a fresh footpath all picked out. We drove less than an hour south from Tucson and then west into pretty ranch country, its rolling green hills peppered with mesquite trees. Cows meandered out onto the winding road, and here and there white-painted fences lined the fields. But as we made our way toward occupied Arivaca, the picturesque rural land-scape turned into a war zone. In a quick fifteen minutes, we counted four Border Patrol SUVs cruising the road, followed shortly thereafter by a fifth hauling a horse in a trailer. Next, a Wackenhut bus carrying captured migrants clattered by. A Border Patrol helicopter droned noisily overhead.

Beyond the town, we found the trail McCullough had in mind. We set off through the trees, the sun glancing off the leaves, yellow butterflies flitting through the grasses. It was monsoon season, and the desert was refreshingly green from the recent rains, but at 101 degrees, it was hot. Make that broiling.

"This is a great time of year!" McCullough exulted as he zipped along, unbothered by the heat or the hills. "And this is a great county for quartz," the geologist in him added, kicking at a white rock. "One of the nice things about being out here is you see Gila monsters, tarantulas, and dung beetles."

And water bottles. They littered the rocky trail, and Ed gave them a once-over with his scientist's eye. He knew all about their life cycle, having once conducted an experiment in his Tucson driveway to test their longevity. He had filled a plastic bottle with water and left it out in the sun to see how long it would take for the plastic to break down. Out in the field, this information helped him calculate the amount of time elapsed since a bottle was dropped.

"In six weeks, it's brittle," he said. He picked up an old bottle from the dirt and squeezed. It cracked. Ancient history. The migrant who quaffed that water had passed through here at least a month and half earlier, in early July. Next, McCullough picked up a man's shirt that was caked with mud. "Now this has been through several rains," he judged; it had probably been dropped more than a week before. Next, he found a footprint, but the storms had smudged its edges. "Every time you get rain, it's like erasing a blackboard," he said.

Ed had a rating system for the trails, 1 to 5, with 1 going to cold routes no longer in use and 5 awarded to hot paths where he encountered live migrants. For now, he gave this path a low 2. It had been traveled, but not recently.

McCullough hadn't forgotten his mapmaking. A GPS unit dangled from a cord looping around his neck, and every three hundred feet he pushed a button on it to record a waypoint. Bit by bit, a virtual trail took shape on the GPS screen. Later, when he got home from his hike, he'd feed the data into a computer and print out an up-to-the-minute map for the activists.

In a never-ending game, once migrant groups began tramping a path in great numbers, the Border Patrol pounced. Then the smugglers changed their routes and bushwhacked through virgin territory. And just as quickly, the agents—and activists—tried to alter theirs. The maneuvering reminded the retired scientist of the adaptations of evolution.

"It's Darwinism," Ed declared.

In 2004, the first summer of the No More Deaths camp, McCullough and his wife, Debbi, an artist, volunteered. Like the other campers, they'd walk the desert, calling out "Hola, amigos, tenemos agua y comida," looking for migrants to help. The walks gave Debbi material for her art: mixed-media pieces she created out of the spoons and holy cards dropped by the travelers. But Ed wasn't satisfied with meandering unsystematically. There wasn't enough information to suit him. No hard data.

"We'd go out onto the trails, but you had no idea where they went," he says. "When you came back in [to camp], you couldn't tell anyone where you'd been. We were just wandering. There was no systematic approach. I didn't like being out there and not knowing where I was."

Likewise, the Samaritans—humanitarians who roam the countryside in vans and walk into the desert—"had no records or maps." So the retired geologist formulated a plan. He would measure and map. "The first thing, I drove the ranch roads in low gear. They're all dirt roads. Some haven't been used for years. My father-in-law went with me. I'd look outside one way; he'd look out the other. When I saw a trail, I'd get out and map it.

"A pattern started to emerge," he says. "The migrants are mostly going out of Nogales and Sasabe, heading northeast to Tucson. Since they were going northeast, I'd drive roads going northwest. And the trails would cross the roads."

Many of his fellow activists were "faith-based," but McCullough was not a churchgoing man. "I was raised Southern Baptist, and that was enough to make me not religious," he said, laughing, his voice still tinged by the soft accents of his native West Virginia. "I was not always interested in immigrant issues, but when people started dying…" His voice trailed off. "What makes me mad is you've got a problem, and nobody is addressing the causes."

The problem was that people were still dying in Arizona's desert cauldrons. On August 29, the day before McCullough mapped the trail near Old Ruggles Road, Juan Montes Mendez, a fifty-one-year-old Mexican, died of exposure a mile southwest of Sells. Sonia Alvarado Soriano, a twenty-five-year-old woman from parts unknown, likewise died of exposure outside Douglas.

The day before that, on August 28, a twenty-two-year-old Mexican named Maria del Carmen Sanchez Hernández from Tlaxcala landed in the morgue at St. Mary's Hospital in Tucson. Ana Maria Yaxon Chavez, twenty-six, late of Sololá, Guatemala, was in the holding freezer at Tucson Medical Center. Ana Maria's cause of death: complications of hyperthermia and dehydration.

Outside the county hospital in Tucson—named for Kino, the wandering seventeenth-century padre—a modest one-story building stands almost unnoticed at the far end of a parking lot. Its walls are a bland patterned cinderblock. A mesquite shelters the front door, and carefully tended cacti sprout from a "lawn" of pink-beige gravel. The place could be any anonymous office anywhere in this desert city, an insurance broker's, say, or a financial planner's.

Only a small tasteful sign, hidden in a corner, hints at the grisly work that goes on inside. That and the generators roaring out back. These monster machines power up the building's refrigerated rooms, where at any given moment some 250 bodies, or parts thereof, lie on cold shelves. The sign reads Forensic Science Center, but what it really is is the Pima County morgue.

All manner of accidents bring the dead to this manicured place.

"Our general caseload is any unnatural death," Dr. Bruce Parks, the Pima County medical examiner, explained. "Homicide, suicide, car crash, any suspicious death. Or any unexpected death." If a ten-year-old with tonsillitis dies on the operating table, say, her corpse finds its way to Dr. Parks. So do the bodies of elderly snowbirds who die while wintering in Arizona, without a doctor of their own to sign their death certificate. "The total number of deaths where we bring the body in is twenty-three hundred to twenty-four hundred a year," he said. In the last ten years, more and more of those bodies have been migrants, harvested from the surrounding deserts and mountains.

"Unauthorized border crossers are a substantial part of what we do," Dr. Parks said. "They represent more than 10 percent of the autopsies we perform. We used to call them UDAs"—undocumented aliens, borrowing a page from the Border Patrol. "Now we call them undocumented border crossers. They're defined as people who entered illegally and died in transit."

On this January day in 2009, during the slow season for migrant deaths ("June and July are the big months"), Dr. Parks had the remains of fifty-six undocumented border crossers in cold storage. They accounted for more than 20 percent of the two hundred and fifty corpses on hand. "Typically at any given time we have over a hundred border crossers, seventy-some unidentified, in addition to the people in the process of being identified." Parks's operation spends an estimated hundred thousand dollars a year on the migrants, what with the autopsies, identifications, and storage.

Parks takes in bodies from all over Pima County, a 9,189-square-mile stretch of dry landscape that includes not only Tucson but Altar Valley and the Tohono O'odham Reservation. He is also under contract to accept dead migrants from Santa Cruz, the much smaller border county to the south that Ed McCullough routinely explored. It was in Santa Cruz—Holy Cross—County that Josseline died, and it was here, to Parks's examining rooms, that her body was brought.

Parks and his staff see 90 percent of the migrant dead from the Border Patrol's Tucson Sector. The only sector border deaths he didn't handle were in Cochise, the southeast county where Silverio Huinil Vail had died. Occasionally he even took crossers from Yuma County, in the far southwest corner of Arizona.

The worst year yet, in the long decade since Parks's office was first deluged with the corpses of dead migrants, was 2005, the year that Marta broke her leg. The morgue got 197 migrant bodies. It ranked as Parks's second-highest year for migrant deaths, but it had the "most heat-related deaths. It was so hot." (Kat Rodriguez's more inclusive tally for all of southern Arizona was 279.) The average high that summer was 99.8 degrees, and on fifty-two days the thermometer shot up above 100 degrees. The summer rains were sparse. Day after day, the heat yielded fresh cadavers, victims of dehydration and heat stroke. "In July, we had an average of two a day, a total of sixty-eight or sixty-nine suspected border crossers in one month. We were so backlogged we had to make a choice *not* to autopsy some of them."

With two or more bodies coming in daily, corpses were crammed onto every shelf, and every spare gurney was pressed into service. At the time, the morgue could hold only

120 corpses, and so many bodies piled up that the doctor ran out of room. "It was a problem that became a big issue," he remembered. It got so bad that finally he had to rent a refrigerated storage truck. He parked the overflow bodies in the truck out back.

The grotesque symbolism of migrant corpses spilling out of the packed county morgue attracted the national media. Ed Bradley of *60 Minutes* came calling, and so did Anderson Cooper of CNN. The Department of Homeland Security came up with sixty thousand dollars to buy Parks a cold-storage truck of his own—at least he didn't have to shell out the nine hundred dollars a week in rent anymore. Eventually, "the county found the funds to construct a stand-alone structure, a refrigerated building" behind the main complex. Now, the doctor said, "We have space for two hundred and ten to two hundred and twenty full-sized adults, if you store more than one body on a shelf. If they are partial remains, skeletons in body bags"—as migrant remains frequently are—"we can put several people on one tray."

Fortunately, the next summer, 2006, was more moderate. The average high was 98.7 degrees—a full degree lower than 2005's—and the desert was drenched by unusually strong monsoon rains. Wild thunderstorms repeatedly flooded southern Arizona (Tucson's Sabino Canyon got eight inches in a single week in July, and rockslides and floods closed the popular recreation area). The deaths dropped, a little, and Parks had 174 border-crosser bodies for the year. Kat Rodriguez logged 205.

But 2007 turned beastly hot again. The average high was 99.7 degrees, just a bit below the number for 2005, and migrant deaths zoomed up again. The bodies of 218 migrants filled Parks's shelves that year, the same year Ed Mc-Cullough took us out on his desert hike. Kat's numbers spiked to 237.

The association of deaths with rising temperatures was

so obvious that Parks teamed up with a University of Arizona emergency-medicine doc to come up with a formula to predict the likelihood of death on any given day. Like Parks, Dr. Samuel Keim, a professor, physician, and researcher, saw the deaths as a public health problem. In the late 1990s, "we began to notice in the local media reports of people dying of heatstroke when they were trying to cross the desert," Keim said. "They were also coming to the emergency room. I do academic research in community medicine, and this was something new."

Working with Parks, Keim began tracking the heat deaths. "We compared the dates of death for four consecutive years, and their association with the ambient high temperature on a given day. We could accurately predict the probability of one or more heat deaths on that day in Pima County." He set up a Web site that calculates the correlation between daily temperatures and the risk of death. In English and Spanish, his site, borderrisk.med.arizona.edu/crossingRisk.html, gives a six-day forecast, and lists the probability of death on each of the days. A day with a forecast high temp of 90, for instance, indicates a 12 percent risk. A prediction of 97, just seven degrees higher, catapults the risk of death up to 27 percent. Keim's goal, quite simply, is "the prevention of further heat deaths." Travelers on the trail obviously couldn't log on to the site, but their rescuers could. When the mercury rose, agents and activists alike could be prepared.

Dr. Parks's office was plain and tidy, a refuge from the catastrophes he dealt with every day. The only personal touch was a collection of family photos on his desk. Tall and runner-lean, he favored plain clothes too, buttoned-down shirts and khakis. His thinning white hair didn't quite match the youthfulness of his face. He hadn't always planned on a career in forensic pathology, he said. In medical school, it was a required course. "I didn't know if I could deal with it. I did an internship for one year, and I was able to get a residency."

Ultimately he decided the work suited his personality —and indeed, he speaks calmly, respectfully, even gently about the most difficult of subjects. As he sat at his desk and looked through Josseline's autopsy file, he spoke of her as "this young lady."

Parks first joined the medical examiners' office in 1986, and became chief ME in 1991. In those days, he almost never saw the bodies of young girls, or adults, for that matter, with histories like Josseline's. The annual number of identified migrant bodies delivered to his lab hovered in the single digits: 6 in 1990; 2 each in 1991 and 1992; 8 in 1993; 1 in 1994.

After the clampdown of the late 1990s, the numbers started edging up. In 1998, 12 dead migrants were brought in; the next year, 17. Then, in 2000, the year that Silverio Huinil Vail died over in Cochise County, Dr. Parks's tally shot up to 65. (In 2000, Parks began counting *all* migrants, ID'd and unknown.) The next year he logged 75, and by 2002, the tally had skyrocketed to 146.

The year 2001 marked "a dramatic rise," he remembered. "It sank in when those fourteen people died in May [of that year] in Yuma County." The travelers, all Mexicans walking in one group, died in agony, victims of extreme heat and coyote error, their bodies strewn across the infamous desert pass known as El Camino del Diablo. Luis Alberto Urrea recounted the tragedy in his book *The Devil's Highway,* a finalist for the Pulitzer Prize. (The fourteen Diablo fatalities set a new record for highest migrant death toll in a single incident, but that record soon fell. Two years later, in May 2003, nineteen border crossers suffocated inside a locked tractor-trailer near Houston.)

The Yuma medical examiner "asked us to take the whole bunch," Parks recalled. "I thought we might have to get a refrigerated truck. Fourteen autopsies all at the same time. It was a disaster. We realized, 'Hey, this is really taking off.'"

———

Each day the dead are brought into Parks's building via the double-wide doors out back, sparing clients of the physical therapy practice across the way the unnerving sight of body bags being unloaded. An inviting little patio divides the nitty-gritty of the morgue from the ordinary offices up front. Hummingbird feeders dangle from mesquite trees, and there's a chair or two for employees fatigued by their deadly labors to sit and watch the tiny red-throated birds darting about. Beyond the patio are several autopsy labs, a "family viewing room," and a storage room for dead migrants' belongings—some pesos, some pictures, a watch.

Dr. Parks brought me into the receiving room, the first stop at the morgue for Josseline and the rest of the dead. It was cool but not freezing. A gridded chart on the wall kept track of all the bodies, each box representing a shelf—and a body—in the morgue next door.

"A person is brought into this room first and logged in," Dr. Parks said. Each is assigned a number. Josseline was placed on a gurney here and given the name Jane Doe #7 and the number 2008-0368.

Parks and his fellow docs autopsy every dead migrant whose corpse comes their way. Exposure is by far the most common cause of death. Josseline died of exposure in winter, but it's the summertime heat that kills most of them. Hyperthermia is a "condition when the core temperature of the body gets to a dangerous level, 106 or 107," Parks said. "When that happens, there's a failure of the body at the molecular level. The heart is beating fast. It tries to pump blood through the dilated vessels, trying to create heat loss. If the body temp continues to climb, the dying person becomes confused and disoriented, and may even hallucinate."

In a winter death like Josseline's, the "body tries to keep warm. Shivering causes the muscles to work, to slide across each other to generate heat. At ninety degrees there's a loss of consciousness, the heart slows down as the temperature goes down. [You get] an irregular heart rhythm." Josseline's death was not painless. "There's some element of discomfort along the way. Eventually the heart ceases to function."

Since her body was not found until weeks after she died, the official cause of death couldn't be precise. The lab's forensic anthropologist, Bruce Anderson, had to be called in, because "when the body is badly decomposed, it's necessary to have a person knowledgeable about bones." Anderson arrived at a probable cause of death via a process of exclusion. "If you don't have a bullet wound, slices in the skin, no hemorrhage of the brain, an apparently healthy person, no cause of death is apparent," Dr. Parks said. "You've got a person out in the environment, and it's cold out at night. It looked like she'd been dead a while. The final determination was probable exposure."

Parks has committed his lab to identifying as many of the border crossers as possible, and boasts a success rate of 70 to 75 percent.

"We first go through all the belongings. We look for secret compartments, pockets, backpacks, insoles in shoes. Sometimes we find ID and money. Sometimes compartments are sewn into the waistbands of pants. Or ID and money are safety-pinned inside bras. We document the brand and size of clothing, tattoos, and scars."

Josseline's wardrobe was duly logged: Rampage-brand blue jeans, size small; one black sock and one white; a black tank top, large; neon-green Fashion Sport Shoes, and Ambiance-brand gray sweats, "Hollywood on rear."

If the workers are "lucky enough to find an ID, the information gets relayed to the Mexican consulate," Parks said. "The majority of them we identify are from Mexico. The consul will track down name and phone numbers and report back to us." Unfortunately, he said, "if they don't have anything with a name or an ID, the odds are slim."

Josseline wasn't carrying an ID, but her identifiable clothes—those pants and those shoes—and the paternal DNA made her case relatively straightforward. In the more intractable cases, investigators comb missing-persons reports and check with the consuls, in case a family member has called to say their "loved one was last seen at such and such a place."

Skeletons that have been drying out in the desert for years have little chance of ever being identified. And the number of skeletal remains has been rising as people venture farther out. A month after we accompanied Ed McCullough on his mapmaking walk in August 2007, bleached bones were found near Sells. They were so far gone that Border Patrol agents couldn't even determine the dead person's gender, let alone name or date of death.

Even when there's little chance of identifying skeletal remains, forensic anthropologist Anderson carefully examines them, in hopes of coming up "with age, race, country of origin, stature, sex, and any suspicious" signs of foul play, Parks said.

For all the unidentified, the doctors sift through the evidence twice, making sure "X-rays have been taken, teeth charted, an anthropological evaluation performed." When nothing more can be done, the docs remove a section of femur, and store it along with the paperwork and scans. "We keep the information and the bones indefinitely." In early 2009 he had 370 bone specimens on file, and was working to get a grant that would pay for DNA tests on them all. The plan was to encourage families with missing loved ones to get themselves tested and compare their results to a database. "We would do a campaign to get the word out to the countries of Mexico, Guatemala, El Salvador."

The detective work is costly and time-consuming, but for Dr. Parks it has a deeply moral dimension. "It's not popular with the public. But we're doing what is the human thing to do," to give a name to the dead, to find their families and to allow them to be laid to rest at home. "So far, knock wood, we have been well supported by the county. We have never been told, 'You're wasting resources on these people by working so hard to ID them.'"

At least Josseline's family got her body back. The undertaker, Funeraria del Angel, came to Tucson and picked her up, and brought her at last to California, in a hearse. The others, the unidentified and the unclaimed, are delivered to a contract funeral home in Tucson. Their bones and bodies are buried in the city's Evergreen Cemetery, in a potter's field, in unmarked graves.

No More Deaths calculates that more than 5,000 migrant bodies have been found across the southwest borderland between 1994 and 2009, in the years since Operation Gatekeeper got under way. Kat Rodriguez of Derechos started counting in 2001; through April 2009 she had 1,588. But those are only the bodies that have turned up.

"We don't have any idea of the actual number of deaths," Kat said, and no real way of ever knowing how many of the dead lie hidden in the backcountry. She calls her list Arizona Recovered Bodies, not Arizona Dead. Josseline, for one, likely never would have been discovered if Dan Millis hadn't happened to take her trail the day he did. Her remains eventually would have washed away down Cedar Canyon in the monsoon rain. Without Dan's chance discovery, Josseline would not have appeared as number 49 on Kat's list for fiscal 2008, or on anybody else's roster.

Academic studies back up Kat's point. "The actual number of migrant deaths is, at present, unknowable," Raquel Rubio-Goldsmith wrote in *The "Funnel Effect" and Recovered Bodies,* the team report published in 2006 by the University of Arizona's Binational Migration Institute (BMI). "Most assume that there are actually far more deaths than have been discovered," especially since so many "occur in the remote, inhospitable areas along the U.S./Mexico border."

Kat's numbers are the most inclusive of all the tallies, BMI wrote, while the Border Patrol chronically undercounts the dead. The agency only counts deaths it has investigated. When eight migrants were killed in an SUV rollover near Sonoita, Arizona, in June 2009, the Department of Public Safety (DPS) rushed to the scene. (Twenty-seven migrants were inside, "stacked like logs," an officer told the *Arizona Daily Star*.) But because the accident was a DPS case, the Border Patrol did not plan to add the eight dead to their list. The bodies were taken straight to Dr. Parks.

Weather and geography were often culprits in migrant deaths, but Kat blamed them primarily on the militarization of the border. "People are forced to shift routes into more dangerous and desolate areas. The deaths spike. Militarization has never been successful in controlling immigration. It only shifts the flow."

The Border Patrol typically sidesteps the correlation between the border buildup and deaths by blaming the fatalities on the coyotes. "Our job is not to lead people out to the desert," said agent Jesús Rodriguez, who shares Kat's last name but not her views. "We're not the ones that take them out to the desert—they [coyotes] just leave them there."

Even so, an analysis by Brady McCombs of the *Arizona Daily Star* in May 2009 demonstrated that the risk of dying had shot up during the crackdown years. The chance of migrants dying en route was seventeen times greater in 2009 than it was in 1998. Apprehensions were dropping, but the numbers of deaths per one hundred thousand captured rose. There were three deaths per one hundred thousand in 1998, and fifty-one deaths in 2009.

Research by Gary Christopherson, director of the Center for Applied Spatial Analysis in the University of Arizona's geography department, also supports Kat. Christopherson regularly pinpointed the locations of migrant deaths, and his maps showed they occurred farther from the roads every year. Humane Borders uses his information to set up its water stations in the most perilous sites.

Likewise, Ed McCullough's data suggested that the increased patrols and surveillance had, in fact, pushed walkers farther away from the roads and deeper into the desert. In the early 2000s, migrants typically walked ten miles, maybe a day's walk from the border, to Arivaca Road, where they met their rides, he said. The evidence was in the three-year-old "drop piles" of backpacks and clothes he'd found alongside the road.

Now, with agents swarming Arivaca, they had to walk much farther, hiking the backcountry for many more miles, and more days, to avoid the patrols. And the longer people were in the desert, the greater the danger. McCullough plotted the death locations on his computer maps, too, and his findings correlated with Christopherson's data: "The peak deaths take place at forty miles," he said. It was a matter of simple math. "Because of the increased number of agents, the farther the migrants have to walk, the more are going to die."

Which was why McCullough trekked so deep into the desert.

On our hike, the farther into the wilderness we went, the more evidence we found of recent human travelers. A Santo Niño de Atocha water bottle—a popular migrant item, bearing the image of the boy Jesus as a pilgrim, dressed for travel in hat and cloak—was fresh and pliable. On a hilltop we discovered an active windmill, watched over by a herd of placid white cows, where migrants could easily pump out fresh water if they could get to the top. "If you were a seventeen-year-old boy you'd have no trouble climbing up there," he told me. Nearby, a fresh cache of water bottles indicated that somebody had recently made the leap. We came across an unrusted can of Red Bull ("the equivalent of five cups of coffee," Ed calculated) and an empty electrolyte bottle, another migrant necessity. "You can drink lots of water," he noted, "but if you get no electrolytes, it don't make no never-mind."

A sock hung in a prickly pear, a shirt in a grove of trees, a pair of worn boots lay in the path. And then the final proof Ed was looking for: a fresh footprint, stamped by a tennis shoe *after* the recent rains. "This was made in the last day or so," he said excitedly. "I'm upgrading this to a number 3. I don't think there's any doubt we're walking a migrant trail."

When he got home, he would certify the path as an active route. Within days, activists would be walking it with water.

Over the years, Ed had met a parade of suffering folks: a young man who was trying to keep his ailing aunt alive; a pregnant seventeen-year-old ready to give up; a fearful husband and father of two. That man wasn't worried about the bandits who prey on migrants, or la migra, who send them back home, McCullough said, but he was "deathly afraid of dying in the desert. That was his big fear, but he came anyway. That tells you something."

Once while tracking in the Altar Valley flatlands—the "alluvial plain," the geologist called it—west of the Sierrita Mountains, McCullough came upon two stranded young men. "One had severe knee problems and couldn't walk," he said. "They'd been there four days. They'd built a fire trying to attract the Border Patrol. Fortunately, they were near a water tank. We called Border Patrol, and they sent a helicopter." The young men "were tickled. Usually people [in that situation] are starting to have a fear of dying out there." If Ed hadn't happened along and summoned help, the pair might not have made it.

He had gotten kindness in return from travelers. One group of robust young people in their twenties, alarmed to find this white-haired grandfather miles from nowhere, offered him their own precious water.

"You can't go out there and run into people and see their situation and not feel something," he said.

As a scholar, McCullough found it disturbing that the human catastrophe of migration had been predicted and then allowed to happen anyway. Plenty of researchers had warned that NAFTA, and the similar Central America Free Trade Agreement (CAFTA), would push poor farmers off the land. And that's what happened. Cause and effect. The displaced workers fled, to take up new American lives as crop pickers and meatpackers, construction workers and cleaners.

"Papers were written, predictions were made that people would come to the U.S.," McCullough fumed. He and his wife, Debbi, had visited Chiapas several times and saw firsthand the villages emptied of working adults. "The whole thing was just ignored."

So McCullough did what he could.

"I have no doubt we've saved a number of people this summer," he said. Still, more lives might have been spared. "Most of the July deaths were on known trails. If we had more volunteers, we could have saved them."

There wasn't time for rumination. He had work to do right now. And off he trotted, at breakneck pace, through creek beds, under low-lying mesquites, around prickly pears, and up into the saddle of a mountain, clicking on his GPS as he went. After all, as he said, "We need more information."

CHAPTER 9

The Last House before the Border

I hate the bastard! It's so ugly.

—Bill Odle, Arizona landowner,
speaking of the border wall

Late on a blustery November day in 2008, Ellen Logue was driving along the bumpy border road, aiming her pickup west toward her own little piece of Arizona paradise. The scenery was beautiful, as long as she trained her eyes on the sunset over the Huachuca Mountains ahead of her, or on the rolling ranchlands on her right. She tried not to look to her left, where the border wall loomed, but it was hard to ignore. So close she could almost touch it, the wall was a fourteen-foot-high stretch of metal, an assemblage of wires and poles and flats the color of rust. Billowing out across the land for miles, it had erased the view that used to go on forever, south into Mexico.

Ellen sighed when she remembered what this valley used to look like. Back in 1998, she and her husband, Bill Odle, bought fifty acres of grassland in southeastern Arizona, thirty-four miles west of Douglas, right up against the international line. They were tired of the noise and crime in San Diego, where they'd lived for years, and they came to this remote land, near the hamlet of Palominas, for respite.

Their place is on the east bank of the San Pedro, the only undammed river in Arizona that flows year-round. Wending its way north from Mexico, the stream is an unimaginable treasure in the bone-dry desert. Thirsty green cottonwoods line its route, and you can feel the mud soft and wet under your feet when you walk its banks. Mammals of all kinds, humans included, migrate along its streambed, and hundreds of species of birds, including the endangered yellow-billed cuckoo, flock to its waters.

From their property, Ellen and Bill could see for miles in every direction. On the Mexican side, over to the southeast, was the great cone of San José, a mountain so high at 8,331 feet that black bears clamber around in its pine forests. West, on the American side, was Montezuma Peak, 7,676 feet up at the tail end of the Huachucas—Thunder Mountains, to the Apaches who used to live here. From these slopes the Spanish explorer Francisco Coronado first took a gander at this landscape in the early 1540s. Up here, at the Coronado National Memorial, you can see that these sky islands and desert valleys are all of a piece, international boundary or no.

The night the couple took possession of their land in this lovely place, "we stood out here with a bottle of champagne," Ellen said. "There were no lights." Just the darkness, the stars, and the quiet.

That was then. Now there was the wall, bollard posts sprouting out of the plants right at the end of their front yard. They had built their house facing Mexico, to take advantage of the views, but now, instead of a sweep of grassland and mountains, all they had was a barrier, stretched east and west as far as the eye could see. With its harsh geometry and raw steel, the wall looked too urban for this rural place, and too warlike for a border between two countries at peace. And it was noisy, a clanging mass of metal that howled and screeched when wind gusted through the valley.

"It's pretty wretched," Bill said. "When the wind blows, this sucker is noisy as all get-out. It's hideous."

In the darkening afternoon, Ellen had stopped her truck when she saw J.C. Mutchler, a sometime neighbor from a ranch nearby, ambling along the road. J.C. had brought my husband, Kevin, and me along unannounced, hoping to find his old friends at home. Following the cordial custom of the country, Ellen invited us to hop into the bed of the pickup and come on out.

"I can give you a ride if you don't mind sitting in the back," she called out the window.

J.C. was a rare enough visitor. He had held onto his land adjacent to theirs after marrying, but he had moved on up to Vail, outside Tucson, and didn't return too often. Ellen and Bill were pleased to see him, but they were so distraught about the new wall that from the minute he jumped out of the pickup they could hardly talk about anything else.

"I hate the bastard!" Bill sputtered, his voice rising almost to a shout. "It's so ugly."

A big man with a wild mane of graying dark hair flopping over bald spots, Bill is retired military, an ex-Marine who's loud and articulate and profane. He was wearing an old camouflage jacket. Ellen is the quiet in her husband's storm, small and soft-spoken, a retired nurse with a long braid down her back, and tidy practical clothes: boots, long-sleeved stretchy shirts, and pants. The twilight soon gave way to inky blackness. Ellen invited us inside. She hurried to make coffee and tea. In the cozy living room, their four big dogs lounged on the concrete floor, looking on calmly at Bill as he enumerated all the depredations the wall had wrought. He was too agitated even to sit down.

The couple had moved out here to live off the grid. They built their house themselves of straw bale, a newfangled sustainable medium that mimics the thick walls and soft curves of adobe. They get their power from the sun and wind, and they pump their own water out of the ground, courtesy of the

San Pedro watershed. But they're not easily pigeonholed. Bill proudly calls himself a gun nut. He's deeply suspicious of the expanding powers of the federal government, particularly as they've been exercised of late on his own land.

"We can't let our system degrade itself by letting powerful people run the show," Bill railed. "There are too many sheep in this country."

The way he saw it, those powerful people, aided and abetted by those sheep, were responsible for the wall now snaking through this historic landscape. The fury around the country over illegal immigration had somehow devolved into one simple demand: wall off Mexico from the United States. To people living nowhere near the border, it was a tidy answer to a messy problem: build a wall, keep the immigrants out, problem solved. Bill declared that people who support the wall should come to the border and see it for themselves, to learn how ugly and damaging and useless it really is.

"People see pictures on TV, and they think it looks great," he said. "There is no doubt, this is all for show. It doesn't work in any sense. It's like the old joke: if it doesn't work and it's too expensive, it must be a federal project."

Opinions about the wall were mixed along the border. The anti-immigrant Minutemen loved it, and even built some fences themselves; some ranchers welcomed it, too, in hopes it would stop the migrant flow. But other residents along the border and just about every environmentalist and human rights advocate hated it from the start. Janet Napolitano, then governor of Arizona, now Secretary of Homeland Security under President Barack Obama, opposed it, famously saying, "You show me a fifty-foot wall and I'll show you a fifty-one-foot ladder."

It wasn't Governor Napolitano's call, though. The international border was the bailiwick of the feds, not the states. In September 2006, Congress passed the Secure Fence Act, ordering the Department of Homeland Security to build a wall—and to build it quickly—in hundreds of miles of open country along the southwest border. With the cities already blockaded, Arizona was to be sealed off. Only the steep hills of its southeast corner were to be spared. The congressional reps set a short deadline for the massive construction project: May 30, 2008. Michael Chertoff, DHS secretary under President George W. Bush, had previously expressed his doubts about the efficacy of a wall, but he got to work in a hurry. And at a staggering cost—from $400,000 per mile for the cheap junk landing-mat segments to the $1.25 million per mile for vehicle barriers to the $4.5 million per mile for the bollard posts. The Government Accounting Office—figuring in the very expensive segment east of San Diego, where the three-and-a-half mile Smuggler's Gulch was filled in with dirt at a cost of $16.5 million per mile—calculated the average price tag at $3.9 million per mile. It was a sweet piece of work for the private companies contracted out to build it. Congress coughed up another $775 million for the border wall in fiscal 2009.

The May 2008 deadline came and went, but work proceeded at a breakneck pace in the waning days of the Bush administration. In December 2008, Chertoff announced that 500 miles now extended along the whole southwest border, short of the congressional demand for 670. President Obama, newly installed in January 2009, kept the bulldozers going, and by June of his first year in office, the barriers extended 625 miles all along the southwest line. Almost half of those miles were in Arizona, according to Dan Millis. Always an outdoorsman, the No More Deaths volunteer had gone to work for the Sierra Club. He was heading its Borderlands Protection Campaign and spreading the word about the violence the wall was doing to the landscape. By Dan's tally, Arizona now had 307 miles of barriers along its 376-mile boundary with Sonora. About 124 of those miles had fourteen-foot "pedestrian fencing"—the benign government-speak name given to the biggest and most impenetrable walls like those adjoining Ellen and Bill's land—and 183 miles had the less intrusive "vehicle barriers," the kind used on the Tohono O'odham Reservation. These shorter posts, four feet apart, stop cars and trucks but allow migrants and wildlife to pass through. Eighty percent of the state was now sliced apart from Mexico.

Crews started in on the stretch near Ellen and Bill's property in October 2007 and ended in February 2008, with a "couple of stops in between," Bill said. Workers rode in on a battalion of bulldozers, earthmovers, graders, and dump trucks, barreling through the fragile desert grasses, raising up clouds of dust, and smashing through the treasured San Pedro. They labored "from can't see to can't see," Bill said, making a racket from dawn to dusk. And when at last they finished, the stark metal they left behind had forever altered the open landscape that Coronado had once marched through. Now it looked like Cold War Berlin, or Gaza today.

"The wall is a symbol of problems we really do have," Bill said, a metaphor for the nation's great divide over uncontrolled immigration. But the barrier itself was all too real. "It's crazy this has occurred. It's beyond surreal. Unfortunately, I don't wake up and say, Man, what a shitty dream. It's not a dream."

To Glenn Spencer, Bill Odle's nightmare was a dream come true. Spencer loved the wall. He lived on the other side of the San Pedro, opposite Bill's house, and he was Bill's opposite number. Spencer had one hundred acres to Odle's fifty, and they faced each other down over the ribbon of green. ("Glenn has camporees with his folks. He's a little too National Socialist for me," Bill said. "He's big on towers, double walls, lights.") The two neighbors had even had a skirmish about access to the river; Bill said he'd had to get papers at the courthouse to prove his right to drive along a river road.

In Glenn's mind, the only thing wrong with the wall was

that there was too little of it. The Secure Fence Act ordered up double rows of fencing all along the border, with a lit-up no-man's-land in between. The only place that got multiple barriers was Yuma, Arizona's westernmost county, and it was so effective that the Yuma "Border Patrol agents sit around doing nothing," Glenn said.

The founder of the American Border Patrol (ABP), a nonprofit that he ran out of his house, Spencer was one of the last of the big-time vigilantes still living along the line. Chris Simcox, of Minuteman Project fame, had transferred his militia operation from Tombstone to Phoenix. Spencer's big worry was the "*reconquista*," the plot he believed Mexico had hatched to retake the United States by sending immigrants to invade and overwhelm. (The Southern Poverty Law Center lists his ABP as an anti-immigrant hate group.) Every day, Glenn walked the border and the San Pedro with his seven dogs, on the lookout for migrants. "I bought a German shepherd and had her bred, and had six pups. Now I have seven German shepherds. We go for runs, jogs along the border two times a day. At three p.m., we go to the river."

Glenn, a retired systems engineer, did more than patrol his own land. He had his own airplane, and he'd been flying over the border for the last two years. "I'm the pilot. I've got two guys in the back with cameras, a video camera and a still camera, tied into GPS. We go from Texas to California. Yesterday we flew out to forty miles south of El Paso," he said in January 2009. He flew regularly to check on whether the feds were really building the walls they claimed they were. The answer, he said, is that they weren't. The DHS tallies of miles built were flat-out lies. "The liberal cabal, including the Department of Homeland Security, the Border Patrol, and the old Immigration and Naturalization Service," was pulling one over on the American public, he said, until Chertoff got wise to them and started really cranking on the construction.

Glenn also commanded troops of Internet volunteers who monitored video cameras set up along migrant trails all over southern Arizona. When the virtual border-watchers spotted live walkers, Spencer posted the video for all America to see: migrants walking through deserts and forests, shot in negative—black figures slipping through a white landscape.

Like Simcox, Spencer was an anti-immigration carpetbagger out of California. He'd preached his gospel on his own right-leaning radio show for years, and he led his own anti-immigrant group, Voices of Citizens Together. He moved to rural Cochise County, Arizona, in 2002, so he could be on the front lines of the invasion. He already knew Roger Barnett, the Sierra Vista tow-truck operator and part-time rancher who's been in and out of trouble with the law for years for apprehending immigrants at gunpoint. Spencer first rented in Sierra Vista, and eventually bought what he wanted, a spread right along the border. Setting up his organization as a nonprofit so that people could donate money to the cause, he modeled his efforts on the work of one of his heroes, a woman named Muriel Watson. She had undertaken a "Light up the Border" campaign in San Diego. She and a convoy of friends regularly drove down to the line at night and aimed their car headlights at the terrified migrants scuttling across. Glenn's Internet project, with videos of migrants scrambling through the wilderness, is a "high-tech version of what she did in California."

No matter how much their neighbor liked it, Bill and Ellen argued that the Great Wall of Arizona doesn't do the job it was so expensively meant to do. Migrants have found ways to jump it, sidestep it, cut it, and climb it. They have a powerful motive to get past it, and they've come too far not to try.

"Some lard-ass in Des Moines thinks it will stop them," Bill Odle said. "*I* can't get over it"—he's in his sixties—"but some twenty-year-old kid from Oaxaca who's hungry can get over it."

Sure enough, no sooner was the wall in place in early 2008 than Napolitano's ladder prediction materialized. Ellen and Bill started finding homemade ladders left behind by migrants, and they regularly propped them up against their house, Exhibit A in their brief against the wall. Two of them were leaning there, like pieces of conceptual art. The ladders were crude, jerry-rigged out of two-by-fours and pegs and rope, and just five or six feet tall. Evidently they did the job, though. They had been discarded on the northern side of la frontera after they'd launched their makers into the United States.

The couple had also found lengths of knotted rope; they believe migrants tie the cord to the wall, hang onto it like mountain climbers as they haul themselves up one side, then toss it over and slide down into Arizona, hand over hand. Rancher John Ladd, Ellen and Bill's neighbor, had recently demonstrated for *Tucson Weekly* writer Leo Banks that a migrant could easily stand on a pickup parked on Mexican soil, and hoist himself over the wall from the truck's roof. A picture of Ladd straddling the barrier landed on the paper's front cover. "People get over that wall in a heartbeat," a female rancher told me. "I'm sixty-eight. I've climbed the wall. If I can do it, anybody can."

Migrants themselves—particularly the agile young ones—say it's not hard. At the migrant aid station in Agua Prieta, the Chevron worker, Carlos Ortiz, twenty-seven, the deportee from Seattle, had laughed when I asked him how he'd done it. "I jumped," he said, using his hands to show how he shimmied up the bars and then leaped over. At the Migrant Resource Center in Naco, Sonora, even closer to Ellen and Bill's land in Palominas, Raymundo Ahuatl Martinez, twenty-four, described another technique. "You can put your foot in the bars. You try it step by step." Sometimes, he said, crossers literally lend a hand to their *compañeros,* entwining their fingers together into temporary steps of flesh and bone. Some segments of the wall, called Sandia fencing, are made of screen strung between poles—a kind of glorified chain link that's excellent for climbing. Peter Young, a painter from the nearby arts town of Bisbee who volunteers at the Naco center, said migrants make little stirrups out of heavy wire and hook them onto the fence's mesh. Then they walk up and down the new-made steps with ease.

Even Robert Gilbert, chief of the Border Patrol's Tucson Sector, acknowledges that the wall slows migrants down by only a few minutes. He argued at a press conference in Tucson in October 2008 that the delay—the "speed bump," as Mike Scioli had it—is enough to make the billions spent worthwhile. (Using common agency parlance, he called the monumental steel barrier a fence, a term more neighborly sounding than "wall.") In the pre-fence days, he said, migrants easily crawled through the barbed wire. Large groups could steal through at the same time, then scatter. Now, Gilbert said, the wall forces crossers to go over one by one, and they're easier to catch. To critics like Ellen and Bill, that sounded like a slight benefit.

The new fourteen-foot wall had indeed curtailed vehicle crossings, but not all. In fall 2008, some enterprising drug dealers tried driving over it on a makeshift ramp. (One rancher said that the new road alongside the wall has been a godsend to drug runners. The traffickers in Mexico toss the drugs over the wall, and cars waiting in Arizona pick up the goods and zip easily away on the expensive new roads.) Bill argued that a less intrusive vehicle barrier would have done the job as well as the giant steel wall. It would have kept cars out, with less expense to the taxpayers, less harm to the environment, and less damage to his cherished view.

"Don't get me started on the U.S. Army Corps of Engineers," Bill said. "We thought the ideal would be a four-foot vehicle barrier, four feet apart, with barbed wire. Something simple that could define the border, that would prevent vehicular traffic and allow animals to go through."

Three deer were idling at the border, two does and a buck with plans to go south. But the new structure was blocking their usual route. The deer had no way of knowing or understanding that their habitat had been split in two, permanently, and they stood there gazing at the metal wall. Elsewhere a porcupine was mulling over a similarly puzzling problem. A trench had been carved into the earth during construction in the exact spot that the animal was accustomed to roaming. The porcupine sat, marooned at the edge of the precipice.

All four animals were photographed by environmentalists intent on documenting the problems the wall was wreaking on nature in the Southwest. (Ellen Logue shared the pictures with me, along with shots of serious erosion along the wall's base and plant debris piled up after the summer's monsoon storms.) Wildlife biologists talk about the dangers of "habitat fragmentation," and it's hard to imagine a habitat more fragmented than one sliced in two by a giant metal barrier.

"The wall is a critical problem," said Paul Hirt, a professor of environmental history at Arizona State University and past president of the Sky Island Alliance, an environmental organization. It's doing damage to sensitive public lands from the Gulf of Mexico to the Pacific. In Arizona, the borderlands are an "ecological melting pot" of overlapping climate zones, as Matt Clark, with the conservation group Defenders of Wildlife, put it. The temperate climate zone sweeps down from the American north while the tropical climate zone pushes up from the Mexican south, creating a hybrid zone that's home to an unusually rich mix of animals. Coatimundi, coyotes, deer, black bear, and, most spectacularly, jaguars travel this country, and the wall has stymied them all.

The prized jaguar is the biggest cat in the Americas, and the return of the luxuriously spotted feline to southern Arizona has delighted biologists and the public for more than a decade. The jaguar died out in the state early in the twentieth century, partly because settlers were shoving their way into its turf, partly because the government waged a campaign to exterminate it. By 1972 the U.S. Fish and Wildlife Service didn't even bother putting the American jaguar on the federal endangered list; as far as its scientists were concerned, the big cat was extinct. The only jaguars anyone knew about in the region were deep in Mexico, in the Sierra Madres, two hundred miles south of the border.

Then one day in 1996, an Arizona cowboy by the name of Warner Glenn was out hunting in the mountains near New Mexico. He was looking for mountain lions, but what he found was a jaguar, a full-grown male. Instead of shooting it, he photographed it. Later that same year, in the Baboquivaris, the same thing happened to another hunter, Jack Childs. He photographed another male. Dazzled, wildlife biologists quickly organized to monitor the animal that Paul Hirt calls a "charismatic megafauna"; they set up cameras and trip sensors in the wilderness. The next year they had enough data to persuade Fish and Wildlife that the jaguar was back, and it was relisted as an endangered species. The jaguar saga was complicated even further in March 2009 when Fish and Wildlife caught and killed Macho B, the jaguar believed to be the only one in the state at the time. During the resulting furor, the wildlife biologists insisted the animal was suffering from untreatable kidney disease and had to be euthanized.

Environmentalists still hoped to protect critical jaguar habitat. "For those who would like to see the survival of these magnificent creatures, the wildlife need to be able to move around the landscape, to adapt to climate change," Hirt said.

"Key conservation goals are to get protected core areas and to get safe-passage corridors between habitats."

The wall threatens both: it isolates the core areas and it blocks safe-passage corridors. If jaguars are traveling up from home base in Mexico, the wall will stop them at the border, and, conversely, it will isolate animals already on the American side. Camera evidence suggests that the wall quickly made an impact. After a section of wall went up in the Altar Valley, east of the Baboquivaris, "for an eighteen-month period no jaguars were seen across the Buenos Aires National Wildlife Refuge," Hirt said. "They stopped getting jaguar photos."

Biologists, environmentalists, and fans of the Old West enraptured by the comeback story were enraged that the ham-fisted Secure Fence Act threatened it. The potential loss of the jaguar, for the second time, is a "kind of symbol" of all the environmental damage the wall has wrought on the fragile landscape, Hirt said. The problems are legion. The Hollywood lights beaming down from high poles alongside the barrier confuse multiple species and disrupt their biorhythms. Bats, for one, are thrown off course and deterred from their important task of helping pollinate saguaros. The steel wall is "impermeable even to a horned toad," Dan Millis said, referring to a ubiquitous—and tiny—desert critter. Some minuscule fauna can't even cross the border road, a swath of sixty-foot concrete. And the road is as damaging to the desert soils as the wall itself.

In the summer of 2008, during monsoon season, the wall triggered serious flooding, and not only in hilly Nogales. In Organ Pipe Cactus National Monument, a spectacular preserve in southwestern Arizona, water accumulated up to seven feet deep. Everywhere along the line, floods carved deep gouges in the soil on either side of the fence, and sticks, plants, and vines piled up. "At Naco, the debris was three to four feet," Ellen Logue said. The wall "will change the water flow."

Archaeologists complained, too. In September 2008, Bill Elliott, the manager of the historic John Slaughter Ranch east of Douglas, showed me excavations of ancient Hohokam dwellings and historic Chinese and Mormon settlements at the southern boundary of the ranch, once part of the legendary San Bernardino spread. He picked up potsherds, fragments of blue-and-white Chinese ceramics, and held them in his hand. They'd been in this ground since the nineteenth century. All of it was about to be plowed under, deemed insignificant. "It matters not," he said in disgust. "They're going to put the fence right through it. The Army Corps of Engineers calls the shots." The Border Patrol had told him it was for his own good: the wall, they assured him, would keep terrorists from overrunning the remote ranch.

Environmentalists and libertarians alike howled when Chertoff's bulldozers began closing in on the beloved San Pedro in 2007. Bill Odle and Ellen Logue were apoplectic that the feds had begun putting vehicle barriers in the riverbed of their cherished oasis. (The bulldozers also unearthed an ancient burial site.)

"The San Pedro is the only free-flowing river still in Arizona undammed," Matt Clark said, speaking in his Tucson office, decorated with a photo of javelinas stopped in their tracks by the wall. "And not only is it the last free-flowing river, but it's a riparian corridor that supports tremendous diversity. It's a ribbon of life" that brings water for 115 miles through parched Arizona. The feds had fast-tracked the required environmental studies and found, not surprisingly, that vehicle barriers in the river would have "no significant impact."

Matt's Defenders of Wildlife joined forces with the Sierra Club, and in October 2007 the two groups sued in federal court to stop construction in the riparian area. A sympathetic judge signed a temporary injunction and the bulldozers went silent for almost two weeks. But Chertoff had another law in his toolkit. The REAL ID Act, one in a suite of post-9/11 security laws that conflated immigration concerns with national security, gave the director of Homeland Security the power to override any and all laws "necessary to ensure expeditious construction of the barriers and roads" along the border. That meant that with a single stroke of his pen, the director—an appointee unelected by any voters—could waylay forty years' worth of laws designed to protect the environment and archaeological and cultural resources. Invoking REAL ID, Chertoff waived nineteen laws that protected the San Pedro. The bulldozers rumbled back to work in the preserve.

"It made our case moot," Matt said. "Without the laws, we had no case." A last-ditch effort, an appeal to the Supreme Court challenging the constitutionality of the REAL ID Act, went nowhere. "They chose not to take up the case."

The following spring, in April 2008, for good measure, Chertoff signed a so-called "megawaiver," abrogating thirty-six environmental and cultural laws covering five hundred miles of border. "Undemocratic" and "egregious" and "harmful," Matt Clark called it. Bill Odle, the libertarian, went further.

"When Congress goes and gives power to the executive branch, they must have read *Mein Kampf*," he raged. "You gotta keep a handle on this, folks. When they can run over laws that have been enacted by our representatives, I don't know why there's not more fury over that."

Workers forged ahead and planted vehicle barriers in the San Pedro streambed. The plan, ludicrous in Matt's eyes, was to haul in cranes every summer, before the monsoons hit, to pluck the barriers back out of the stream and prevent flooding. Even without the barriers, the San Pedro was in trouble. A growing local population was drawing on its waters, and overpumping "is still a concern," Matt said. Now, with the big bollard walls wrapping around the riparian area in both directions, migrants were being funneled into the delicate riverbed. "Habitat fragmentation, funneling of migrants, border enforcement, it's a triple whammy," he said. "I never imagined something like this happening so fast and so furious. I have never been so disappointed in my own government."

Chertoff scoffed at the concerns of environmentalists who had been cheering the return of the jaguar, of desert dwellers who cherished the flowing river, of historians who prized the archaeological record, of landowners like Ellen Logue and Bill Odle who mourned the permanent loss of the landscape's beauty. He framed his actions as an effort to save migrants, and claimed his critics were prizing animal over human life. In waiving legal protections for the San Pedro, he said, "I have to say to myself, 'Yes, I don't want to disturb the habitat of a lizard, but am I prepared to pay human lives to do that?'"

Maybe not, but the new wall didn't stop migrants from dying. At least a dozen people perished in the deserts and mountains near Ellen and Bill's house in the months after their segment of wall was complete. Arturo Cortez-Rodriguez, twenty-seven, died on Valentine's Day 2008 near Bisbee, not far from Palominas. Cause of death: strenuous physical activity. Sixty-one-year-old Miguel Jimenez followed on March 27, dying of exposure outside Bisbee. Five died in Sierra Vista in April and May. Torrid June claimed two, an unidentified woman in Bisbee and Jorge Lopez Cervantes, thirty-two, in Hereford, a short distance from Palominas, both of exposure. Three more died in August, two of them near Bisbee and one, Valatin Martinez Zavala, right up the road in Sierra Vista. Valatin died of exposure in the summertime inferno.

———

The Palominas Trading Post Country Diner is a hole-in-the-wall restaurant *cum* lending library a mile north of Ellen and Bill's place. Pam Waters, the chef and owner, is famous in these parts for her pies—on a Saturday a few weeks before Thanksgiving, customers were coming in to order one of her blueberry or banana cream pies in advance, to guarantee they'd have it for the celebratory table. But if you wanted to have Thanksgiving dinner at the Trading Post you could do that too. And it'd be free, turkey on the house for the holiday.

Locals also turn up for the diner's books. Pam's husband, John Waters, keeps hundreds of paperbacks on shelves on one side of the dining room, the likes of John Grisham and Agatha Christie. When a newcomer to town, a woman named Victory, wandered in in search of pies, she was startled to hear of the diner's literary side dish. "Take as many as you want," John boomed to her. "Keep as many as you want. Bring back some if you want. We've given away three thousand books. Why throw a book away?"

John Waters jokingly calls himself Juan H2Os, spelling the letters out. He loudly presided over a table of his buds, old-time ranchers in their sixties and seventies who liked to tease and banter. One man, who gave his name only as Lee, was the very model of a cowboy, complete with white handlebar mustache, neck bandana, and cowboy boots and jeans. When he stood up, you could see he was as bowlegged as Yosemite Sam. J.C. Mutchler, likewise in full cowboy regalia—ten-gallon hat, canvas jacket, boots—introduced himself as a neighbor. Would they consent to an interview with the strangers he'd brought along? The men agreed with a practiced air; they were used to reporters. This was Minuteman country.

The Palominas Trading Post was a Minuteman meeting place back in the movement's heyday; John and Pam had even let the citizen volunteers camp outside the diner in their RVs. The region had been host to a number of home-grown militias, from Ranch Rescue to the Barnett brothers, operating with greater and lesser degrees of fury directed at migrants. In the aftermath of 9/11, Californian Chris Simcox had transplanted himself to Tombstone in 2001 and invited American patriots to lend their ears and eyes to the border as part of his new Civilian Homeland Defense. Then in 2005, he'd joined forces with another Californian, Jim Gilchrist, to create the Minuteman Project. The pair showily invited armed volunteers from all over America to come down and play soldier on the border. Local officials feared an outbreak of violence. The international media swooned over the story, so much so that on the first day of the Minuteman patrols, the reporters outnumbered the armed volunteers.

Even so, the Minutemen tapped into deep anger among the locals. The Arizona ranchers were barely scraping out a living as it was. Then their government ordered up Operation Gatekeeper and Operation Safeguard, the new policies that pushed Latin America's poorest right into their backyards.

To a man, the diner denizens were incensed about the invasion of "illegals" across their property. "People are tired of it," John Waters declared. "We don't know the meaning of the word 'illegal' anymore. I call them international travel-ers." Lee brought up a recent news article about migrant-rights groups asking the courts not to use the word "illegal" in hearings, since it tends to prejudice the listeners. When American citizens break the law, Lee argued, they pay for their crime. "I've been illegal many times myself," he dead-panned. "But whenever I am, I do my time."

Waters is not from these parts originally. He was an elec-trical engineer in Tucson, and, like Ellen and Bill, he and his wife moved here to get out of the big city. Pam was "raised in a restaurant"—her parents owned the old Arroyo Café in Tucson—and in the early 1990s bought the roadside trading diner in tiny Palominas. In 1950 the café's first owners hauled the buildings south from Fort Huachuca, as the base cast off army surplus after World War II. It was still peaceful more than forty years later when the Waterses turned up. "There were hardly any houses down here then," John sighed. Now nearby Hereford was a burgeoning suburb of Sierra Vista; subdivisions populated by retirees, military and otherwise, were rapidly filling the once-rural landscape.

If the Waterses' peace was already being disturbed by the incursion of new houses, it vanished altogether once the migrants converged on the San Pedro Valley. Border crossers cruise through mostly at night. "We've had sleep deprivation," John said. "The dogs barked all night long. They [migrants] paraded like they owned the place. When you call the Border Patrol, they blow you off."

The wall, he conceded, is "slowing down vehicles." But like Rev. Mark Adams down in Agua Prieta, he believes more migrants than ever are crossing Cochise County, the Border Patrol's claims notwithstanding. "Congress and the Senate have no idea what they're doing. Is the Border Patrol helping? It depends on which week."

The one thing that had made a difference was the Minutemen. "Everything changed when the Minutemen came in. Boy, did that help. They spurred the Border Patrol. At first the Border Patrol was mad, but then they shook hands" in gratitude for the militia group's efforts. The volunteers didn't harm the international travelers, he said. Positioned on lawn chairs facing south, they used binoculars to spot migrants crossing and to report their whereabouts to the authorities. "They did not harass them. They called the BP. The Minutemen interrupted the flow."

Border crossers had always passed this way, but before 2000 their numbers were far fewer. Waters believes the earlier migrants were harder working and less disruptive than the current crowd. "Used to be they came across, you feed them, give them water, they work. Now they cut the hose."

Ben Hemenway, seventy, was eating lunch at the other end of the table with his daughter, Kathy, forty-eight. He calls her Punkin. "She's a little slow," he said. He looks after her on Saturdays and Mondays while his wife works, and he took care to see that she had just the right amount of hot sauce and cheese on her Mexican tacos. Husband, wife, and daughter live on the remains of the old Hemenway family ranch, a half mile north of Palominas. Just five acres are left. After he "failed as a cowboy," Ben left home to work industrial construction. He came back around 1999 and bought the homeplace from his mother. His prodigal return coincided with the incursion of migrants into Arizona, and he wasn't happy about the change.

"Border Patrol says apprehensions are down but that means they're not catching them," he said. "I'm seeing as many people crossing as ever. The dogs bark. Every once in a while there's a knock on the door for help. People are hungry, thirsty, hot, sick."

Ben had the same nostalgia as John Waters for a better model of Mexican. When he was a young cowboy, he worked for a big ranch that straddled the border, and rode side by side with Mexican vaqueros. "I knew Mexican cowpunchers from the other side of the border," he said. "We all worked for the same outfit. There wasn't this big invasion." He contends the newcomers "suck down social services." They're not here to work, he went on, but to freeload on the free health care and schools in America.

The whole area, he said, is wracked by petty theft, and he blames the border crossers. Once when he found a migrant trying to break into his truck, he pulled out his rifle. The terrified man ran toward a passing Border Patrol vehicle, naturally preferring arrest to getting shot. Another time, when a neighbor had a stereo stolen, "My hound dog treed the wetback in a tree. One got away with the stereo. My neighbor called the Border Patrol and they said we can't prove who stole what."

Like almost everyone else locally, from J.C. Mutchler to Bill Odle, Hemenway believes the agents are under orders to let in enough workers to meet the needs of U.S. business. "I have heard that they're told to keep the numbers down."

The Border Patrol is not much help to the locals, he said. They're outsiders, from "Philadelphia or Trenton, New Jersey. I don't know where." They arrive in town oblivious to local conditions, he claimed, asking, "'Where's the border?'" Once he called the Border Patrol after he noticed walkers dropping a load into a waiting truck at the schoolyard every third night. He figured it for a regular drug operation, but couldn't interest the agents in checking it out. And he's called in the middle of the night to report "an army of illegals walking up Palominas Road. Dispatch will say, 'It's dark out there.' I'll say, 'Follow the sound of the dogs.' Then dispatch says, 'We can't hear them.'"

Bill Odle didn't see eye to eye with the diner denizens on much, but they were in agreement about the Border Patrol. The quiet and solitude he and Ellen had cherished was obliterated by Border Patrol cameras trained on their property, by agency vehicles roaring by on the new roads night and day, by copters rattling overhead. "Helicopters fly over sometimes," Bill said. "There was one this morning. On a quiet night, when it's a dead night, you can hear the unmanned aerial vehicles."

A Border Patrol agent had driven right over Ellen's plants ten feet inside their property line, and agents have more than once shined a light on the couple in their hot tub. "We've had more trouble with the Border Patrol than with anyone trying to cross the border," Ellen complained. "They don't respect your property."

It infuriates both that federal officers claim the right to come onto their land. "The Border Patrol says they can go anywhere," Bill said. "I've caught them out on my land. If they're in hot pursuit, that's understandable. But just snooping around is not. I have curtilage"—an old legal concept defining the sanctity of a home and its surrounding land. "It's your living space, the space outside, where you expect to have privacy. If I'm doing something, get a goddamn warrant. Good police work doesn't need all that."

Their neighbor J.C., a cowboy with a Yale PhD who teaches history at a satellite campus of the University of Arizona in Sierra Vista, bought his forty acres and a "crappy" house for $75,000 in 2003, right when the action was at its most extreme. "As an Old West thing, I loved it: the Minutemen, the gunshots, the helicopters," he said. "I would see one hundred migrants a week. They were hauling ass to get to the San Pedro or picked up on Highway 92."

But like Bill and Ellen he was none too pleased about Border Patrol incursions on his land. One time he saw a four-wheel-drive vehicle on his property, and thinking it might be a drug smuggler, he said, "I go tearing down there and find two guys in camouflage digging holes, putting sensors on my land. They told me, 'Get the hell out of here. It's none of your business.'" And he hated the way young agents hotdogged around on the ranch roads: "You get a kid, twenty-five, in a four-wheel drive, get your adrenaline up, get a gun."

Bill Odle doesn't go down to what he calls the "redneck café," but he and the proprietor agreed on the need for compassion. Waters has had all the players in the drama in his café: "illegals," Minutemen, Border Patrol. The travelers, like them or not, were human beings, he said. "If they need water, if they've got babies with them… I've had the sheriff bring them in here in winter. I give them coffee, cocoa. You try to be humanitarian."

John blamed corruption in Mexico for many of the border crossers' problems. He found it understandable that a man would migrate to the much wealthier nation right next door, especially if he had a family depending on him. "If I lived on the other side of the fence, I'd probably cross, too."

Bill was of the same mind. "No matter what your position is you have to have a heart," he said. "An Indian lady from Michoacán was crying at the fence one day. It was hot. Her group had left her. The dogs were barking at her. We got her food and water. We've seen folks sick.

"I don't have any problem with people coming up to work. It's great that they want to work. These shitheads up here don't. Why not have them come up lawfully, as guest workers?" He hated the way the migrants' illegal status kept them in a shadowy underclass. "Eighteen in an apartment. What kind of crap is that? They're hiding, they're not treated well. This is the United States of America. It shouldn't be happening."

Deep into the evening, Ellen and Bill's dogs were whimpering for their supper. One of them, Jake, had his own issues with the border. He was a Mexican dog who'd migrated over from the other side, following the San Pedro. He showed up one day, seeking shelter from a storm, sat himself down on the patio, and made the decision then and there that Palominas was where he wanted to live, *al Norte.* He still didn't understand the international protocols. He routinely went back to the green riverbed and splashed through the water, walking under the cottonwoods right back to Sonora. Then he'd circle back east along the wall opposite the Logue-Odle acres and bark, baffled that he could be so close to home and yet so far, stranded on the Mexican side of the steel.

"He gets trapped over there," Bill said in frustration. But he had a plan. The wall wasn't going to stop his dog much longer. "If he does it one more time, I'm gonna cut a hole in the fence."

CHAPTER 10

The Case of the Panda Express Eleven

I told my husband I loved him, and to take care of the baby. I said, "I think it's Immigration."

—*Roselia Araceli Torres Ruiz, Tucson restaurant worker*

Marlen Yobana Moreno-Peralta snuggled in bed with her baby early on a March morning. Freddy, just shy of eight months, was her only child, and she always tucked him in beside her as she slept. It had been rainy and cold a few days before, and Marlen had a scratchy throat. She was planning to sleep in.

A loud banging at the door suddenly woke up mother and son. It was 7 a.m., too early for visitors, and the knocking was insistent. Marlen's parents, Isabel and Martin, were asleep in their room at the opposite end of the family trailer on Tucson's south side, and they didn't hear it. So Guadalupe, sixteen, stumbled out of bed to answer the door.

Guadalupe was shocked at what she saw. Outside, just beyond the chain-link fence and her mother's garden patch, was a platoon of cars from the Department of Public Safety. The Arizona agency chases down speeders on the highway, but it also runs high-level criminal investigations of drug dealers, gun smugglers, and the like. Now two DPS officers were standing on the Moreno front steps. And they were demanding to speak with her big sister, Marlen, twenty-four.

No one in the house had ever had trouble with the law. The family was from Cumpas, Sonora, a little town south of Douglas. Only the oldest son had legal residency in the United States, but they'd been living peacefully in Tucson for ten years, since 1998, when Marlen was fourteen years old. Martin had had good jobs in construction, and his son was working as a mason. The whole family was proud that Marlen had graduated from Cholla High School, back in 2002, and that she'd worked so hard ever since.

Once she picked up her diploma, Marlen had gotten a job scrubbing the sticky-popcorn floors at a movie theater in Sahuarita, south of the city; then she'd moved on to cleaning the bathrooms and changing the soiled sheets at a Super 8 Motel in town. Next up was a waitressing job at the House of Cheng. Finally, in 2004, she'd hired on at Panda Express. Ever since, she'd been a counter server at the popular Chinese fast-food chain, slinging Beijing beef and kung pao chicken for hungry diners. When the lunch crowds dwindled, she'd go on cleaning detail, washing tables and swabbing down the toilets.

Now on this morning in 2008, something was seriously wrong. Guadalupe hurried into Marlen's room. "The police are here for you," she cried out. Startled by all the commotion, Freddy began wailing. His aunt took him from his mother's arms and tried to soothe him, bouncing him on her hip. Marlen hurried out to the living room in her pajamas. "I was in shock, afraid," Marlen said later. "I was afraid for my child."

Her voice was hoarse, but she asked the agents what was going on. They told her they wanted to talk to her about her car out front, and she let them into the house. She'd bought the Ford Mustang so she could cut down on her commuting time to Panda—the bus ride, with transfers, took two hours—and she'd taken out a huge loan to pay for it.

Once inside, the officers changed the subject. "We know you work at Panda Express," one said, as Marlen later told me the tale. "And you're using the name of Marlen Martinez. You're coming with us."

The officers arrested the young mother on charges of using someone else's name—Marlen Martinez—and someone else's Social Security number, to work and to get the car loan. The crimes she was accused of were apparently so serious that there was no time for her to get dressed. She'd have to go into custody in her pajamas. Put on a sweater, the officers told her, and put on some shoes.

"They didn't let me eat. They didn't give me papers or read me my rights," Marlen recalled months later, sitting at the kitchen table of the trailer with her mother, who wept at the memory of the police in the house. "They treated me like a dangerous person."

She asked for permission to brush her teeth, and got it only after the agents had conferred at some length. She managed to snatch a bra from her bedroom and sneak it into the bathroom. She put the bra on under her pajama top; that way, at least, she could maintain a modicum of modesty as she was led away in her nightclothes.

Freddy was still wailing, and the officers ordered Guadalupe, at sixteen still a minor, to tend to him. Then they hauled Marlen outside, where a female officer frisked her and handcuffed her behind her back. The neighbors were out and about, going to work, taking their kids to school. They saw her get cuffed, saw her car being towed away. And then they watched as the young waitress was hustled into the back of a police car and driven away to the sound of Freddy's screams.

By the time Marlen saw her baby again, after 112 days in the Pima County Jail and three weeks in a for-profit immigration detention center in Eloy, Arizona, Freddy had already passed his first birthday. He'd fussed for weeks after she disappeared, and he had trouble sleeping, even though his grandparents tucked him in between them at night. But by the time his mother came home more than four months later, he had no memory of her. When she tried to hold him, or even touch him, he'd hit her and cry.

He had no idea who she was.

Across town from Marlen's trailer park, over on Tucson's near-north side, the Arizona Department of Public Safety was setting a trap.

The Panda Express was in a generic shopping plaza, north of a Walgreens and south of a Sleep America, with a sliver of a view of the Catalina Mountains to the north. It hardly seemed like a crime scene, but in a parking lot out back, the DPS cops set up a stakeout. The restaurant normally opened at 10:30 a.m. for early-bird lunchers, and the staff came in around ten to polish up the faux-marble tabletops and to start sautéing the veggies. The day that Marlen was rousted out of bed just after dawn, most of the workers had arrived early, around 9:30. They had been told to expect a visitor from corporate, and they wanted the place to look as good as it could.

"We were waiting for our boss from California," remembered Roselia Araceli Torres-Ruiz, twenty-five, months later, after she got out of jail and detention. "Everybody was cleaning." Araceli was scheduled to work her usual twelve-hour shift, from ten in the morning to ten at night, but she didn't mind putting in the extra half hour. She'd been working at Panda five years at least, and she was "lead counter," head of the women who dished up food from the buffet. (Panda Express divided jobs along traditional gender lines; men were the chefs, women the servers.)

Araceli and her coworkers didn't know yet that Panda Express had been actively cooperating with DPS for weeks. Nor did they know, as they arrived for work dressed in their uniforms—little black caps and polo shirts embroidered with pandas—that Marlen was already in custody. Or that as they stepped off the Sun Tran bus or pulled their cars into the parking lot, they were under surveillance by agents surreptitiously surrounding the store.

Darío Cruz-Diaz, fifty-five, had gotten there even earlier than the other workers. He turned up at eight to wash the big plate-glass windows. "He was good at that," Araceli said. The rest of the team "went in twenty minutes early. We were joking around, laughing. I went to the bank. I came back."

Assistant store manager Omar Espino-Lara, twenty-five, was in a good mood. He was just back from a corporate strategy session in Phoenix the day before, and he'd gotten the welcome news that sales this year were up. A father of four, he'd be working the twelve-hour shift with Araceli. Rudy Garza-Salas, thirty-eight, on the job three years, had begun cooking in the open kitchen, stir-frying broccoli and grilling strips of chicken. Rosa Nohemi Gutierrez Parra, twenty-eight, was readying the heat trays on the line. A college graduate with a degree in chemistry, she was a tireless volunteer at Duffy Elementary School, where her six-year-old son, Jorge, was in kindergarten. She'd been working at Panda just three months.

At precisely 10:30 a.m., "I opened the register, opened the store," Araceli said. "I saw what I thought was my first customer." She turned to the woman with a smile, but this was not somebody with a late-morning craving for crispy shrimp. It was a DPS agent, the advance guard of the workplace raid. Araceli cried at the memory. "It's the last day I saw my team," she said, wiping away tears. "We were happy. I liked that job."

Outside, two agents ordered Darío to put down his

sponges and get inside. They followed him into the store, and Araceli saw one turn and lock the door. "I told Omar, 'These are police.' I got nervous. I had a bad feeling." Araceli trembled as she remembered her mounting fear. "I called my mother. I told her to take care of my daughter," three-year-old Giselle. "I said, 'I don't know what's happening but I love you guys.' I called my husband, told him there were police all over the store. The back door was closed. Something was going on. It was not looking good.

"I told him I loved him, and to take care of the baby. I said, 'I think it's Immigration.'"

The five cornered workers didn't know it, but a whole troop of DPS agents was circling around outside. (In all, eighteen DPS cops participated in the raid.) Inside, officers handed Omar a search warrant and ordered everybody to sit at the customer tables, underneath the cheerful posters of pandas in every possible pose. Just then, in a spectacular piece of bad luck, Juan Trujillo, twenty-two, turned up. He was late for work, and he pulled open the front door and hurried in, oblivious to the drama inside. He walked right into the trap.

"What's up?" he asked his work buddies, puzzled, at first, to find them all sitting when they should have been working. His friends looked up with despairing faces, and the officers told him to sit down too. It took Juan a few seconds to understand that a raid was under way and that he'd been caught. Now DPS had snared six suspects. The agents separated them into groups of two. Araceli and Darío were seated together and read their Miranda rights. The officer intoned the familiar words, "You have the right to remain silent… " But then, Araceli said, he kept right on questioning her: "Are you legal or illegal?"

Araceli was feisty, used to managing the line, and she replied, "I have a right to keep silence. I don't want to answer."

Then, "he got really mad. He took his badge and said, 'You're being arrested for ID theft. I'm going to ask you one more time. Are you legal or illegal?'"

When she again refused to answer, the man replied, "There's only one answer."

A woman handcuffed her and, according to Araceli, pulled hard on her hands and berated her, complaining to the other officer, "She doesn't want to cooperate with us."

The man agreed. "She doesn't want to answer me."

Araceli finally succumbed to the pressure. "All these people were around me. I said, 'I'm illegal.'"

The corporate visitors Araceli and the staff had been expecting turned up in time to see their workers being led away in restraints. By 1 p.m., according to the DPS report, the "restaurant was turned over" to Apichai Vitayaprachasakul, Alan Huang, and Ricky Tong of Panda Express. Alongside startled would-be customers who had arrived in search of sweet-and-sour pork or Mandarin chicken, the Panda Express brass watched as the cooks and waitresses were driven away in a procession of law enforcement vehicles. The restaurant workers had a tough afternoon ahead. They were interrogated by law enforcement of all kinds, over many hours, in facilities all over town, from the Border Patrol headquarters near the Air Force base to the DPS center on Tucson's heavily Hispanic south side. Finally they landed at the Pima County Jail on the west side, where suspects accused of crimes from DUI to murder were held.

DPS fanned out across Tucson to round up four other staffers at their homes. Norberto Hernández Ochoa, a chef, had cooked at Panda ten years. A thirty-four-year-old father of three little boys, Norberto was married to an American citizen, Maria, who worked nights at a nursing home. Francisco Domingo Mondaca Duarte, twenty-two, was a Pima Community College student hoping to become a computer engineer. He had been working at Panda part-time, in between classes. Artemio Marin Bustamante, twenty-three, had a pregnant wife and a toddler at home in Mexico, and José Guadalupe Pichardo Rivera, twenty, was a single guy who worked long hours at Panda and held a second job at Oregano Pizza.

Late in the day, the eleven workers reunited, tearfully, at Pima County Jail. Six of them were still wearing their jaunty Panda work shirts, and Marlen was still in her pajamas. Soon, they would trade these clothes in for prison garb: the humiliating orange jumpsuits that marked them as outlaws.

"We were with all these people who were really, really criminal," Araceli said. "We couldn't realize we were going into jail. I started to cry. That's the last day I saw my daughter."

The case of the Panda Express Eleven erupted in Tucson on March 18, 2008, the day after St. Patrick's Day. While the city's Irish Americans were at a parade and festival remembering yesterday's immigrants, their state government was plotting a raid on today's.

Headlines about the case splashed across the newspapers. Eleven Mexican nationals had been arrested, and Arizona attorney general Terry Goddard noted darkly, and falsely, in a press release that all eleven were "associated with a Tucson identity-theft ring."

It was big news. Just sixty-four miles from the border, Tucson was filled with immigrants, documented and otherwise. Individual workers without papers regularly got caught, detained, and deported, but the city had largely escaped the workplace raids that had become commonplace up in Phoenix. Joe Arpaio, sheriff of Phoenix's Maricopa County—dubbed America's Toughest Sheriff by the national media—had made a kind of blood sport of detaining Latinos, staging telegenic midnight raids to catch workers in the act of working, their incriminating mops and brooms in hand. And in the waning years of the Bush administration, the federal Immigration and Customs Enforcement agency (ICE) had been conducting near-paramilitary raids on a huge scale, complete with helicopters hovering over factories. Armed agents snatched up hundreds of Guatemalan seamstresses in New Bedford, Massachusetts, in 2007 (they sewed backpacks for the U.S. military, among other customers). Two months after the Panda Express raid, the feds apprehended almost four hundred meatpackers in Postville, Iowa.

"By design, the raids are an assault against working men and women," attorney Margo Cowan declared in the summer of 2008. "The Bush administration wants to wreak as much harm as possible before the sun sets on their power to do so." A longtime immigration activist and volunteer lawyer with No More Deaths, she is also a staff attorney with the Pima County Public Defender's Office. She takes on so many cases and works so many hours in her day job that "it's like working for three attorneys," her assistant told me. Margo explained the breakdown. "The Panda case is part of my public defender job. My volunteer work is just my small effort to relieve some of this terrible suffering that results from our immigration policy." She paused. "It's a war on the poor."

In Tucson, Barbara LaWall, the Pima County Attorney, didn't see large-scale operations to round up fast-food workers as a particularly good use of taxpayer money. As one of her prosecutors put it, she preferred to spend staff time and money on people committing real crimes. But the Panda Express case was a state operation, green-lighted by the state attorney general and conducted by the DPS Organized Crime Unit. Accustomed to tracking down major drug traffickers, the officers on the case had even taken the TV-drama precaution of staging a dawn drive-by of Marlen's trailer in the hour before they pounded on her door.

"What has happened is shameful, a travesty," Cowan said. "These people made this community better, as immigrants to this country have been doing for two hundred years."

The Panda Express Eleven could have come right out of an Econ 101 textbook: they were classic low-wage workers in a service economy. For eight to ten dollars an hour, they cooked and served food for the California-based corporation (which has twelve hundred restaurants altogether), and washed toilets and floors. Marlen's pay, after four years, was $8.70 an hour. In their report, the DPS detectives tallied up all she had ever earned at Panda. In the course of four years of dishing food and swabbing floors, she had earned a total of $50,324.92. That's an average of $12,580 a year, paid by a thriving corporation whose mission statement calls it an "organization where people are inspired to better their lives."

Ironically, it was the low Panda wages that circuitously led to the investigation and the arrests. Once Freddy was born, Marlen's small paycheck was stretched too thin, and she applied for benefits at the Arizona Department of Economic Security. Freddy is an American citizen, born July 20, 2007, in Tucson, and he was entitled to get help.

"My child qualified for food stamps and ACCESS [the Arizona health care system for the poor]," Marlen said. "The problem began when I asked for food stamps for Freddy."

Marco Liu, a program administrator at DES, said U.S. citizen children of undocumented immigrants are entitled to get such benefits, if the family qualifies financially. Normally, staffers don't tip off authorities if they encounter undocumented applicants—in fact DES tries to dispel that fear in the community—but "if there's an intentional program violation we refer it up to state and legal counsel."

A DES investigator went out to Marlen's house, and the case went up to the state attorney general. "Our office had this referred to us with concerns of welfare fraud," said Anne Hilby, the attorney general's spokeswoman. "That one individual applied for benefits with a Social Security number that was not hers."

In February, DPS served a subpoena on the Panda Express offices in Phoenix, demanding information on Marlen and all the workers at the Swan Road restaurant. Panda Express was only too happy to give up its loyal workers, some of whom, like Norberto, had worked for the company ten years. Joyce Martinez, with Panda's California headquarters, called DPS on February 20 to say the company "wanted to assist in complying," according to the DPS report. Lyle Forcum telephoned two days later, reiterating Panda's readiness to help, and then shipped off a list of the employees' names, birthdates, and Social Security numbers. A DPS investigator forwarded the information to the Social Security Administration; a check revealed that the names and numbers did not match.

I asked Hilby why the attorney general's office went after all the workers. The investigators originally targeted only Marlen, she agreed, "but if you come across evidence of other crimes, our office has the responsibility to investigate. We became aware of it, and we had to move forward with prosecution."

By March 18, DPS was ready to pounce.

Despite its finding that no fewer than twelve out of the store's fourteen workers were undocumented and working illegally with fraudulent Social Security numbers, DPS hastened to assure the media that Panda would not be charged with any crime.

"This didn't have anything to do with Panda Express," DPS spokesman Quentin Mehr told the *Arizona Daily Star.* "This is not a reflection on the Panda Express," he reiterated to the *Tucson Citizen.* "They are not being investigated." And Panda's corporate counsel, Monte Baier, asserted in a written statement, "Panda Express has and continues to be in full compliance with all federal and state laws."

Not so, one worker told me. The Panda Express managers knew their staffers were undocumented, the worker said, and even advised them to make up new Social Security numbers if an old one bounced back as invalid. Still, Hilby insisted that the attorney general's office "found no evidence that Panda Express was aware of the fraudulent Social Security numbers."

And in any case, the company benefited from a ready-made loophole. Arizona's tough Legal Arizona Workers Act—an employer-sanctions law that can take away a business's license on a second offense of hiring illegal workers—would not have applied even if investigators had found Panda violations. It didn't go into effect until January 1, 2008—after the workers were hired.

Panda Express wasn't taking any chances. After the raid, "out of an abundance of caution," as company spokeswoman Thien Ho put it, the company conducted a purge at its eleven other Tucson restaurants. Managers checked every employee's papers, and everyone who was illegal got fired.

Once they were seized, the Panda Express workers inadvertently became poster children for the state's harsh new anti-immigrant laws. They had had the bad luck to be arrested after a 2005 change in Arizona law that made using a fake ID in order to work a felony. During a three-month investigation that began in December 2007, the DPS Organized Crime Unit amassed a sea of documents on all fourteen employees working at the Panda Express on Swan Road. Detectives concluded that twelve out of the fourteen were using Social Security numbers that were not theirs. The twelfth worker happened to be on vacation the week of the raid; she was never caught or charged.

Three women and eight men were indicted on a class-three felony charge of aggravated identity theft.

"None of them had any idea it was a crime," Isabel Garcia, Pima County legal defender and Marlen's attorney, told the court. For generations, undocumented workers had bought fake numbers and cards so that they could work and feed their families; they thought of them as working papers, Garcia said. Social Security taxes were taken regularly out of their paychecks, but they would never see that money in their old age. Instead, the money they'd contributed would go toward other retirees. "The baby boomers are benefiting," Garcia noted.

Because the Panda Express Eleven had been charged with a felony, they were facing an immigrant catch-22. They were not eligible for bail, even though none was accused of a violent crime and most had local family ties. Thanks to Proposition 100, still another anti-immigrant measure, this one voted into law by the people of Arizona in 2006, a defendant accused of a felony and believed to be in the country illegally can't get bail. No exceptions. People accused of murder, rape, and drug dealing have a chance at getting bail and going home to await trial. By contrast, judges have no discretion in immigrant felony cases. Trapped in a guilty-until-proven-innocent nightmare, the restaurant staff had to sit in jail for four months until the trial began. As the mother of an infant child, Marlen begged for release, but Pima County Superior Court judge Frank Dawley turned her down. He had no choice but to enforce the law.

The judge was flooded with letters from the community testifying to the workers' good characters. The kindergarten teacher who had Nohemi's son in his class wrote that she was a wonderful mother; she worked with the boy on his lessons at night and regularly helped out in the classroom with the other children. A pastor detailed Omar's volunteer work with his church's teen members. "These people you're getting to know are fine people, victims of the federal government's inability to do immigration reform," attorney Cowan told Dawley. "They are victims of state laws that criminalize them for working."

The Panda Express Eleven languished long months in jail, most of them separated from young children. In the end, despite the high drama of the stakeouts, the headlines, the front-page photos of them in their prison garb, not one of the Chinese-food workers was convicted of a felony. After some masterful lawyering by Cowan and company, the state attorney's office agreed to a plea bargain. All eleven pled guilty to the far lesser charge of criminal impersonation, admitting only that they were "pretending to be a lawfully employed member of the Panda Express restaurant crew."

Dawley ruled the infraction a misdemeanor and sentenced the defendants to fees and time served. The court never found that the workers had stolen anyone's identity, nor that they had hurt anyone in any way. The numbers they'd used were made up; only one had belonged to a real person, and she was deceased. In fact, Dawley reproached the prosecutor, saying, "You don't have any specific example of harm."

At a rally for the workers—picketed by anti-immigrant protesters—Garcia held up the foot-high stack of DPS documents. She disgustedly told the audience, "This investigation was a complete waste of taxpayer money."

But the government was not through with them. The former Panda workers still had their immigration woes to contend with. Dawley ruled that they had done enough time at the county jail, but they were not free to go home. They were picked up in July by the feds—ICE agents—and taken in chains from the county jail to immigration detention centers in Eloy and Florence, isolated communities an hour and a half from Tucson. (Nina Rabin, a University of Arizona law professor, has written that immigration detention centers are invariably in remote locations that are hard for families and attorneys to get to.) The Panda workers were held in federal detention for weeks while their cases were adjudicated. Darío Cruz-Diaz, the diligent window-washer, stayed the longest. Norberto Hernández Ochoa never got as far as detention. He had a previous criminal conviction, dating back many years, and was deported almost immediately after his sentencing.

By January 2009, eight of the workers were back in Mexico. Some of them didn't see that they had much of a shot at arguing their right to stay, so they accepted voluntary return. In a curious twist, Artemio, Rudy, Juan, José, and Nohemi were all sent back to Mexico before their criminal sentencing, and Dawley agreed to conduct them via cell phone from their homeland. (José joked to me at his Mexico hearing—in an office in Nogales, with norteño music playing outside— "Too bad I didn't take that job at Chipotle," referring to the Mexican restaurant chain in Tucson.)

Marlen, Araceli, and Omar all filed petitions to stay, and they were released from detention after local activists raised the money to pay their bonds. Margo Cowan thought they had a pretty good case. Omar was married to a legal resident. All three were brought to Tucson as children and grew up in the city, and all three have kids of their own who were born in the United States and had automatically become U.S. citizens.

Then in May 2009, the highest court in the land did the Panda workers a good turn. In *Flores–Figueroa v. United States,* the Supreme Court ruled unanimously in favor of an undocumented Mexican who had been charged with identity theft in Illinois under a federal statute. The steelworker was using a Social Security number that turned out to belong to somebody else. The law, the justices wrote, required that such a defendant had to *know* he was using the ID of a real person. If he didn't, he couldn't be convicted.

Margo was delighted. "A great ruling," she called it.

"Knowing means knowing." It wouldn't overturn the Arizona law, but it would put a greater burden of proof on prosecutors next time they felt inclined to round up undocumented waitresses and cooks. And it might sway the deportation judge.

Araceli was optimistic about her chances.

"I consider myself part of this country," she said. "Even though I don't have papers, I've done a lot of positive things in this country."

A month after Araceli Torres went back home to her husband and child, I visited her at their modest cinderblock house in midtown Tucson. Her daughter, Giselle, four by then, was rocketing around the bare living room, calling to her mom, tugging on her sleeve, doing whatever she could to get her attention. Araceli still seemed fragile. She sat at the dining table and wept more than once when she talked of all that had happened.

"I've lived seventeen, eighteen years in Tucson," she said. "My family came from Oaxaca. I came in ninety-two, around the age of seven. My mom was here already. She came in eighty-nine, ninety. My aunt, two cousins, and a friend brought me." They had no trouble crossing the border that she can remember. "We came straight to the house, my uncle's house, and I reunited with my mom." She had an older brother born in Mexico and a little sister born in the United States.

Araceli's mother enrolled her in the Tucson public schools, starting her out at Cragin Elementary, in my own neighborhood. My daughter, Linda, went there, too, I told her in surprise. "Let me see if she's in my yearbook," Araceli exclaimed. She hurried off to fetch the book from her bedroom. Sure enough, there in the Cragin Cougars yearbook, in the house of this young woman in danger of being deported, was a picture of my child, age eight, near a little Araceli, age ten.

"I must have seen you running around on the playground," I said. I was stunned. The coincidence brought home to me how long she'd been in Tucson, how much a part of the community she was, and how different her opportunities in life were from my daughter's. Linda had just graduated from college; Araceli had just gotten out of jail.

Araceli was embarrassed that she had dropped out of high school one and a half credits shy of graduation, but she had to work. She had started a job washing dishes in a restaurant. Then she switched to telemarketing, where she used her Spanish to sell prepaid phone cards. Next up was Sears at the Tucson Mall, where as a customer service rep she deployed her excellent English, as well as Spanish skills, to help Anglos and Latinos alike exchange their purchases. When she got the job at Panda Express, she settled in for the long haul.

Omar Espino-Lara, her friend and coworker, had a similar history. Sitting in a conference room at attorney Margo Cowan's office, his mother, Juana, by his side, he told me his family had come up to Tucson from Guanajuato when he was nine. They had stayed only two years. They'd gone back to Mexico for another three years, but the family's seven children didn't adjust well. "My dad realized it was better for us to be here." So the Espinos returned permanently, in 1997, when Omar was fourteen. They had a harrowing crossing. The coyote divided them into two groups, and Juana was separated from her husband and children. She fell and broke her ankle in the desert near Nogales, and the rest of the Espinos had some anxious hours waiting for her to turn up. When they finally arrived in Tucson, she was afraid to go to the doctor. She didn't walk again for a long time.

Long, lean, and athletic, Omar became a soccer star at Sunnyside High School. He graduated in 2002, and went on to Pima Community College to study accounting. But when his father was badly injured in a bicycle accident, Omar dropped out of college to support the family.

First he worked at Carl's Jr. and then went over to Panda Express, where he rapidly rose to assistant manager. He married and had a son, and took his responsibilities as a stepfather to his wife's three children seriously. Their father was an American citizen, but he "doesn't care about them," Omar told me. A pillar of Iglesia de Dios, the Church of God, on Tucson's south side, he coached the congregation's youth soccer team on weekends. He's an *hijo bravo,* a wonderful son, his mother told me through tears. "Never, never"—*nunca, nunca*—"did I think I would see him in jail."

On a summer day in August, a few weeks after she was released from the immigration detention center, Marlen Moreno-Peralta bustled around her immaculate kitchen, loading up a plate with cookies. She was delighted to be at home again. Tucson immigration activists had raised the money to pay the bond to get her out of detention, and she was awaiting word on her petition to stay in the United States. She never did get her car back, or any of the money she had paid on it.

Marlen is a big, soft-spoken young woman with a cascade of light brown curls. She was smiling, even though her son, Freddicito, as she calls him, was staring at her warily from the safety of his grandmother's arms.

She seemed less traumatized than Araceli. But when she looked over at her son, she said, "It's very unjust what they did to us." Five months after being torn from his mother's arms, he was still refusing to come to her. "They took us away from our children, separated us from our families. I will never forget. It was only for working. They treated it as a crime."

Marlen was humiliated to have been imprisoned with people accused of serious offenses. At Pima County Jail, she was with "drug dealers, DUI people. Three women were accused of murder." She was afraid too. "The places are always dangerous. The women fought." The detention center in Eloy, run for the feds by the for-profit Corrections Corporation of America, was "very dirty. There was no privacy in the bathroom. There was a lot of contraband, people smoking drugs, very different from the people in my regular life."

Jail was painful for Omar, too. An athlete all his life, he suffered as a result of being locked up in a small space. He was allowed outside only "one hour a week, on the basketball court."

He struggled to keep up his spirits. "I didn't eat at all for the first six days. I didn't take a shower for ten days. The place was dirty....I didn't want to live anymore. I spoke to no one." The detention center in Eloy was "not better." The place was infested with gangs, he said, and he had to fend off their demands that he join.

Araceli said some of the officers were kind. They were used to much tougher customers in jail and they sympathized with the plight of the Panda prisoners. But others were harsh; one officer scolded her for speaking Spanish. A fellow inmate taunted her that she'd be deported, but Araceli defended herself. "I have done more positive things for the country than you," she shot back at the woman. "I love this country. I'm here because I was working. You're here for stealing. I'm proud of myself and did a lot of good things."

Worst of all was the separation from their children. At Pima County Jail, only visitors with legal status can visit, and even then, they see their loved ones not in the flesh but via a video on computer. The setup was particularly unsuitable for kids. I visited Norberto in jail one day with his wife, Maria. Their three-year-old, Angel, came along, but he paid almost no attention to his dad's image flickering on the tiny screen. Norberto sat slumped and sad, and Maria pleaded with Angel to "say hello to Daddy." Angel ignored her and his dad both, and rolled around on the floor, restless and distracted. Omar's two-year-old son, Gianlucca, named for an Italian soccer player, would come to prison with his mom, but he was confused, too, Omar said.

"What are you doing there?" he would ask, peering at his dad on the computer screen. "When are you coming out of the office?"

The jail performs rigorous screening of visitors. I had to fill out a lengthy form, answering questions about employment, arrest history, and so on (I declined to give my Social Security number), and I had to surrender my notebook, pens, cell phone, and purse. Without legal status, Marlen's family was fearful about visiting her, and so they couldn't bring her son Freddy to see her. Araceli refused to have her daughter Giselle visit; she didn't want the little girl to see her mother in jail. Unlike Freddy, Giselle was big enough to remember her mom during the long absence, and big enough to be mad that she was gone.

"Where are you, Mommy?" she'd ask her on the phone. "When are you coming home?" Sometimes, though, "She was too angry to talk to me," Araceli said. "She'd run and cry." It was hard for both mother and daughter; the worst was when Giselle got sick while her mom was locked up.

The Panda Express prisoners had twelve young children among them. Most of the kids were U.S. citizens, deprived for months of their parents' loving care and financial support. In June, the three mothers in the group—Marlen, Araceli, and Nohemi—wrote a plaintive letter to the public from inside the prison walls.

Under U.S. immigration law, the women wrote, "working has been transformed into a crime." *Trabajar se ha convertido en un delito.* "Because of this law, we remain here, far from our families and children. Our children are the most affected. They were suffering the absence of their mother and fathers, who one day went out to work and never came back."

The Birth of Jesús

The Child Jesus helped me. I named the baby
for him.

—*Lilian Escalante Abrego, migrant mother*
from Honduras

The weekend before Christmas 2008, temperatures dropped
sharply across southern Arizona. By midnight on December
21, the border town of Douglas was shivering in the low 40s.
By the time a baby boy was born in the desert a few hours
later, it was down to 34, so cold the soft earth had hardened
and the cactus spines were crackling.

The baby's mother, Lilian Escalante Abrego, had been
hiking the wilderness for three days, in a group of *quince
compañeros caminando*, "fifteen friends walking": five women,
a nine-year-old girl, and nine men. Lilian had started out
with a friend in their native Honduras, and the two of them
had met the rest of the migrants along the way. The journey
lasted weeks, and the travelers had become close. That night
they were in the foothills of the Perilla Mountains, ten miles
east of Douglas, hoping to make it to a road and a ride. Lilian
wasn't expecting her baby until January. But in the wee hours
of December 22, she went into labor.

Unlike those who walked with Josseline, Lilian's *compañeros* didn't even consider going on without her. They shook off their backpacks and spread a yellow blanket on the cold desert floor, trying, vainly, to find a spot free of rocks and prickers. "I lay down on the ground," Lilian said later, and the wayfarers gathered around under the stars to await the birth of the child. They were in ranch country, and cattle were lowing. With *Navidad* on her mind, Lilian prayed to the Christ Child.

This was her fifth baby and the labor was short. After only two hours, Lilian brought her baby to the light, *lo dio a luz*, as the Spanish term for childbirth has it. At three thirty in the morning, near where Silverio Huinil Vail had died eight years before, Arón Jesús Escalante Abrego was born.

"One of the *muchachas*"—the women—"cut the umbilical cord with a knife," Lilian said. Both the baby and his mother were in trouble. Arón Jesús was dangerously small and Lilian was bleeding vaginally. She had banged up her legs during the trip, and her feet were badly blistered. "I couldn't run," she said. "I couldn't even walk. I wanted help from la migra." So someone lit a fire. The birthplace was in lonesome country, and the agents never saw the flames blazing in the winter night. When no help came, ten of the migrants set out to find it.

"A man stayed with me in the desert," Lilian said. "A Mexican *compañero*. He told me, 'I'm not going to leave you alone.'" Nicknamed Capulina, he had already teasingly asked the widow Lilian to marry him. She'd teased him right back, saying he was too old, forty to her thirty-nine, but at her moment of crisis he was there at her side. "He cried when the baby was born."

At daybreak, the others found a solitary ranch house and banged on the door. The owner peered out and, hearing of the birth in the desert, put in an emergency call to the Border Patrol. When la migra arrived, the migrants regaled them with the story of the Christmas baby. The agents hurried out, and in the morning light tracked the walkers' footprints back to the yellow blanket. They found Arón Jesús and Lilian swaddled in sweaters and trembling in the cold. The paramedics from the Douglas Fire Department were on their way, so one agent positioned Lilian on a quad—a four-wheeled motorcycle. Just a few hours postpartum, she sat astride it with the officer, and bounced three miles out to the road. Capulina refused to surrender Jesús to anyone else. He followed on foot, cradling the baby in his arms.

When paramedic Frank Honne got to Lilian, she was "cold and exhausted," he said a few weeks later. "Mom was bleeding. We were able to control it. She got stable. We took care of her." As for the newborn, "The infant was extremely cold. He appeared tiny." Frank and his partner, George Alba, strapped oxygen masks on mother and son and started them on IVs. Then they whisked them by ambulance to Southeast Arizona Medical Center.

"We did our job," said Frank, thirty, father of a seven-year-old girl. A Douglas native born and bred, he'd been with the fire department seven years. "In my career, I've had close to fifty calls about migrants, especially in the extreme weather in the summer and winter. It's usually a body recovery. Sometimes it's depressing, but some are happy calls. I'll remember this one."

At the hospital, Capulina was mistaken for Lilian's husband and the baby's father. He was permitted a final glimpse of the pair before he was led away. Like Raúl Cruz Uribe, another Mexican who'd saved another Honduran—Marta Gomez Garcia—Capulina was sent back to Mexico, his hopes of disappearing into the United States dashed. Lilian didn't know his town or even his real name.

"He was an angel," she said. "He sacrificed everything to take care of me." The rest of the *compañeros* also paid a price for saving her. All but one were sent back to their home countries. Only the woman who'd midwifed the baby was able to elude la migra's grasp.

The Douglas doctors were worried about Arón Jesús. He was dehydrated, he weighed a little over four pounds, and his birth—complete with knife—had been far from sterile. The community hospital was not equipped to treat a baby in such danger, so the docs rushed him by helicopter to Tucson, to the neonatal intensive care unit at University Medical Center. Lilian followed by ambulance on the ground, arriving that night. She was put in a bed in the maternity ward, a floor below the baby. Instead of an infant at her side, she had a series of uniformed Border Patrol agents, male and female, posted round the clock in a chair in her room. Her case was different from Marta's. Because she wasn't critically ill, under Border Patrol policy she had been kept in custody, under guard. She would be arrested later.

"It's a very sad story," Lilian said the next day, her eyes filling with tears. "I'll cry a lot when I tell him" how he was born. Yet there was much to be grateful for. "Thanks be to God"—*Gracias a Diós*—"I'm alive and he's alive. The Child Jesus helped me. I named the baby for him."

Alerted by a celebratory Border Patrol press release—"Border Patrol Agents Rescue Mother and Newborn"—I tracked Lilian to her hospital bed the day after the birth. It was December 23, the cusp of Christmas, and Tucson was gearing up for the holiday. Up the street from the hospital, at the Arizona Inn, a historic hotel in pink adobe, well-heeled visitors were sitting by the fire in the library, drinking late-afternoon tea. (Arizona's cold Decembers surprise tourists and migrants alike.) A Christmas tree stood in the window. Outside, Mexican luminarias were twinkling in the rainy twilight.

Lilian's hospital room was all the grimmer for the contrast. She lay back weakly in a metal bed, dressed in a thin gown, her wavy black hair falling out of the straggly bun atop her head. Nearby, a young female agent sat tight-lipped and unsmiling. The room was dark, with no lights on, no TV, and no baby. Tiny Arón Jesús was still upstairs in intensive care, tethered to IVs blasting him with antibiotics. His blood-platelet count was low, the nurses said. Lilian's milk was coming in, but she wasn't allowed to sit by his incubator for long stretches to try to get him to nurse. She was permitted only infrequent visits. He was *bonito*, she said. "Pretty, very pretty, with lots of black hair."

Lilian was glad, if a little surprised, to have a visitor. Her family in Honduras had no idea where she was. She was eager to unburden herself, to explain how she'd ended up alone, in a foreign hospital with a sick baby, two days before Christmas.

"I live in a little town that's very poor," she said. "I have no house and no job." *No tengo ni casa ni vivir.* "I had to come to the U.S. to provide a living for my family."

She was from San Antonio de Cortés, in the northwest part of the small Central American country. There were four children at home, "all boys," she said with a laugh, thinking of her latest. The oldest, Alfredo, twenty, and Carlos, eighteen, had long since been working in the fields. Then came Merlin, fifteen, and Juan Inez, seven, her *pajarito*, little bird. Her niece, Adria, was caring for them and for Lilian's mother, eighty-two and ailing. This was the third time Lilian had crossed into the United States to support this tribe. She'd lived in Raleigh, North Carolina, working as a cleaning lady, scrubbing houses and buses. In fact, Juan had been born in a hospital in Raleigh. She'd been caught by the immigration authorities and deported, and she'd been back in Honduras ever since.

Her husband, Juan, had died in the last year. His brother had been killed, she said, and in his despair Juan drank himself to death. Lilian pulled out a picture of her family in happier days; it showed a smiling trio, Lilian, little Juan, and big Juan, grinning behind his mustache. "I loved him very much," she said, her eyes reddening. The way she saw it, after her husband's death she had to go back to the United States. Honduras has maquilas, she said, clothing factories run by Chinese and Americans, but they don't hire anyone forty or over. With that big birthday coming up for Lilian the next June, she decided to go north.

"I work for my children," she said. "I don't see them."

She left Honduras on Sunday, November 9; it took her six weeks to get to the American desert where her youngest child would be born. The way was long, as it had been for Josseline, and for Silverio. She had to cross part of Honduras, all of Guatemala, and the whole of Mexico from Chiapas to Sonora. Along the way, she joined up with fellow Hondurans, Nicaraguans, Salvadorans, Guatemalans, and Mexicans, the group of *compañeros* growing as the journey progressed. In Mexico, people were invariably kind when they saw she was pregnant. *Muy buena gente,* she said: "Very good people." A family in Chihuahua begged her to stay with them, and when she refused, they showered her with sweaters and blankets to fend off the cold. "I wore five sweaters at a time," she said, and over her big belly, "I looked fat!"

Lilian rode to America by train. "How much did it cost?" I asked. "Six weeks," she replied. "No, no, I mean how much for the ticket?" She looked at me steadily. "Nothing." Nada. She hadn't paid. She'd jumped the train.

In her hospital bed, Lilian demonstrated with her arms how she would run alongside a train as it was pulling out on the tracks, then grab a railing and swing her body aboard. The trains are notorious. It's easy to miscalculate a jump, easy to fall. More than a few migrants have lost their limbs or their lives to the steel wheels churning below. Lilian avoided the roofs, where bandits prowl and the nimblest ride. "I couldn't climb up to the top with my belly," she said, curving her hand to show where her pregnant abdomen had swelled. She rode inside, in the boxcars. Twice she'd badly hurt her legs trying to get in. She pulled up the hospital blanket to show me the cuts the train had carved into her flesh.

Once, she almost didn't make it. She was slipping until a fellow migrant seized her arms and hauled her into the moving train. "I thought I was going to die."

At least for now she was safe. And she was hungry, ready to fuel up the milk production in her breasts. Dinner, a nurse had told her, would be at six thirty.

On Christmas Eve, the upward arc of Lilian's story—and the heartwarming tale of the Border Patrol's rescue of a new baby in Christmas week—spiraled back down. In the early afternoon, I found her dressed and sitting on the edge of the hospital bed, discharge papers in hand. A new Border Patrol agent was standing by. Now that she was medically able to travel, the agent had orders to take her to the station. Never mind that she was a nursing mother with a newborn son in intensive care. And never mind that it was Christmas Eve. The agent tried to be conciliatory. He was quite sure Lilian would be back by the end of the afternoon.

Lilian was well into a bad cold, coughing up mucus from deep in her lungs, and she had a pain in her chest. Two days postpartum, she was still suffering the pangs of afterbirth, and she was still having problems walking. Yet the hospital discharged her, and for good measure withheld the wheelchair customarily used to take patients to their cars. She had to make the long walk down the hospital corridors, past the Santa decorations, past the Christmas tree in the lobby. She trudged along haltingly, flinching with every step, a new mom leaving the maternity ward with no baby—and under arrest. A few people noticed. They averted their eyes at the sight of the departing patient escorted by an agent in green. I stood and watched until Lilian and her captor disappeared at the far end of the parking lot.

The agent leading Lilian away didn't seem like a bad sort. He was a family man himself. He was going to have to work on Christmas, he told me, so he and his wife had already celebrated the holiday with their three-year-old son. Yet the law demanded that this pleasant young father separate this once-and-future cleaning woman from her newborn child.

The Border Patrol did not return Lilian to her baby that day.

On Christmas Eve night, a nurse told me by phone the good news that Arón Jesús had improved enough to step down to the pediatrics unit, and the bad news that Lilian had not been brought back as promised. His mother's breasts were engorged with wholesome mother's milk, but the nurse had to give him a bottle of formula. While the city was celebrating the Christmas story in candlelit midnight services, the Border Patrol was holding a flesh-and-blood new mother at its barren headquarters. She was made to stand long hours, postpartum status notwithstanding, she reported later, and an agent taunted her that her baby had not really been born in the United States. She was given a cold cheeseburger to eat. There were no cots. She lay down on a patch of floor, with only dirty blankets to warm her. She cried for her baby through the night.

On Christmas morning, she was released. A kindly agent drove her back to the hospital; on the way, he stopped at McDonald's and insisted on buying her breakfast. ("¡Papas!" she said the next day, wonderingly. *Potatoes!*) She had a joyful reunion with her infant. Free for the moment of her Border Patrol guards, Lilian had been told to report to an immigration judge in a few days. If she didn't show up, they'd be back to arrest her. She was much the worse for wear from her night on cold concrete. Her cough was deeper, and her belly and back ached badly. The tenderhearted pediatric nurses gave her a comfy cot in her baby's room ("She had a rough night," one said) and promised her three nutritious meals a day and a place to stay as long as the baby was a patient. "It's what we *can* do," a nurse said. Tucson's Samaritans had gotten wind of her plight and organized a round-robin of visitors. A Samaritan doctor checked her out and gave her antibiotics for what by now was a serious respiratory infection in her sinuses and both ears. Santa Claus came by on Christmas Day and gave the baby a bear. Lilian phoned her family in Honduras, and on Christmas night her seven-year-old, her little bird, asked her to come home. His baby brother, rooming at last with his mother, took to nursing like a champ.

The arc had swung up again, slightly. Lilian couldn't help but mourn the failure of her journey. She didn't yet know how the legal tangle would unspool, whether she'd be detained up in Eloy or Florence, where the Panda Express Eleven were held, whether she'd be deported immediately or whether she'd find a way to slip free.

"I wanted my children to have a better life," she said sadly as she cradled baby Arón Jesús in her arms. "But I didn't succeed."

Acknowledgments

This book could not have been written without the help of the migrants whose stories it tells. Many of them were suffering through the worst days of their lives when I happened to come along. Yet they answered my questions with patience and sometimes even good cheer. Often they were puzzled that anyone would be interested in their private tragedies. I thank them for allowing me to bring their heroic tales to light.

I am also grateful to the women from West Africa and the Caribbean who cared for my mother in Philadelphia for the last ten years with exuberance and grace, particularly Pinkey Johnson of Jamaica and the late Edith Adams, who died on the job, never to return to the home she longed for in Trinidad. They taught me much about the privations of immigrant life.

Many people helped me gather material for this book. I thank the Border Patrol agents who took me on ride-alongs, Edmundo Erik Moncayo, Vince Hampel, and Mike Scioli, and the activists who led me into the desert, Daniel Strauss, Ed McCullough, Maryada Vallet, Gene Lefebvre, Steve Johnston, and Mike Wilson. Thanks also to Rev. Mark Adams, Miriam Maldonado Escobar, Tommy Bassett, Adrián González, Margo Cowan, Anthony Damelio, Peter Young, translator extraordinaire Michael Brescia, mapmaker Andy Mosier, and Dr. Bernard Fontana. Thanks too to my *compañeros del viaje*, Héctor Acuña, Jay Rochlin, J.C. Mutchler, Will Gosner, and Kevin Gosner; to Laila Halaby, who helped introduce me to Beacon Press; to my editor Gayatri Patnaik, who took a chance on me; to Beacon director Helene Atwan for her encouragement; to assistant editor Joanna Green, managing editor Susan Lumenello, and senior production coordinator Sarah Laxton, for their patience and for the care they gave the manuscript; and to *Tucson Weekly* editor Jimmy Boegle, who published some of the pieces in this book in a somewhat different form.

A raft of friends encouraged me as I wrote: the members of the Steve Cox Retirement Support Group—Steve Cox himself, Jay Rochlin, Tom Miller, Tim Vanderpool, Cynthia Jordan, Beth Henson, Adele Conover, and David Laird; John and Anne Gerbner, Ellen Foos, Eileen Kenna, Carolyn Cooper, Hannah Glasston, Eileen Devlin, Barbara Kremer, Matt Rosney, Brian Byrne, Janet Cadogan, Doug Biggers, Jim Nintzel, Beulah Ruby Jordan, and all the Parkettes. I must also thank my mentor, Chris Satullo, who guided me into the writing life, and the late Sister Teresia, SSJ, who taught me to read.

Love and gratitude always to my family: my sibling support team—Mary, Billy, Anne Marie, Eileen, Michael, Paul, and Jimmy Regan; my in-laws, Pam Gosner, Marilou Regan, Doug Magee, Tim Smith, Patricia Regan, Sandra Riley, and the late Alice Swaboski; my daughter, Linda Regan Gosner, who was too busy excavating an Egyptian temple in Luxor and Roman ruins in the Mediterranean to join in the family border trips, but whose work ethic and feisty determination are an unceasing source of inspiration; my son, Will Gosner, the only Arizona native in the family, and a fine young scholar who gave me provocative insights on border issues, astute writing advice, and able research assistance; and my husband, Kevin Gosner, for his cheerful willingness to live within the orbit of my writerly disorder, for his thoughtful editing of this book, and for his unwavering belief in me.

Finally, I thank my beloved parents, the late Mary G. Regan, the most loving and gentle of mothers, who modeled compassion and kindness to her nine children and never turned a stranger away from her table, and the late William L. Regan, a grand storyteller in the Irish tradition who enthralled me when I was a child with tales of our own immigrant past. Their love and pride made me what I am.